TREATY INTERPRETATION, THE CONSTITUTION AND THE RULE OF LAW

BY

JOHN NORTON MOORE

OCEANA PUBLICATIONS, INC.
Dobbs Ferry, New York

Information contained in this work has been obtained by Oceana Publications from sources believed to be reliable. However, neither the Publisher nor its authors guarantee the accuracy or completeness of any information published herein, and neither Oceana nor its authors shall be responsible for any errors, omissions or damages arising from the use of this information. This work is published with the understanding that Oceana and its authors are supplying information, but are not attempting to render legal or other professional services. If such services are required, the assistance of an appropriate professional should be sought.

You may order this or any other Oceana publications by visiting Oceana's website at http://www.oceanalaw.com

Library of Congress Control Number: 2001132457

ISBN 0-379-21443-1 (alk. paper)

Manufactured in the United States of America on acid-free paper.

To

Philip C. Jessup

Who Would Have Us
Not Forget That A Treaty Is An
International Agreement

Treaty Interpretation, The Constitution And The Rule of Law

By
John Norton Moore*

---

* Walter L. Brown Professor of Law & Director of the Center for National Security Law and the Center for Oceans Law & Policy at the University of Virginia. Professor Moore served as Counselor on International Law to the Department of State and, among seven Presidential appointments, as the founding Chairman of the Board of the United States Institute of Peace and as a United States Ambassador to the Third United Nations Conference on the Law of the Sea.

The author initially worked on this subject during the 1980s as a consultant to the Arms Control & Disarmament Agency in advising the Director of the Agency on the "Broad-Narrow" Issue in Interpretation of the ABM Treaty. The 4000 page study by the author on this overall issue has not yet been declassified. An unclassified 607 page volume of this study reviewing the constitutional arguments on all sides of this debate, however, will be published in the near future as a separate monograph, JOHN NORTON MOORE, THE NATIONAL LAW OF TREATY IMPLEMENTATION (2001).

I should like to express my thanks to Malvina Halberstam, A. E. Dick Howard, and John C. Jeffries, Jr., for their helpful comments on a draft of this article and to Ms. Joanna C. Murdick for her helpful editorial suggestions.

About the Author

John Norton Moore is one of the best known international lawyers in the world. His writings on international law and constitutional dimensions of foreign policy have been read literally around the world. He has served as a U.S. Ambassador, as the Counselor on International Law to the U.S. Department of State, as a Deputy Special Representative of the President and Chairman of a National Security Council Interagency Task Force, and as a Consultant to the U.S. Arms Control and Disarmament Agency and the President's Intelligence Oversight Board. Among seven presidential appointments, most recently Professor Moore served for two terms as the Senate-confirmed Chairman of the Board of Directors of the United States Institute of Peace. At the University of Virginia School of Law, Professor Moore is the Walter L. Brown Professor of Law and Director of the Center for National Security Law. He has written and testified extensively on constitutional issues and the conduct of United States foreign policy. He has worked on the treaty power as the Counselor on International Law to the State Department and as a consultant to the Arms Control and Disarmament Agency. As Counselor on International law, he participated in the drafting of Circular 175 on United States treaty practice. He has also testified at Senate hearings on executive agreements and treaty termination.

I.
Introduction: Great Case and Bad Law

> *"Great cases like hard cases make bad law. For great cases are called great, not by reason of their real importance in shaping the law of the future, but because of some accident of immediate overwhelming interest which appeals to the feelings and distorts the judgment. These immediate interests exercise a kind of hydraulic pressure which makes what previously was clear seem doubtful, and before which even well settled principles of law will bend."*[1]
>
> *Mr. Justice Holmes, dissenting in* Northern Securities, *1904*

Imagine a new doctrine in the foreign relations law of the United States. This new doctrine would require, whenever it were applicable, either that the United States violate its treaty obligations or that it be held to obligations not incurred by our treaty partners. Never mind *pacta sunt servanda* or mutuality of obligation. It would adopt the practice toward other nations of following internal deliberations in our domestic ratification process rather than the treaty as internationally negotiated and binding. Never mind the general international law rule limiting invocation of internal law to violations that are "manifest and concern . . . a rule of . . . internal law of fundamental importance."[2] If other nations were to follow our lead on this practice, they, in turn, could assert that they were not going to adhere to an

1 Northern Securities v. United States, 193 U.S. 197, 400-401 (1904) (Holmes, J., dissenting with the concurrence of the Chief Justice, Mr. Justice White, and Mr. Justice Peckham). The common law maxim, of course, is "hard cases make bad law."

2 *See* Article 46 of the Vienna Convention on the Law of Treaties, *opened for signature* May 23, 1969, art. 46, 1155 U.N.T.S. 331, *reprinted in* 8 I.L.M. 679. And see the even stronger general rule embodied in Article 27 of the Vienna Convention, subject only to this Article 46 exception. It provides: "A party may not invoke the provisions of its internal law as justification for its failure to perform a treaty. This rule is without prejudice to article 46."

agreement as negotiated with the United States or other nations since their Executive, or members of their Duma or equivalent, had stated a different interpretation at the time of internal consideration.

This new doctrine would declare as binding, domestic conditions attached in internal ratification debates absent conveyance to the other party for their agreement, or even absent identification of the interpretation as a domestic condition attached to a resolution of advice and consent. It would mandate that the United States not follow international law interpretations of international courts if such interpretations were inconsistent with even expressed views of participants during internal advice and consent deliberations. Its most extreme version would actually bar the Executive Branch and United States Courts from reviewing treaty interpretation materials not before the Senate during the internal advice and consent process, as is frequently the case with *travaux préparatoires* and foreign language versions of treaty texts, and as is usually the case with subsequent practice of the parties.

This remarkable new doctrine would do all of this in the face of a long history of Supreme Court decisions treating treaties not as legislation, but as contracts or compacts among nations, and adopting the intent of the parties to a treaty as the basic standard for interpretation, much as is reflected in the contemporary international law of treaty interpretation.[3] It would proceed despite the 1898 Supreme Court decision refusing to apply an unpublished proviso to a treaty and stating what one would assume to be the common sense understanding, that it "shocks the conscience [to put forth a treaty] . . . as embodying the terms of an arrangement with a foreign power or an Indian tribe, a material provision of which is unknown to one of the contracting parties."[4] Indeed, it would do all of this in the face of absolutely no authority for the new doctrine prior to its recent appearance.

Other strange departures for the new doctrine would include domestic lawmaking by Executive Branch testimony or statements of a few members of the Senate, quite counter to the normal requirements for domestic federal legislation as reflected in Article I Section 7 of the Constitution and the *I.N.S. v. Chadha*[5] and recent *Clinton v. City of New York*[6] cases, and with little or no regard for the two-thirds of a quorum for treaty approval require-

---

3 *See, e.g.*, the line of Supreme Court cases from United States v. Schooner Peggy, 5 U.S. (1 Cranch) 104 (1801); The Amiable Isabella, 19 U.S. (6 Wheat.) 1 (1821); Geofroy v. Riggs, 133 U.S. 258 (1890), to the present. And for the international law rules, *see, e.g.*, Articles 31-33 of the Vienna Convention on the Law of Treaties, *supra* note 2.

4 New York Indians v. United States, 170 U.S. 1, 23 (1898).

5 Immigration and Naturalization Service v. Chadha, 462 U.S. 917 (1983).

6 Clinton, President of the United States v. City of New York, 524 U.S. 417 (1998).

ment as reflected in the classic *Fourteen Diamond Rings* Case.[7] It would seek to make binding national law through examining legislative intent in the absence of any domestic legislative vehicle to which the intent could attach. It would convert a constitutional "veto" in the advice and consent process into an undefined domestic lawmaking power. No doubt this effect of the new doctrine would come as a surprise to the House of Representatives, which has assumed it was part of that general domestic lawmaking process, and to the President, who has failed to realize that his "veto" power would presumably also carry with it an undefined general domestic lawmaking power should the general theory of the new Senate power be followed. It would assert this domestic conditions lawmaking power despite the fact that in apparently the only case in which this issue of the validity of domestic conditions has actually been fully argued and briefed to a court, the Court of Appeals for the District of Columbia Circuit held, in a two-to-one opinion by Judge Bazelon, that even a clear "reservation" attached to a treaty by the Senate which concerned only domestic policy had no legal effect,[8] and this despite the domestic condition being formally conveyed to and accepted by the other treaty party *and* its being simply a "non-self-executing" condition, certainly the strongest such setting for the permissibility of "domestic conditions." And this new doctrine would require departure from the international legal obligations of the United States with minimal evidence of general intent to do so, quite counter to the normal requirement in the foreign relations law of the United States for even a solemn legislative act, not to interpret it as in violation of the international law obligations of the United States "if any other possible construction remains. . . ."[9]

Perhaps most remarkably, this new doctrine would be zealously espoused to remedy the problem of a President intentionally lying to a Senate during the advice and consent process as to the meaning of a treaty, a problem said to be urgently in need of a remedy despite absence of a single example of the problem occurring in the constitutional history of the United States.[10]

---

7 Fourteen Diamond Rings v. United States, 183 U.S. 176 (1901).

8 *See* Power Authority of the State of New York v. Federal Power Commission (the Niagara Reservation case), 247 F.2d 538 (D.C. Cir. 1957); *vacated as moot sub. nom.* in American Pub. Power Assn. v. Power Authority of the State of New York, 355 U.S. 64 (1957). Further, even the dissent in this case made it clear through his reasoning that his support for the condition only went to its status as a "non-self-executing" condition. *See* the dissenting opinion of Circuit Judge Bastian 247 F.2d at 544-53, particularly at 547 and his conclusion on page 552.

9 Murray v. Schooner Charming Betsy, 6 U.S. (2 Cranch) 64, 118 (1804). *See also* RESTATEMENT (THIRD) OF THE FOREIGN RELATIONS LAW OF THE UNITED STATES § 114 (1987).

10 Despite the heated debate about interpretation of the ABM Treaty in the "broad-narrow" dispute, no one argued that President Nixon had sought to mislead the Senate about the meaning of the ABM Treaty when submitting the Treaty to the Senate in

And it would be pursued in the face of numerous available options to protect the integrity of the advice and consent process, including the quite powerful remedies of subsequent legislation, public hearings, future noncooperation, invoking existing criminal sanctions against lying to the Senate, or in extreme cases of intentional effort of a President to mislead a Senate, the impeachment process. And it would be pursued for the purpose of protecting the intent of the Senate during the advice and consent process even though its implementation would never be able fully to carry out the intent of any consenting Senate as to both *meaning* and *bargain*, and, even more perversely, its implementation would seem in many, if not most, cases to comply less well with likely priorities in Senate intent given the choices then available, than the traditional rules looking to the intent of the parties. Most remarkable of all, in light of the above effects on the foreign relations law of the United States and the Nation's ability to comply with its international legal obligations, this new doctrine would be said by its proponents to serve the rule of law.

It seems likely that few neutral observers would find merit in the proposed new rule or agree that it would serve the rule of law. Yet astonishingly, and almost certainly without recognizing some or all of the above problems, the United States Senate has begun a practice of routinely attaching an ambiguous condition to advice and consent of important treaties, which if it does anything, would largely have the effects discussed above.[11] Even more as-

---

1972. Nor has anyone in the debate cited a single example of a President intentionally lying to the Senate about the meaning of a treaty when submitting it for advice and consent.

11 The first such condition, emerging from the background of the "broad-narrow" debate, was known as the "Biden Condition," and was attached to the INF Treaty in a process significantly polarized along party lines. *See* ACDA Briefing Memorandum, Final Senate Action on the INF Treaty (May 31, 1988); *Senate Approves Historic INF Treaty on 93-to-5 Vote*, WASH. POST, May 28, 1988, at 1, col.5. The condition was adopted by the Senate on May 26, 1988, and provides in relevant part:

> that the Senate's advice and consent to ratification of the INF Treaty is subject to the condition, based on the Treaty Clauses of the Constitution, that—
>
> (1) the United States shall interpret the Treaty in accordance with the common understanding of the Treaty shared by the President and the Senate at the time the Senate gave its advice and consent to ratification;
>
> (2) such common understanding is based on:
>
> (A) First, the text of the Treaty and the provisions of this resolution of ratification; and
>
> (B) Second, the authoritative representations which were provided by the President and his representatives to the Senate and its Committees, in seeking Senate consent to ratification, insofar as such representations were directed to the meaning and legal effect of the text of the Treaty; and
>
> (3) the United States shall not agree to or adopt an interpretation different from that common understanding except pursuant to Senate advice and consent to a subsequent treaty or protocol, or the enactment of a statute; and

tonishingly, leading scholars in our profession, unquestionably committed to the rule of law, have supported this Senate action and, again I believe without recognizing some or all of the associated problems, have offered

---

> (4) if, subsequent to ratification of the Treaty, a question arises as to the interpretation of a provision of the Treaty on which no common understanding was reached in accordance with paragraph (2), that provision shall be interpreted in accordance with applicable United States law.

See also 27 I.L.M. 1406, 1407 (1988) for the condition as attached to the I.N.F. Treaty.

In announcing ratification of the I.N.F. Treaty, President Reagan made an ambiguous statement with respect to the Senate "condition" on treaty interpretation, the thrust of which seems to be to affirm that treaties are international agreements to be interpreted in accordance with the international law standard as traditionally applied by U.S. and international courts, and to deny that the Senate can unilaterally alter these principles of treaty interpretation or other rights and duties under the Constitution. Thus, the President's statement included the following points:

> The Senate condition relating to the Treaty Clauses of the Constitution apparently seeks to alter the law of treaty interpretation. The accompanying report of the Committee on Foreign Relations accords primacy, second only to the treaty text, to all executive branch statements to the Senate above all other sources which international forums or even U.S. courts would consider in interpreting treaties. It subordinates fundamental and essential treaty interpretation sources such as the treaty parties' intent, the treaty negotiating record, and the parties' subsequent practices.
>
> Treaties are agreements between sovereign states and must be interpreted in accordance with accepted principles of international law and U.S. Supreme Court jurisprudence. As a practical matter, the Senate condition only can work against the interests of the United States by creating situations in which a treaty has one meaning under international law and another under domestic law. Unilateral restrictions on the United States should be avoided, especially in a treaty affecting vital national security interests. . . .
>
> . . . the principles of treaty interpretation recognized and repeatedly invoked by the courts may not be limited or changed by the Senate alone, and those principles will govern any future disputes over interpretation of this treaty. . . . I am compelled to state that I cannot accept the proposition that a condition in a resolution to ratification can alter the allocation of rights and duties under the Constitution . . . .

27 I.L.M. 1406, 1413 (1988). The President's statement, however, also contained a vague and ambiguous statement about "authoritative" executive statements, apparently designed to appease the Senate treaty condition hawks. *Ibid.* Administration spokesmen were forced into several other ambiguous statements over the course of the full "Biden Treaty Interpretation Condition" debate. For the full context *see* JOHN NORTON MOORE, *supra* note *.

From 1992 to 1996, in the Start I, Open Skies, and Start II Treaties, the Senate attached this treaty interpretation condition as a "declaration" attached to the resolution of advice and consent, as opposed to an attached "condition." Possibly this reflected some Senate doubt about the legal basis of the use of "domestic conditions." *See* 102 CONG. REC. S15956, S15957 (Oct. 1, 1992) (Start I); 103 CONG. REC. S10800 (Aug. 6, 1993) (Open Skies); 104 CONG. REC. S461, S462 (Jan. 26, 1996) (Start II).

During 1997 and 1998, however, the Senate reverted to attaching the treaty interpretation condition to treaties as a "condition." Such a condition was attached to the Chemical Weapons Convention, the CFE Flank Agreement, and the NATO Protocols on the accession of Poland, Hungary and the Czech Republic. *See* 105 CONG. REC. S3651, S3656 (April 24, 1997) (Chemical Weapons Convention); 105 CONG. REC. S4476, S4477 (May theoretical justification for it.[12] One Federal District Court Judge reached out to embrace the doctrine in the absence of the parties fully briefing or ar-

---

14, 1997) (CFE Flank Agreement); 105 CONG. REC. S4217, S4220 (May 4, 1998) (NATO Protocols).

The current blanket treaty interpretation condition seeks to establish that its rules of interpretation apply to *all* treaties, not just those to which it is appended. It reads: "The Senate affirms the applicability to all treaties of the constitutionally-based principles of treaty interpretation set forth in condition (1) in the resolution of ratification of the INF Treaty. . . ." *See, e.g.*, 105 CONG. REC. S4220.

This general condition will be referred to from time to time in this article as the "Biden Treaty Interpretation Condition"or simply the "Biden Condition," after the practice of one of its principal authors. For Senator Biden's use of the term "The Biden Condition" to describe this condition, *see* Joseph R. Biden, Jr. & John B. Ritch III, *The Treaty Power: Upholding a Constitutional Partnership*, 137 U. PENN. L. REV. 1529, at 1544 (1989).

12 *See, e.g.*, David A. Koplow, *Constitutional Bait and Switch: Executive Reinterpretation of Arms Control Treaties*, 137 U. PENN. L. REV. 1353 (1989). This volume of the *University of Pennsylvania Law Review* contains a variety of views on the treaty interpretation issue, written at the height of the "broad-narrow" debate about the proper interpretation of the ABM Treaty, including views of the principal protagonists in the debate, Abraham D. Sofaer and Senators Sam Nunn and Joseph R. Biden, Jr. For a view supporting the traditional approach to treaty interpretation, *see, e.g.*, Eugene V. Rostow, *The Reinterpretation Debate and Constitutional Law*, 137 U. PENN. L. REV. 1451 (1989). And for the views of three Senior-Attorney Advisors in the Office of Policy Development, United States Department of Justice, critical of Professor Koplow's approach, the position of the *Restatement (Third)*, and the "dual" approach to treaty interpretation in general, *see* Lawrence J. Block, Lee A. Casey & David B. Rivkin, Jr., *The Senate's Pie-in-the-Sky Treaty Interpretation: Power and the Quest for Legislative Supremacy*, 137 U. PENN. L. REV. 1481 (1989).

For other supporters of the "dual" approach to treaty interpretation, including the power of the Senate to achieve a domestic lawmaking effect solely through informal legislative history not even embodied in the resolution of advice and consent, *see* Sam Nunn, *A Common-Sense Definition of "Common Understanding,"* 137 U. PENN. L. REV. 1523 (1989); Joseph R. Biden, Jr. & John B. Ritch III, *The Treaty Power: Upholding a Constitutional Partnership*, 137 U. PENN. L. REV. 1529 (1989); Michael J. Glennon, *The Constitutional Power of the United States Senate to Condition Its Consent to Treaties*, 67 CHICAGO KENT L. REV. 533 (1991).

For a note sympathetic to the Biden Condition, but suggesting a modified condition, *see* Gary Michael Buechler, *Constitutional Limits on the President's Power to Interpret Treaties: The Sofaer Doctrine, the Biden Condition, and the Doctrine of Binding Authoritative Representations*, 78 GEORGETOWN L. J. 1983 (1990). This note also discusses some of the subsequent positions effectively coerced from Judge Sofaer and the Executive Branch following the full court press on this issue against Judge Sofaer, the then Legal Adviser of the Department of State, and the threat of Senate non-consent to the INF Treaty. The most important of these Executive Branch statements, which, in some cases, are only marginally preferable to the Biden Condition itself, is the Letter from Arthur B. Culvahouse, Jr., White House Counsel, to Senator Michael G. Lugar (March 17, 1988); a statement effectively coerced from the Administration during Senate consideration of the INF Treaty at the height of the Biden Condition excitement. *See generally* on this letter and its background, JOHN NORTON MOORE, *supra* note *.

For the principal Congressional hearings on these issues, *see The ABM Treaty and the Constitution: Joint Hearings before the Committee on Foreign Relations and the Committee on the Judiciary, United States Senate*, 100th Cong. 1st Sess. (Comm. Print 1987).

guing it, and was apparently unaware that the only prior precedent was in his D.C. Circuit where, as we have seen, the Court of Appeals went the other way.[13] Even the United States Supreme Court became involved, again interestingly in a case where apparently the issues were not briefed or argued to the Court. Here, however, the test the Court seemed to apply, as opposed to an ambiguous footnote dictum attached to the majority opinion, was the traditional rule of treaty interpretation rooted in the intent of the parties. Further, two Justices, Kennedy and O'Connor joined in a concurring opinion in which they highlighted this issue as not even ready for implicit comment, and Justice Scalia concurring, explicitly rejected an approach to treaty interpretation rooted in the intent of the legislature of one of the parties rather than agreement between the parties.[14] Perhaps saddest of all, the *Restatement (Third) of the Foreign Relations Law of the United States* seems to give aid and comfort to this extraordinary new Senate assertion, although not focusing on the key issue, and almost certainly without embracing all of the effects I believe the doctrine would produce.[15] And an exuberant defense of the *Restatement (Third)* position against Justice Scalia's criticism of it in this Supreme Court battle of the dictum was featured in the pages of *The American Journal of International Law*, sadly, without alerting the reader to the real issue in what is a most serious struggle for the rule of law in United States treaty practice.[16]

It would be tempting to brand this Senate assertion of a new constitutional doctrine of its treaty powers as part of an all too frequent "neo-know-nothing-ism" in foreign policy that has produced, among other lapses, the

---

13 *See* Rainbow Navigation, Inc. v. Department of the Navy, 699 F. Supp. 339 (D.D.C. 1988) (merits). Importantly, this decision by Judge Harold H. Greene in Rainbow Navigation was overturned by a unanimous Court of Appeals which included Judge Ruth B. Ginsburg, now a Justice of the Supreme Court. *See* Rainbow Navigation, Inc. v. Department of the Navy, 911 F.2d 797 (D.C. Cir. 1990). The Court of Appeals did not address the constitutionality of "domestic conditions" but did apply the traditional treaty interpretation rule of "the intent or expectations of its signatories" to decide the case. 911 F.2d at 800. And it said in response to Judge Greene's argument that Executive Branch statements made during Senate consideration were binding: "Ambiguous ratification history cannot be allowed to obscure the meaning of clear Treaty language." 911 F.2d at 802. The Supreme Court denied certiorari in 1991. *See* 499 U.S. 906 (1991).

14 *See* United States v. Stuart, 489 U.S. 353 (1989). For a detailed analysis of this case, including its ambiguous footnote 7, the concurring opinions of Justices Kennedy and O'Connor, and the concurring opinion of Justice Scalia in which he emphasized that the appropriate standard for treaty interpretation is "what the two or more sovereigns agreed to, rather than what . . . the legislature of a single one of them, thought it agreed to" (489 U.S. 374), *see* John Norton Moore, *supra* note *. *See also* Part VI (C) of this article.

15 *See* RESTATEMENT (THIRD) OF THE FOREIGN RELATIONS LAW OF THE UNITED STATES § 303 cmt. d and Reporters' Note 4 and § 314 (2), cmts. b & d. *See also* cmt. a and Reporters' Note 1 to § 326.

16 *See* Detlev F. Vagts, *Senate Materials and Treaty Interpretation: Some Research Hints for the Supreme Court*, 83 AM. J. INT'L L. 546 (1989) (Editorial Comment).

non-payment of United States financial obligations to the United Nations. That, however, would be wrong, as paradoxically the original motivation of its movers in the Senate was to promote United States adherence to its treaty obligations. No doubt it was, at least in part, a product of a general resurgence of congressional activism in foreign affairs in a post-Vietnam era, in which we have seen similar congressional efforts to mark off turf in the war powers, treaty modalities, treaty termination, information flow, executive privilege, and the conduct and control of intelligence and secrecy matters.[17] That this background struggle between the branches is still with us is evidenced by the recent address of a Chairman of the Senate Foreign Relations Committee to the United Nations followed by hearings before the Senate Committee for foreign national representatives to the Security Council.[18] In the words of my colleague Robert F. Turner, we live in an age in which the original understanding concerning the primary authority of the President in foreign affairs has been lost as though there were a collective hard drive crash about previous conceptions of constitutional authority and practice.[19] Yet again, while playing a role, this too is not the principal source of the Senate asserted new doctrine. Rather, the principal source of the new doctrine takes meaning from the common law maxim "hard cases make bad law," or Mr. Justice Holmes's even more appropriate variation "great cases like hard cases make bad law." For this doctrine was rooted in the contentious great debate during the 1980s about the correct

---

17 Eugene V. Rostow, former Dean of the Yale Law School and a former Under Secretary of State and Director of the Arms Control and Disarmament Agency, concluded in his 1989 critique of Professor Koplow's support of the "dual" approach that "[the ABM interpretation debate] became part of the campaign by Congress and particularly by the Senate to take over large areas of presidential power in the field of foreign affairs." E. Rostow, *supra* note 12, at 1453.

18 That there was a problem with this hearing in United States foreign relations practice seems implicit in the thin veneer that such representatives were before the Committee solely in their individual capacities, a veneer not followed at least by the Representative of the Netherlands. In fairness to the Chairman of the Senate Foreign Relations Committee, these activities seem to have had the blessing, or even encouragement, of the Administration, and particu-larly the United States Ambassador to the United Nations.

19 Robert F. Turner, currently the Associate Director of the Center for National Security Law at the University of Virginia School of Law and formerly the Deputy Assistant Secretary of State for Congressional Relations, completed his SJD at Virginia on the respective powers of the President and Congress in foreign affairs, and has written and spoken widely on the separation of powers in foreign affairs. Indeed, he has written more on this issue than any other and is responsible for the modern "rediscovery" of the Executive power clause in art. II, § 1 of the Constitution. *See, e.g.*, ROBERT F. TURNER, NATIONAL SECURITY AND THE CONSTITUTION: AN INQUIRY INTO THE SEPARATION OF POWERS (unpublished 1996); ROBERT F. TURNER, *The Constitutional Framework for the Division of National Security Power Between the Congress, the President, and the Court*, *in* NATIONAL SECURITY LAW (John Norton Moore, Frederick S. Tipson & Robert F. Turner eds., 1990), ch. 17.

interpretation of the 1972 Anti-Ballistic Missile (ABM) Treaty with the then USSR, adopted in Salt I by President Richard Nixon.

This debate, which has come to be known as the "broad-narrow" debate about the meaning of the ABM Treaty, remains the single most complex and contentious legal debate in the history of United States foreign policy. It was truly a "great debate" in our national life. The core of the debate concerned whether it was legally permissible under the Treaty to test and develop mobile ABM systems based on "other physical principles" (OPP), such as lasers or particle beams. It occurred in the context of President Ronald Reagan's speech, dubbed "Star Wars" by the media, in which he raised the possibility of an effective missile defense of the United States, quite possibly involving space based, and thus mobile, ABM systems. At its height this debate had split both the Executive Branch and the Senate. It became most public and personalized, however, with respect to the debate between its two principal antagonists, Senator Sam Nunn and Judge Abraham Sofaer, both of whom produced massive analyses to support their positions. Senator Sam Nunn, the powerful Chairman of the Senate Armed Services Committee, supported by most academic commentary, most of the arms control community, and some of his colleagues in the Senate, believed that the correct legal interpretation was that testing and development of such OPP based mobile systems were not permitted, a view known as the "narrow" interpretation of the Treaty. Judge Sofaer, on the other hand, a former Federal District Judge and then Legal Adviser of the Department of State, supported by Senator Hollings, some arms control experts in the Administration, and some academics, believed that the correct legal interpretation permitted testing and development of OPP based mobile systems, a view known as the "broad" interpretation.[20]

The constitutional dimension of this debate was presented when proponents of the "narrow" view noticed that an Executive Branch spokesman had supported the "narrow" interpretation during the Senate consideration of the ABM Treaty and that several Senators seemed also to have held that view during the hearings or floor statements. In view of that record, Senator Nunn and other Senators strongly objected to the March 26, 1987, testimony of Judge Sofaer concerning these views to the effect that: "When . . . [the Senate] gives its advice and consent to a treaty, it is to the treaty that

---

20 This abstruse issue was made all the more difficult for even the expert observer by the ease with which it could be confused with issues of *research* on OPP based systems, mobile or fixed; development and testing of *fixed* land based systems, OPP based or otherwise; development, testing or deployment of *mobile systems not based on OPP*; *deployment* of OPP based mobile systems; and research, testing, development or deployment of *theater* systems, among other complexities all presenting different issues under the ABM Treaty.

was made, irrespective of explanations it is provided."[21] This was taken as a denigration of the Senate's role in advice and consent, requiring response. And, of course, the existence of a separate constitutional argument for their conclusion on the merits offered an additional and independent argument for their position, regardless of the underlying dispute about the correct international legal interpretation. That is, if the proper constitutional standard for treaty interpretation is the view believed to be correct by the Senate during advice and consent hearings, or even the view of an Executive Branch spokesman or individual Senators during such hearings, as opposed to the internationally binding meaning rooted in the intent of the treaty parties, then this would serve as an alternate basis for their position and would also, they seemed to believe, give proper deference to the Senate role. Since they believed the correct international legal interpretation was the "narrow" interpretation they believed this new doctrine would also serve the rule of law in United States adherence to the ABM Treaty. They did not seriously reflect, as far as I can tell, on the fact that, regardless of the correct interpretation of the ABM Treaty in the "broad-narrow" dispute, this new doctrine would only have legal effect where it *differed* from the correct international legal interpretation, and that in those settings where it mattered, it would either require the United States to violate its treaty obligations or hold the United States to a higher obligation than bargained for under the treaty. It was this highly charged legal debate, and a climate in which proponents believed they were serving the rule of law, which almost certainly triggered the attention of Judge Harold Greene in the *Rainbow Navigation* case,[22] and which subsequently was likely responsible for the peripheral debate in dictum within the Supreme Court in the *Stuart* case.[23] Sadly, proponents of the new constitutional doctrine in treaty interpretation seem not to have understood in any of these settings the real legal effect of the new doctrine as undermining rather than supporting the rule of law.

A second ingredient in the mix leading to the new Senate espoused doctrine is a little noticed debate going back to apparently still the only case to have fully argued and addressed the authority of the Senate to attach "domestic conditions," that is, those affecting only domestic law, to a treaty before the Senate. This case, the *Niagara Reservation* case, was decided in the Court of Appeals for the District of Columbia Circuit in 1957, and, as has

21 *See* the letter from Senators Robert C. Byrd and Sam Nunn to Secretary of State George P. Shultz, Feb. 5, 1988, *reprinted in* JOHN NORTON MOORE, *supra* note *.

22 Rainbow Navigation, Inc. v. Department of the Navy, *supra* note 13. For a full discussion of the interrelation of the decision by Judge Harold Greene in this case with the then "broad-narrow" debate about the ABM Treaty, *see* JOHN NORTON MOORE, *supra* note*.

23 United States v. Stuart, *supra* note 14.

been seen, Judge Bazelon wrote an opinion for the two-to-one majority holding that even a clear reservation by the Senate concerning domestic law had no legal effect.[24] This case seems, at least indirectly, to have pitted Professors Philip C. Jessup and Oliver J. Lissitzyn, then senior international law faculty at Columbia, against Professor Louis Henkin, then a more junior member of the faculty but one who became one of the Nation's top experts on the foreign relations law of the United States. Professors Jessup and Lissitzyn argued in a lengthy brief for the New York Power Authority in the case that: "the operation of a treaty as the supreme law of the land cannot be dissociated from its existence as an agreement or contract between nations. . . ."[25] Professor Henkin, however, in a law review article dated before the decision of the Court and cited favorably by the dissenting Justice, disagreed and posed "several grounds for questioning the conclusion that the provision [the domestic condition] . . . is invalid."[26] Some years later, the *Restatement (Third) of the Foreign Relations Law of the United States*, with Professor Henkin as Chief Reporter, adopted the views that: "The Senate may also give its consent on conditions that do not require change in the treaty but relate to its domestic application . . . .",[27] and:

> When the Senate gives its advice and consent to a treaty on the basis of a particular understanding of its meaning, the President, if he makes the treaty, must do so on the basis of the Senate's understanding.[28]

---

24 Power Authority of the State of New York v. Federal Power Commission (the Niagara Reservation case), *supra* note 8.

25 P. Jessup & O. Lissitzyn, Opinion of Philip C. Jessup and Oliver J. Lissitzyn With Respect to the United States Senate's Attempt to Repeal the Federal Power Act in its Relation to the Niagara Through the Use of the Treaty-Making Power (Power Authority of the State of New York, Dec. 1955).

26 *See* Louis Henkin, *The Treaty Makers and the Law Makers: The Niagara Reservation*, 56 Col. L. Rev. 1151, 1181-82 (1956).

27 Restatement (Third) of the Foreign Relations Law of the United States § 303 cmt. d (1987). This comment does seem to limit the scope of such domestic conditions to those "having plausible relation to the treaty," although it does not explain how a power rooted in "the Senate's constitutional authority to grant or withhold consent to a treaty" (as explained in Reporters' Note 4 to § 303) which it seems to regard as the basis of this power, can be so limited. Nor does it seem to be aware of the implications of even this test that, for example, the Senate could attach domestic implementing legislation to its resolution of advice and consent. This would seem likely a considerable surprise to the House of Representatives, which has assumed it had a role to play in such domestic implementing legislation.

28 Restatement (Third) of the Foreign Relations Law of the United States § 314 (2) (1987). *See also* § 339 cmt. a, which takes the position that the Senate could condition a treaty on requiring the consent of Congress or the Senate for termination of the treaty. This further assertion of a Senate "domestic condition" power is accompanied by an even more startling conclusion in relation to the asserted subsequent termination power of the Senate. In connection with this termination power, the *Restatement* fails to address the question of whether such a *unilateral Senate treaty terminating power* would be exercised by a simple majority, or a two-thirds majority, of the Senate and, if by a

Thus, the new *Restatement (Third)* seems to tilt toward both at least some Senate lawmaking power to attach "domestic conditions" to treaties, and that even informal Senate understandings as to the meaning of a treaty, not embodied in the Senate resolution of advice and consent, would be binding. Again, however, there is no identification or discussion of the real crunch issue for the rule of law, that is, which interpretation governs when the Senate and internationally correct interpretations differ.

The "dual" approach to treaty interpretation under the foreign relations law of the United States, that is, an approach that would follow a conventional approach under our international legal obligations and, if it differed, an approach based on Senate intent as binding on both the President and domestic courts, is wrong as a matter of both law and good policy as to what that law ought to be. The correct approach is that there is but a "unitary" standard for treaty interpretation under the foreign relations law of the United States and that standard is coextensive with the international legal standard for assessing the obligations of the Nation. I believe also that this issue is of the utmost importance for the rule of law among nations. And, as an issue raised incidentally by this primary "unitary-dual" theory debate, I believe that the Senate does not have an independent lawmaking power to attach "domestic conditions" to treaties during the advice and consent process.[29] When these issues are squarely presented to the United

---

majority, how it would be consistent in general with the treaty power approval requirement or, if by a two-thirds majority, how it would be consistent with the Framers' intention to make it difficult to enter into treaties as opposed to exiting from them. This is yet an additional difficulty with the theory that the Senate has general domestic lawmaking power attached to its treaty advice and consent power as espoused in the treaty termination setting by the *Restatement*.

29 The one exception may be the ability of the Senate to declare a treaty non-self-executing, that is, as requiring subsequent legislation for domestic lawmaking effect. In general, I believe that the best standard for determining whether a treaty is self-executing is also the intent of the parties, but this seems to be a sufficiently *sui generis* category as to make an exception at least arguable. Most such statements by the Senate concerning the self-executing effect of a treaty, of course, would seem to fall within one of the categories of settings where there would be no separate legal effect under domestic law varying from the treaty itself. Thus, to the extent that the Senate statement that the treaty is non-self-executing is simply consistent with the intent of the parties under the treaty, it is not really a reflection of a separate domestic lawmaking power. Similarly, if the statement is conveyed to the other treaty parties and accepted by them as an accurate description of the treaty it simply reflects the normal process of treaty approval. Finally, if the statement reflects a highly visible requirement under the Constitution, for example, perhaps the art. I, § 7 requirement concerning the House role in raising revenues, which then meets the Vienna Convention requirement of "manifest and concerned a rule of its internal law of fundamental importance," again, there would be no discrepancy between the international treaty obligation and the Senate statement. Moreover, as noted in the dissent in the *Power Authority* case, the effect of even a self-executing real domestic condition is generally not to permanently bypass the constitutional framework for lawmaking by the House and the Senate and presentment

States Supreme Court, I believe they will reach these same conclusions. The remaining sections will discuss these issues, which most sharply arose in this emotive "Dionysian moment" of the great ABM Treaty interpretation debate.

---

to the President, but rather to postpone the domestic legal effect of the treaty pending such subsequent legislative action.

To the contrary, however, it should be noted, even on this question of a limited domestic condition power to declare a treaty non-self executing, that the only case to yet address this issue, the *Power Authority of the State of New York v. Federal Power Commission* (the *Niagara Reservation* case), set out above, declared a domestic condition as of no legal effect even though it related solely to whether the treaty with Canada would be self-executing or would take effect in the United States only subsequent to an Act of Congress, and even though it was a special variant of a Senate non-self-executing condition actually conveyed to the other party as a formal "reservation" and so accepted by the other party. This may well be the better rule even with respect to this limited form of "condition." Further, one problem with Senate non-self-executing conditions when inconsistent with the intent of the parties that the treaty be self-executing but not conveyed to and accepted by the other treaty parties, is that such conditions may place the United States in violation of its international legal obligations, at least if subsequent implementing legislation is unreasonably delayed or never enacted. For a fuller discussion of non-self-executing "domestic condition" issues, *see* the text at section IV(D) of this article.

There has been increasing criticism directed at Senate declarations to the effect that particular treaties are not self-executing, on the grounds that the Senate has in many such cases not acted consistent with the treaty or any other basis viewed as appropriate. *See*, for example, Lori Fisler Damrosch, *The Role of the United States Senate Concerning "Self-Executing" and "Non-Self-Executing" Treaties*, 67 CHI.-KENT L. REV. 515 (1991). And for a clear rejection of the power of the Senate with respect even to "non-self-executing" "domestic conditions," *see* Stefan A. Riesenfeld & Frederick M. Abbott, The Scope of U.S. Senate Control Over the Conclusion and Operation of Treaties, 67 CHI.-KENT L. REV. 571 (1991). *See also* Thomas Burgenthal, *Modern Constitutions and Human Rights Treaties*, 36 COLUM. J. TRANSNAT'L L. 211, 222, n.36 (1997); Jordan J. Paust, *Customary International Law and Human Rights Treaties Are Law in the United States*, 20 MICH. J. INT'L L. 301, 324-35 (1999).

Professor Malvina Halberstam takes the position that "a non-self-executing declaration with respect to a treaty (or treaty provision) that would be self-executing by its terms is a violation of Article VI of the Constitution." Letter of December 5, 2000, from Professor Malvina Halberstam to the author (on file at the University of Virginia School of Law). And *see* Malvina Halberstam, *United States Ratification of the Convention on the Elimination of All Forms of Discrimination Against Women*, 31 GE. WASH. J. OF INT'L LAW & ECONOMICS 49, 64-70 (1997).

For the *Restatement* view as to when an international agreement of the United States is "non-self-executing," *see* § 111 (4). RESTATEMENT (THIRD) OF THE FOREIGN RELATIONS LAW OF THE UNITED STATES § 111(4) (1987). The *Restatement* specifically adopts the position that the Senate may give its consent on the domestic condition "that the treaty shall not be self-executing." *See id.* at § 303, cmt. d. Its flat comment here provides no immediate cross-reference to the *Niagara Reservation* case, which held to the contrary, as even ambiguously discussed in § 303, Reporters' Note 4.

For a thoughtful analysis of policy issues in a combination of treaties as both "self-executing" and of "higher status . . . than later-enacted statutory law," the latter of which is not the United States rule, *see* John H. Jackson, *Status of Treaties in Domestic Legal Systems: A Policy Analysis*, 86 AM. J. INT'L L. 310 (1992).

A more recent debate about the self-executing and non-self-executing nature of treaties has been triggered by Professor John C. Yoo, who has argued, initially based largely on his analysis of the origins of the treaty power in the Constitutional Convention and the state ratification debates, and subsequently in rejoinder to criticism advancing textual and structural arguments, that despite the Supremacy Clause, treaties were not intended to be self-executing. That is, he seems to be arguing for a rule analogous to that in the United Kingdom in which treaties must be incorporated into domestic law through subsequent Acts of Parliament. *See* John C. Yoo, *Globalism and the Constitution: Treaties, Non-Self-Execution, and the Original Understanding*, 99 COL. L. REV. 1955 (1999); and John C. Yoo, *Treaties and Public Lawmaking: A Textual and Structural Defense of Non-Self-Execution*, 99 COL. L. REV. 2218 (1999). I regard this admittedly "revisionist" thesis about the foreign relations law of the United States, as with many such "revisionist" theses generally, as *clearly* wrong as a statement of the law (as this article urges in Part III [A] constitutional interpretation involves more than historical analysis, and certainly includes the principal flow of decisions of the United States Supreme Court and constitutional practice). It is also *clearly* wrong as to what the law ought to be, and historically inaccurate as to the author's principal conclusion. For example, there is a huge difference between Madison's understanding that the reality of the legislative power in Congress would serve to "influence" the exercise of the treaty power, and Yoo's at least initial implication that contrary to the clear text of the Supremacy Clause, treaties were never intended to have direct effect in the courts of the United States. For a rebuttal to the Yoo thesis, *see, e.g.*, Carlos Manuel Vazquez, *Laughing At Treaties*, 99 Col. L. Rev. 2154 (1999). A core effort in the now quaintly dated Bricker Amendment debate of the early 1950s was to prevent treaties from ever being self-executing, as well as overturning Missouri v. Holland, 252 U.S. 416 (1920), as to the scope of the federal treaty power. Hopefully, not every generation has to refight this battle, whether presented as a proposal for a constitutional amendment, as in the Bricker debate, or as a newly discovered constitutional interpretation which escaped the Bricker generation. For the testimony of the then Administration in opposition to the Bricker Amendment, *see* the Statement by the Honorable Herbert Brownell, Jr., Attorney General of the United States, before the Senate Committee on the Judiciary, on S. J. Res. 1 & S. J. Res. 43, 83d Cong., 1st Sess. (April 7, 1953), *reprinted in* TREATIES AND EXECUTIVE AGREEMENTS, HEARINGS BEFORE A SUBCOMMITTEE OF THE COMMITTEE ON THE JUDICIARY, UNITED STATES SENATE, 83d Cong., 1st Sess., on S. J. Res. 1 & S. J. Res. 43 at 901-34 (with interspersed comments from Committee members and a further dialogue on pages 934-47) (1953). The concern reflected in the ratification debates about avoiding a general legislative power lodged in the Senate via the treaty power, as opposed to the constitutional legislative process, and the concern as to the protection of state interests, however, *would* seem to support the conclusion of this article that there is no general unilateral "domestic conditions" lawmaking power in the Senate incident to the treaty advice and consent power. *See* the discussion in Part IV of this article.

II.
Issues and Non-Issues: The Wheat, the Chaff, and the Hidden Virus

So much confusion has surrounded the debate about treaty interpretation and the Constitution, and there has been so little understanding of the really important core of the issue, that it is useful to briefly state what the debate is *not* about as well as what it *is* about.

The debate is not really about whether United States Courts have cited or referred to Senate materials in treaty interpretation cases. They have, and the collection of cases breathlessly revealed by Professor Detlev Vagts in his uncharacteristic tilting at the windmill of overly broad language in Justice Scalia's concurring opinion in the *Stuart* case contain examples.[30] It is no more remarkable for United States courts to refer to Senate materials than it is for them to refer to law review articles or scholarly treatises. The question is whether in either case they do so because they regard the issue for decision as turning on the intent of the review or treatise writer or the intent of the Senate, as opposed, in an interpretation case, to the intent of the parties. The former *would* be truly remarkable in a treaty interpretation case and is not born out by Professor Vagts's cases. But Senate materials, as with law review articles or treatises, may contain the transmittal message of the President to the Senate, the Department of State article by article analysis of the treaty, statements of negotiators as to meaning, evidence of practical construction by the parties or other relevant information concerning the intent of the parties. Citing or referring to such materials in Senate sources is simply to use a convenient source for quite ordinary interpretative materials. Because of the potential for misperception of this editorial comment in the *American Journal* by so able a scholar as Professor Vagts, I will revisit his

30 *See* Detlev F. Vagts, *Senate Materials and Treaty Interpretation: Some Research Hints for the Supreme Court*, 83 Am. J. Int'l L. 546 (1989). *See, e.g.*, Immigration and Naturalization Service v. Stevic, 467 U.S. 407 (1984) (although not itself principally a treaty interpretation case). *See* the discussion of *Stevic*, infra Part VI (E) of this article. For a full discussion of Justice Scalia's concurring opinion in *Stuart* and Professor Vagts's comment on it, *see infra* Parts VI (C), (D), and (E) of this article.

comment later in this article, despite the trivial importance of the point it makes in the overall debate.[31]

Nor is the debate about whether the record of Senate non-formal action in consideration of a treaty is entitled to *no weight* in treaty interpretation. Any competent international lawyer, familiar with the looseness of Articles 31-33 of the Vienna Convention on the Law of Treaties, generally said to reflect customary international law in treaty interpretation, can find a host of ways to get before even an international Court most relevant information from such settings.[32] For example, the need to take it into account to establish a "special meaning" of a term, or where an interpretation otherwise "leaves the meaning ambiguous or obscure." Again, however, this is *not* the

31 Indeed, apparently a number of writers did uncritically accept the Vagts critique of Justice Scalia's separate opinion in the *Stuart* case, focused by Professor Vagts on a single sentence excerpted out of the full context of the Justice's opinion, and thus miss the real story in the *Stuart* case of the cardinal plea made by Justice Scalia for the rule of law. *See, e.g.*, Daniel M. Price, *Summary Casenote on* United States v. Stuart, in Peter D. Trooboff, *International Decisions*, 83 AM. J. INT'L L. 918, 923 & 923 notes 32 and * (1989) ("an associate reporter of the *Restatement* has found much to fault in Justice Scalia's reasoning and research.") (The casenote author notes in a footnote, however, "[t]hese views of the author, who recently joined the Office of the United States Trade Representative, are not necessarily those of the U.S. Government."); Nicholas S. Zeppos, *Legislative History and the Interpretation of Statutes: Toward a Fact-Finding Model of Statutory Interpretation*, 76 VA. L. REV. 1295, 1297 n.9 (1990) (*See* Vagts "[f]or an insightful critique of Justice Scalia's use of textualism in treaty cases. . . .") (This article is focused on statutory interpretation and is devoid of any discussion of the real issues in *Stuart*). Hans W. Baade, *"Original Intent" in Historical Perspective: Some Critical Glosses*, 69 TEXAS L. REV. 1001, 1102-03 n. 727 (1991) ("Mr. Justice Scalia's acknowledgment of inability to discover a single case in which the Court had consulted the Senate debate, committee hearings, or committee reports was bitingly castigated by Vagts. . . .") (Professor Baade, however, judged that the majority in *Stuart* referred to Senate debates in aid of interpretation, not to ascertain the intent only of the United States, but rather that of both treaty parties. And, unlike the Vagts analysis, he perceptively singled out for quotation the core of Justice Scalia's concern that "whatever extra-textual materials are consulted must be materials that reflect the mutual agreement (for example, the negotiating history) rather than a unilateral understanding."); Stephen B. Burbank, *The World in Our Courts*, 89 MICH. L. REV. 1456, 1479 n.121 (1991) (*See* Vagts "[f]or an amusing and convincing demonstration that Justice Scalia needs help in his campaign to ban resort to 'pre-ratification Senate materials for the interpretation of a treaty.'") (This reference *en passant* to the Vagts critique is devoid of any discussion of the real issues in *Stuart*. Paradoxically, the author expresses concern for "the costs of dishonoring our treaty obligations" [1480 n.132] and says "treaties partake of the nature of contracts." [1480]). *See* the discussion of the Scalia opinion and the Vagts editorial comment in Parts VI (C), (D) and (E) of this article.

32 Professor W. Michael Reisman, one of the Nation's top international lawyers, points out in this connection:

> International law does not have restrictive rules of admissibility. In my view, *anything* aired in advice and consent procedures that becomes available is going to be used in international performance interpretation. Of course, in all matters of evidence, questions of admissibility are distinct from those of credibility and weight.

W. Michael Reisman, *Necessary and Proper: Executive Competence to Interpret Treaties*, 15 YALE INT'L L. J. 316, 322 (1990).

same as looking at the Senate materials for the purpose of ascertaining the Senate intent of one of the parties as the basis for decision, as opposed to the shared intent of all the parties, as is well established under both international law and the foreign relations law of the United States.[33]

Conversely, the issue is not whether materials not before the Senate during advice and consent can be taken into account in treaty interpretation. Of course they can, and United States Courts have repeatedly done so. The implication to the contrary of early testimony during Senate hearings in the context of the "broad-narrow" dispute by Professor Laurence Tribe is both uninformed as to the foreign relations law of the United States and plain silly.[34] Indeed, *travaux* and foreign language texts are not reliably before the

---

33 There are, of course, continuing debates concerning the best approaches for interpreting statutes or constitutions or ascertaining the shared intent of treaty parties, including particularly the weight to be given to "text" and full "context," and these debates continue apace in both international and domestic law. That is, again, not the core issue here. Rather, the issue is whether the referent for interpretation is the intent of the Senate or an Executive statement to the Senate of one of the parties, or the shared expectations of *all* the parties.

34 Professor Tribe says in his prepared statement for the ABM Treaty interpretation resolution hearings:

> Whatever one's view as to the proper place of legislative history that is theoretically public but practically unavailable, there can be but one answer to the question of what place an indisputably secret negotiating history can have in the meaning of any law—whether domestic legislation passed by Congress and signed by the President or passed by a two-thirds vote over his veto, or a treaty negotiated by the President and consented to by a two-thirds vote of the Senate. *Such secret histories cannot be taken into account because they were not part of the record on which the legally decisive votes were taken.*

Prepared Statement of Laurence H. Tribe, *in* THE ABM TREATY AND THE CONSTITUTION: JOINT HEARINGS BEFORE THE SENATE COMMS. ON FOREIGN RELATIONS AND ON THE JUDICIARY, 100th Cong., 1st Sess. 412, 416 (1987) (emphasis added).

One commentator characterizes Professor Tribe as arguing "that treaties constitute a contract between the executive and the Senate, and that the intent of only those parties can determine its meaning." Paul B. Stephan III, *Revisiting the Incorporation Debate: The Role of Domestic Political Structure*, 31 VA. J. INT'L L. 417 (1991) (footnote omitted with the reference to Professor Tribe's testimony in relation to the ABM "broad-narrow" dispute cited above. Professor Stephan adds a "[b]ut see" reference in this footnote to Eastern Airlines, Inc. v. Floyd 499 U.S. 530 (1991), and adds a commentary to this *Floyd* case describing it as "interpreting treaty by reference to understanding of other State Parties and the negotiating history").

Eastern Airlines v. Floyd, is, in fact, a superb example, and post *Stuart*, of a unanimous Supreme Court applying the French text of a treaty, its negotiating history, subsequent practice, the meaning of the treaty terms in question under French law (including an analysis of French treatises and scholarly writing), and even interpretations of the treaty by another signatory. Moreover, the Court used these materials in its interpretation after pointing out merely that an English translation of the text had been before the Senate when it ratified the Convention in 1934. There is no revisiting of footnote 7 from the *Stuart* case nor any apparent inquiry as to whether these other materials were before the Senate. 499 U.S. at 535-52.

Senate,[35] and subsequent practice, by its very nature, is rarely before the Senate. Yet these sources are frequently taken into account in treaty interpretation. Thus, the decision of the Supreme Court in the 1985 case of *Air France v. Saks*[36] referred extensively to the *travaux préparatoires* of the Warsaw Convention, and specifically it looked to the French text of that Convention even though it pointed out that the official American translation of the text was before the Senate when it ratified the Convention. The Court said: "We look to the French legal meaning for guidance as to these expectations [the shared expectations of the contracting parties] because the Warsaw Convention was drafted in French by continental jurists."[37] Similarly, in 1967 in *Block v. Compagnie Nationale Air France*,[38] the United States Court of Appeals for the Fifth Circuit declared that "[t]he binding meaning

---

Professor Tribe also might want to read the article by Professor Bederman reviewing the extensive use by the Supreme Court of *travaux préparatoires* and evidence of subsequent practice, as well as the view of the Executive Branch, in treaty interpretation cases. *See* David J. Bederman, *Revivalist Canons and Treaty Interpretation*, 41 UCLA L. Rev. 953, 992-96, 1002-1006 (1994). Professor Bederman describes the use of subsequent practice in treaty interpretation cases as "now an accepted tool of treaty interpretation." *Id.* at 972. This article also provides a useful overview of treaty interpretation practice and issues.

35 One of the best descriptions of records concerning Senate consideration of treaties is contained in the Introduction to 1 Christian L. Wiktor, Unperfected Treaties of the United States of America (1976). Christian Wiktor writes concerning foreign language texts in Senate executive documents:

> The printed text includes the English version only. The foreign language text was included during the years 1825 to the mid 1860's, but was then discontinued.

Id. at xx.

36 470 U.S. 392 (1985).

37 470 U.S. 392, 399 (and *compare with* 397). Elihu Root, one of the most experienced international law and foreign policy experts the United States has produced, made an elegant speech to the Senate in 1914 reflecting the importance of *travaux* and full context in treaty interpretation. He urged:

> If you would be sure of what a treaty means, if there be any doubt, if there are two interpretations suggested, learn out of what conflicting public policies the words of the treaty had their birth; what arguments were made for one side or the other, what concessions were yielded in the making of a treaty. Always, with rare exceptions, the birth and development of every important clause may be traced by the authentic records of the negotiators and of the countries which are reconciling their differences.

Speech in the Senate by Elihu Root (May 21, 1914), *quoted in* 2 C. C. Hyde, International Law Chiefly as Interpreted and Applied By the United States, 1471-72 n.3 (2d rev. ed. 1947). This statement is a far cry from urging that treaties should be interpreted, not by the intent of the parties, but rather by the intent of the Senate of one of the parties, or that materials, including *travaux*, not before the Senate can not be taken into account in treaty interpretation. Elihu Root would likely turn in his grave at either prospect.

38 386 F.2d 323 (1967).

of the terms [of the Warsaw Convention] is the French legal meaning,"[39] even though it simultaneously noted that "the text that was read to the Senate, and to which the resolution of ratification was directed, was a text in English originally published in a Treaty Information Bulletin of the Department of State."[40] And, of course, the fifty year pattern of subsequent practice considered by the Supreme Court in, among other cases, the 1984 decision in *Trans World Airlines, Inc. v. Franklin Mint Corp.*,[41] clearly took into account information not before the Senate when it gave its advice and consent to the Warsaw Convention in 1934.[42] The opinion of Mr. Justice Brennan, writing for the Supreme Court in the *Stuart* case, also expressly relies on subsequent practice, as well as the meaning attributed to treaty provisions by government agencies charged with their negotiation and enforcement, without inquiring whether such materials were before a consenting Senate. Indeed, they almost certainly were not. Just how seriously out of touch the Tribe view is with the historic practice of the Supreme Court in considering a wide range of materials in treaty interpretation without inquiry as to whether they were before the Senate, is indicated by an excerpt from the classic compendium of United States international practice by Charles Cheney Hyde.[43] He writes in a section on treaty interpretation focused specifically on "The Attitude of the Supreme Court of the United States":[44] "the conclusions of the Court as to the designs of contracting States have been expressed in terms revealing deference for what the evidence established rather than for any other consideration."[45] And with respect to "Preparatory Work" he says:

> The Supreme Court is not disposed to forbid recourse to, or to decline itself to rely upon, diplomatic exchanges or correspondence indicating the views of negotiators of a treaty. . . . The significant thing is the readiness with which the Court turns to such forms of preparatory work as reasonable and applicable sources of interpretation. It relied upon them, for example, in construing Article II of the treaty with Russia of March 30, 1867, providing for the cession of Alaska; Article III of the treaty with Spain of February 22, 1819, establishing the boundary west of the Mississippi . . . ; Article I of the treaty with Japan of April 5, 1911; Article VII of the treaty with Denmark of April 26, 1826; and Article I of the extradition convention with Great Britain of July 12, 1889. In the case of *Cook v. United States*, decided January 23, 1933, the Court made fullest use of data leading up to the conclusion of the con-

---

39 386 F.2d 323, 330.

40 386 F.2d 323, 330 n.19.

41 466 U.S. 243 (1984).

42 *See also* Day v. Trans World Airlines, Inc., 528 F.2d 31, 35-36 (1975).

43 2 C. C. HYDE, *supra* note 37.

44 2 C. C. HYDE, *supra* note 37, at 1478.

45 2 C. C. Hyde, *supra* note 37, at 1481 (footnote omitted).

vention with Great Britain for the Prevention of Smuggling of Intoxicating Liquors of January 23, 1924, as an effectual means of ascertaining the design of the contracting parties.[46]

The Tribe view is also inconsistent with the *Restatement of the Foreign Relations Law of the United States*, which does not restrict materials to be taken into account in treaty interpretation solely to those known to or before the Senate during consideration of advice and consent.[47] Finally, at least prior to 1919, during a period when the normal Senate practice was to consider treaties in closed session, apparently such consideration did not produce a full, if any, public record of Senate deliberations that normally would be available to a subsequent decision-maker in the interpretive process. That is, during the constitutionally formative period of the treaty power, the normal mode of Senate consideration itself did not even produce a public record as thought of today. Indeed, it was not until the 97th Congress in 1981 that Senate treaty history became routinely and broadly

---

46 2 C. C. Hyde, *supra* note 37, at 1482 (footnotes omitted). There is no indication from Hyde that the Court used these materials in interpretation only after ascertaining that they were before the Senate during consideration of advice and consent. Hyde further shows that the Court did not hesitate to use a Spanish language version of a treaty over the English version. *Id.* at 1484. And he further points out: "[i]t may well be doubted whether the views of particular departments of a government, such as the legislative or executive, long subsequent to the negotiation and conclusion of a treaty are necessarily probative of the sense in which terms were employed when the arrangement was consummated." *Id.* at 1485 (footnote omitted).

In *United States v. Percheman*, 32 U.S. (7 Pet.) 51 (1833), Justice Marshall, writing for the Court, relied on the Spanish version of an 1819 treaty of amity, settlement and limits with Spain, changing his position first enunciated in *Foster and Elam v. Neilson*, 27 U.S. (2 Pet.) 253 (1829), then relying on the English version of the treaty. In doing so, Justice Marshall said:

> In the case of Foster v. Elam, 2 Peters, 253, this court considered these words as importing contract. The Spanish part of the treaty was not then brought to our view, and we then supposed that there was no variance between them. We did not suppose that there was even a formal difference of expression in the same instrument, drawn up in the language of each party. Had this circumstance been known, we believe it would have produced the construction which we now give to the article.

27 U.S. at 89. In doing so, Justice Marshall made no inquiry as to whether the Spanish version of the treaty had been presented to the Senate with the English version. Indeed, since the treaty was ratified by the United States in 1821, any Senate consideration preceded the period of 1825 to the mid 1860s, which Christian Wiktor says was a period in which foreign language texts of treaties were included in Senate executive documents. *See* Christian Wiktor, *supra* note 35, at xx.

47 *See* Restatement (Third) of the Foreign Relations Law of the United States (1987). Reporters' Note 5 to § 325 does not restrict such materials to those before the Senate. Similarly, the comments to § 325 include a cornucopia of materials to be taken into account in treaty interpretation, with no restriction appearing that they must have been before the Senate. These include the Vienna Convention Article 31(2) concept of context of agreement (cmt. b), subsequent practice and interpretations by the parties (cmt. c), *travaux préparatoires* (cmt. e), and non-English language texts (cmt. f).

available to the public through inclusion in the Serial Set and the depository library program.[48]

---

48 According to Christian Wiktor: "Treaties are considered in the Senate first as in the Committee of the Whole. Since 1919 the sessions have usually been open." Christian Wiktor, *supra* note 35, at *xiv*. Wiktor also notes: "All major hearings are printed, as well as many less important ones. The first printed hearing appears to be those held on the Commercial Convention with Cuba of December 11, 1902." Christian Wiktor, *supra* note 35, at *xiii*.

The Librarian of the United States Senate confirms that hearings on treaties "as a printed item" seem to be available roughly from the turn of the Twentieth Century. There is, for example, a "CONFIDENTIAL" "Report No. 1 Executive" concerning "Cession of Danish Islands in the West Indies" from the Committee on Foreign Relations of the 57th Congress, 1st Session of Feb. 5, 1902. Early Senate action in consideration of treaties was apparently recorded in summary form in the *Journal of the Executive Proceedings of the United States Senate*. Conversation of the author with Gregory Harness, Librarian of the United States Senate, November 8, 2000.

The Introduction to the *CIS Index to US Senate Executive Documents and Reports* gives the following description of the arcane practice with respect to the record of Senate consideration of treaties and the significance of the 1981 changes:

> Prior to 1930, documents and reports issued before a treaty was ratified or a nomination was confirmed were usually considered as confidential when printed. Consequently, they were rarely distributed beyond a small circle of Senators and Presidential assistants. Those printed subsequent to 1930 were not considered confidential, but remained nondepository items and continued to be printed and distributed in limited numbers. In addition, although the Senate assigned them document and report numbers from the second quarter of the nineteenth century onward, this numbering was inconsistent, and the collection was never catalogued or indexed.
>
> The lack of control, combined with the tendency to shroud these documents in confidentiality and print them in small numbers, has rendered historical Senate Executive Documents and Reports virtually inaccessible. Outside of Washington, D.C., they survive only as very incomplete holdings in a few historical library collections.
>
> . . . .
>
> . . . the Senate established two series of Executive Documents: one published in the Serial Set composed of materials on executive branch matters in general; and a separate series composed of confidential materials exclusively concerned with treaties and nominations.
>
> The dualism in the Senate's use of "Executive Documents" ended in 1895. At that time, as part of a general reform of publishing and distribution policies, the Senate began publishing broadly defined executive materials included in the Serial Set as "Senate Documents," while continuing to print executive materials relating to treaties and nominations as "Senate Executive Documents and Reports", not included in the Serial Set. (By that date, some 4,772 Senate Executive Documents had been published in the Serial Set, with only a small percentage concerning *nonconfidential* treaties and nominations. These publications are excluded from this index, as they are covered in the *CIS U.S. Serial Set Index* and companion microfiche collection.
>
> Reports of Senate Committees on Presidential Messages became Senate Executive Reports. Unlike the Senate Executive Documents, however, Senate Executive Reports had no like-named counterpart in the Serial Set.

Further reflecting on this erroneous view expressed by Professor Tribe during the height of the ABM treaty interpretation debate, the author has observed in over a quarter of a century of working on constitutional issues in foreign relations that all too frequently some of the Nation's most respected constitutional generalists get it wrong when talking about constitutional issues concerning the foreign relations law of the United States.[49] To provide

---

> Prior to the Civil War, the Senate began to experiment with various systems of sequential numbers for Executive Documents and Executive Reports. The need for a controlled system of identifying numbers was clear and by the post-Civil War era the system had settled basically into the current pattern of assigning sequential letters to treaty documents for each session and sequential numbers to executive reports for each Congress.
>
> In 1914, the Senate passed a Resolution in which it mandated more uniform control over the collection by organizing Senate Executive Documents and Reports into a set of "Regular Confidential Documents". At that time, the Senate ordered the Government Printing Office to print and bind fifty sets of all Executive Documents and Reports issued from the earliest Congresses. Thereafter, the "Regular Confidential Documents" series was maintained on a Congress-by-Congress basis.
>
> In 1930, the Senate lifted the injunction of secrecy from the Documents and Reports as they were printed. However, the Senate continued to exclude these items from the U.S. Serial Set and did not designate them for distribution to depository libraries. Thus, despite their newly unclassified status, their distribution remained very limited.
>
> At the beginning of the 97th Congress in 1981, the Senate replaced the old Executive Documents series with Treaty Documents and revised the numbering scheme to parallel that of Senate Documents in the Serial Set. Treaty Documents include the same type of information as their predecessors. The Senate also continued to issue Senate Executive Reports in their old format. Most significantly, however, the Senate at long last began to include the Documents and Reports in the Serial Set and in the depository library program. After 190 years of relative obscurity, these materials finally became routinely available to the public.

CIS *INDEX* TO US SENATE EXECUTIVE DOCUMENTS & REPORTS COVERING DOCUMENTS AND REPORTS NOT PRINTED IN THE US SERIAL SET 1817-1969, vii, viii-ix.

49 Other examples, just to pick on top constitutionalists, would include Professor John Hart Ely's failure to even discuss the general grant of "The executive Power" in Article II, section 1, as a basis of Presidential power in foreign affairs in his important work on the war powers. It would be understandable, even if wrong, to argue against this grant of power as including the general foreign affairs power. But given the views of Madison, Hamilton, Jefferson, Washington and Jay, to the contrary, it seems simply indefensible to not even raise the issue. *See* JOHN HART ELY, WAR AND RESPONSIBILITY (1993). Ely writes: "Article II grants the president but four powers bearing on foreign relations—the power to receive ambassadors (which is his alone), the powers to appoint ambassadors and make treaties (each of which must be exercised jointly, with the advice and consent of the Senate), and the power to act as commander in chief. . . ." *Id.* at 139 n.3. For a fuller discussion and critique of Ely on this point, *see* Robert F. Turner, *War and the Forgotten Executive Power Clause of the Constitution: A Review Essay of John Hart Ely's* War and Responsibility, 34 VA. J. INT'L L. 903 (1994); For general background on the views of Madison, Hamilton, Jefferson and Washington on the Article II, section 1 grant of "The executive Power," *see* JOHN NORTON MOORE, *supra* note *. Similarly, the author has never appreciated the title of Professor Harold Koh's book on selected constitutional issues concerning national security and foreign affairs,

another example in the foreign relations law forays of Professor Tribe, it may be instructive to quote Professor Bruce Ackerman, Sterling Professor of Law and Political Science at Yale, with respect to the ill-fated efforts of Professor Tribe to assert the unconstitutionality of the two-House procedure in approving United States participation in the World Trade Organization. He writes, with Professor David Golove:

> As in the case of NAFTA, much of the debate [as to the permissibility of "executive-congressional" agreements or what the Department of State's Circular 175 now calls "international agreements pursuant to legislation"] took the modern constitutional consensus for granted. But this time an odd coalition led by traditional protectionists like Jesse Helms and consumer advocates like Ralph Nader made a last-minute challenge to the Senate's decision to consider the WTO under the two-House procedure of the Trade Act. And they enlisted a group of distinguished constitutionalists, led by Professor Laurence Tribe, to join the effort to reassert the senatorial monopoly over "advice and consent." This campaign prompted a vigorous response

---

entitled *The National Security Constitution.* Quite simply and obviously, there is no "National Security Constitution," there is only "The Constitution of the United States." *See* HAROLD HONGJU KOH, THE NATIONAL SECURITY CONSTITUTION (1990). Professor Koh's accusation in support of his own revisionist views of congressional preeminence in foreign affairs are also quite remarkable, to the effect that those who believe, as did Madison, Hamilton, Jefferson, Washington and Jay, that the principal foreign affairs power under the Constitution was lodged in the Executive "are forced to engage in revisionist history to contend that the Framers did not originally draft the Constitution to promote *congressional* dominance in foreign affairs." *Id.* at 225 (italics in original). Koh might benefit from reviewing "Jefferson's Opinion on the Powers of the Senate Respecting Diplomatic Appointments" in which Jefferson wrote in 1790:

> The Constitution has divided the powers of government into three branches, Legislative, Executive and Judiciary, lodging each with a distinct magistracy. The Legislative it has given completely to the Senate and House of representatives: it has declared that "the Executive powers shall be vested in the President," submitting only special articles of it to a negative by the Senate; and it has vested the Judiciary power in the courts of justice, with certain exceptions also in favor of the Senate.
>
> The transaction of business with foreign nations is Executive altogether. It belongs then to the head of that department, *except* as to such portions of it as are specially submitted to the Senate. *Exceptions* are to be construed strictly.

16 THE PAPERS OF THOMAS JEFFERSON 378-79 (Julian P. Boyd ed., 1961) (footnotes omitted). The notes to this memorandum in this edition of Jefferson's papers go on to record:

> Three days after TJ wrote the above opinion, Washington recorded in his diary: "Had some conversation with Mr. Madison on the propriety of consulting the Senate on the places to which it would be necessary to send persons in the Diplomatic line, and Consuls; and with respect to the grade of the first—His opinion coincides with Mr. Jay's and Mr. Jefferson's—to wit—that they have no Constitutional right to interfere with either, and that it might be impolitic to draw it into a precedent, their powers extending no further than to an approbation or disapprobation of the person nominated by the President, all the rest being Executive and vested in the President by the Constitution."

Id. at 380.

from the Administration in defense of the congressional-executive agreement, kicking off a spirited debate. In the months before the Senate voted for the WTO in late November 1994, Professor Tribe launched an accelerating barrage of letters and memoranda on behalf of his new cause. Unfortunately, Professor Tribe did not enter the debate with a fully informed opinion. Not only was his new position at odds with the most recent edition of his treatise, but his legal views shifted from month to month as he learned more about the history and complexity of the issues. As the Senate vote neared, Professor Tribe's emphatic certainties had dissolved into doubts:

> In short the issue is a close one. Although I continue to believe that the constitutional concerns that I have previously raised are deeply important, I cannot say with certainty that my prior conclusions should necessarily be adopted by others or are the ones to which I will adhere in the end after giving the matter the further thought that it deserves.[50]

Professors Ackerman and Golove describe this as a "retreat into uncertainty."[51] One can only hope that on the even clearer issue of the permissibility of the Executive and the courts considering a full range of material bearing on the intent of the parties to a treaty, and not just material considered by a Senate during the process of advice and consent, that "after giving the matter the further thought that it deserves," Professor Tribe will reach the right conclusion.

The issue also is not whether the United States would continue to be bound internationally by reference to the international law standard of treaty interpretation should we adopt some other rule for domestic law. Of course we would, unless, of course, the rule of internal law in question met the understandably high requirements for notice to other parties embodied in Article 46 of the Vienna Convention on the Law of Treaties. That is not remotely the case with the proposed new "dual" mode of treaty interpretation which would not even require anything attached to a resolution of advice and consent to create a binding requirement for the President to depart from the international meaning of the treaty. Indeed, this point of still being internationally bound by the meaning agreed between the parties is the gravamen of the problem, and why the "dual" approach would

---

50 Bruce Ackerman & David Golove, *Is NAFTA Constitutional?*, 108 HARV. L. REV. 799, 917-18 (1995) (footnotes omitted). At the time this article was published, David Golove was an Associate Professor of Law, University of Arizona College of Law. Currently, he is an Associate Professor of Law at Benjamin N. Cardozo School of Law, Yeshiva University. For an excellent short editorial comment on this WTO "international agreement modality" issue, *see* Detlev F. Vagts, *The Exclusive Treaty Power Revisited*, 89 AM. J. INT'L L. 40 (1995).

51 Bruce Ackerman & David Golove, *supra* note 50, at 918. The authors then generously write: "Professor Tribe's aggressive intervention had served the public interest." *Id.* at 918.

so seriously undermine the rule of law as it mandated non-compliance by the United States with its internationally binding treaty obligations as one of the logical consequences of the rule.

The issue is not whether the President and the Executive Branch in general have a good faith obligation to present the meaning of a treaty to the Senate as accurately and honestly as possible. Of course they do! Despite the great debate surrounding the "broad-narrow" issue in interpretation of the ABM Treaty, to my knowledge no one has been able to produce a single example of a President seeking to mislead a Senate at the time of Senate consideration for advice and consent in the entire foreign relations history of the United States. This would simply seem a non-problem despite the implications to the contrary from the "broad-narrow" debate. As has been seen, should it ever be a problem, powerful remedies already exist including criminal liability and impeachment.

Nor is the issue whether the President has authority to interpret treaties. Of course the President has such authority. The Executive power, including the general foreign affairs power, and the obligation to "take Care that the Laws be faithfully executed . . . ," among other Presidential powers, clearly include such authority. Nor is this in the slightest controversial. According to Section 326 (1) of the *Restatement (Third)*:

> The President has authority to determine the interpretation of an international agreement to be asserted by the United States in its relations with other states.[52]

Moreover, according to the *Restatement,* "Courts in the United States . . . will give *great weight* to an interpretation made by the Executive Branch.[53]

Nor is the principal issue whether a subsequent interpretation of a treaty unilaterally by a Senate *after* it has given advice and consent would be authoritative. The decision of the Supreme Court in the classic treaty case of *Fourteen Diamond Rings v. United States*[54] at minimum establishes that even

---

52 Restatement (Third) of the Foreign Relations Law of the United States § 326(1) (1987).

53 Restatement (Third), *supra* note 47, at § 326(2) and cmt. b (emphasis added). *See also* Kolovrat v. Oregon, 366 U.S. 187, 194 (1961) ("great weight," citing "Factor v. Laubenheimer, 290 U.S. 276, 294-295").

It is yet another paradox of the asserted "dual" approach to treaty interpretation, that under that approach, interpretations by the Executive, principally charged with the foreign affairs of the Nation, including the negotiation of treaties, and the duty to "take Care that the Laws be faithfully executed," would not be conclusive in domestic courts but would only be entitled to "great weight," whereas an even informal interpretation of the Senate at the time of advice and consent would apparently be binding.

54 183 U.S. 176 (1901). *See also* Jones v. Meehan, 175 U.S. 1 (1899).

a formal resolution of interpretation subsequent to ratification (and even by from only less than one to eight days in this case depending on whether the concurring or majority opinions of the time are accepted) will have no legal effect short of adoption by a two-thirds vote. And the case has been widely accepted, and probably should be, for the broader proposition that later efforts at unilateral treaty interpretation by the Senate are not legally binding.[55] The opinion of the Court in *Fourteen Diamond Rings* said:

> We need not consider the force and effect of a resolution of this sort, if adopted by Congress. . . . It is enough that this was a joint resolution; that it was adopted by the Senate by a vote of 26 to 22, not two thirds of a quorum: and that it is absolutely without legal significance on the question before us. The meaning of the treaty cannot be controlled by subsequent explanations of some of those who may have voted to ratify it. What view the House might have taken as to the intention of the Senate in ratifying the treaty we are not informed, nor is it material; and if any implication from the action referred to could properly be indulged, it would seem to be that two thirds of a quorum of the Senate did not consent to the ratification on the grounds indicated.[56]

This case is also important in that it seems to imply that in a treaty interpretation case where the intention of the Senate may be relevant, the search for intention must be a search for the intention of an at least two-thirds of a quorum voting for the treaty and necessary for advice and consent. It is also relevant in this case that in his concurring opinion, Mr. Justice Brown said: "In its essence [a treaty] . . . is a contract. It differs from an ordinary contract only in being an agreement between independent states instead of private parties. . . ," and:

> the treaty must contain the whole contract between the parties, and the power of the Senate is limited to a ratification [sic—advice and consent] of such terms as have already been agreed upon between the President, acting for the United States, and the commissioners of the other contracting power. The Senate has no right to ratify the treaty and introduce new terms into it, which shall be obligatory upon the other power, although it may refuse its ratification, or make such ratification conditional upon the adoption of amendments to the treaty. . . .[57]

---

55 *See* Restatement (Third) of the Foreign Relations Law of the United States, Reporters' Note 1 to § 326, concluding: "later interpretations [of a treaty] by the Senate have no special authority."

56 183 U.S. 176, 180.

57 183 U.S. 176, 182-84.

Mr. Justice Brown also quoted with approval the classic statement from the *New York Indians*[58] case that:

> There is something . . . which shocks the conscience in the idea that a treaty can be put forth as embodying the terms of an arrangement with a foreign power or an Indian tribe, a material provision of which is unknown to one of the contracting parties. . . .[59]

Finally, the issue is not whether a Senate can, as a condition of advice and consent, attach understandings, reservations, international conditions to be agreed by the other party, or even require substantial amendment and revision of the treaty. Of course it can! In such cases the President must, where amendments or international conditions are present, obtain the consent of the other party or parties before the treaty can be ratified. And even in settings reflecting permitted reservations or understandings viewed as congruent with the treaty, the President would publicize the United States reservations and understandings at the time of ratification. As such, there is always a modality available to a Senate which regards a particular amendment, reservation or understanding as important, to protect that interest in a legally effective and honorable way.[60] Indeed, it is *only* through such

---

58 New York Indians v. United States, 170 U.S. 1 (1898). Some seek to dismiss this case as only applying to treaties with Indian tribes, but the language of the Court was explicit in referring to "foreign power[s]" as well as Indian tribes. Moreover, the moral, and sound foreign policy principles at stake are equally applicable to the two settings.

59 183 U.S. 176, 183-84.

60 If, for example, the Senate wants to ensure that a treaty will not take effect in the United States until subsequently approved or implemented by Act of Congress, it can insist on an *amendment* to the treaty that the treaty itself will not take effect until subsequent passage of the Act of Congress. When conveyed to and accepted by the other nation, such an amendment modifies the time of entry into force for *both* parties and thus avoids the necessity of any "domestic conditions" separate from the treaty. For an example, *see* United States v. American Sugar Co., 202 U.S. 563 (1906) ("The treaty was a reciprocal arrangement and intended to go into effect coincidently in the United States and Cuba. The two nations provided for this. . . . This coincident operation is of the very essence of the convention.") 202 U.S. at 579. Note that the Senate action in this case, that the treaty should not take effect until approved by a subsequent Act of Congress, was effectuated as an *amendment* to the treaty, *ratified and approved by the other treaty party*. 202 U.S. at 567. It was not a "domestic condition" separate from the treaty. It seems likely that the House of Representatives concern for its authority in tariff matters, pursuant to its power over "Revenue," as reflected in art. I, § 7 of the Constitution, may have been a factor here in Senate insistence on non-entry into force until the Congress had acted.

Similarly, the Senate can simply specify in its resolution of advice and consent that the President should delay ratification on behalf of the United States until domestic implementing legislation is enacted. This would seem the preferred modality particularly for a multilateral treaty in which Senate insistence on an "amendment" might not be appropriate. Indeed, an approach along these lines seems to be the modern practice, as reflected in Senate consideration of the Genocide and Torture Conventions in 1986 and 1990 respectively. See Louis Henkin, Richard C. Pugh, Oscar Schachter & Hans Smit, International Law 627-28 (3d ed. 1993).

open and public action that the intent of the Senate can be really effective, for unknown understandings can have no effect on the international legal obligation. That is, in the real world they will be completely ineffective in the all too frequent struggle for law. One of the strange aspects of the Senate insistence on the "dual" approach in the apparent belief that it will protect its interest, is that the only way to fully protect the interest of the Senate is to achieve effect on the *international* as well as the domestic legal plane. If the Senate believes that its interest can be protected solely by making an understanding binding under domestic law, it is very much mistaken, unless one assumes that members of the Senate, in considering advice and consent to a treaty, find of no consequence the international legal obligation to be created. That is, the "dual approach" seems to reflect a parochial view that it is protecting the Senate that is important, not the Nation, which can only be protected through affecting the international meaning of the treaty.

Having examined what the issue is not, it is easy to state what the issue is. It is: will the United States have a "unitary" approach to treaty interpretation which is rooted in the intent of the treaty parties? Or will the United States have a "dual" approach which will follow the intent of the parties and the standard foreign relations law in treaty interpretation, unless evidence of Senate intent or an Executive Branch statement during the Senate advice and consent process (with, not incidentally, an extraordinarily vague referent as to when either would be present) suggests a different interpretation, in which case the United States will be bound by one standard internationally and another domestically? We should also be clear about what such a "dual" approach would inevitably mean. Whenever it is relevant, that is, in settings in which the "Senate intent" differs from the correct international meaning, then it will *always* either require the United States to violate its solemn treaty obligations internationally or to be held to obligations not binding on the other treaty party or at least not bargained for.[61] *This* is the

---

61 In a debate with the author on June 13, 1994, in Charlottesville, Virginia, Professor David A. Koplow, a principal proponent of what is here labeled the "dual" approach, took the position that the "dual" approach did not exist insofar as requiring *violations* of international law, but only in adding *additional constraints* on the United States. The author fails to understand how the logic of the approach supported by Professor Koplow limits the effect of the "dual" approach solely to adding additional constraints on the United States. If the intent of the Senate is controlling then it would equally control in both cases. Nor is it clear that in the real world this limitation would any more clearly carry out the intent of a consenting Senate. *See* the discussion of this latter point in Part V (C) of this article.

Similarly, Senator Biden and John B. Ritch III, a co-author with the Senator of an article supporting the "dual" approach, don't seem to get it. They write:

> Of course, it is possible to *hypothesize* a "two treaties" scenario in which the Executive, perhaps inadvertently, presents an overly restrictive interpretation to the Senate. Indeed, one can imagine such a case even under the Sofaer Doctrine, since it

hidden virus underlying much of the debate about these issues, but amazingly one not usually brought into the open in the debate. For example, in its at least arguable tilt toward the "dual" approach, the *Restatement (Third)* never reveals what is really at stake in the event of different international and "Senate intent" meanings. Perhaps the Reporters have simply not focused on this issue and would be horrified by the real implications of the "dual" approach. One can only hope so.

To make matters worse, it is probable that most real-world settings posing this issue under the "dual" approach would be settings of simple mistake. That is, our Executive Branch spokesmen or individual Senators thought the meaning was one thing when it turned out to be another when examined more thoroughly years later, or when we were surprised by developments, such as subsequent international practice or adjudication, which establish a different meaning. In such settings *nothing* can ever fully implement the original Senate intent because, when considering a treaty, the Senate intent always has a dual element. Thus, it believes the meaning is X, but it also believes that X is, as well, the meaning binding on the other party to the treaty. To focus on carrying out meaning X then, when internationally it turns out to be Y, forces us to either violate our treaty obligations or to be held to higher obligations than the other party, neither of which was the intent of the Senate. And to focus on the internationally binding meaning Y is to ignore the meaning X, also not the intent of the consenting Senate. And in most settings, even setting aside the treaty would not carry out the intent of the Senate, which may have regarded the issue as relatively small in relation to the whole treaty relationship. That is, since a treaty, unlike legislation, is a *contract between nations* or, as John Jay wrote in *Federalist* 64,[62] a *bargain*, the Senate has an intent as to *meaning*, but it also has an intent as to the *bargain* or nature of the agreement between the nations. Settings in

---

allows that some, albeit very little, executive testimony may be binding. But in practice "two treaties" has not proven to be a problem, and it was profoundly revealing that Sofaer and others were never able to point to a real-world example.

Joseph R. Biden, Jr. & John B. Ritch III, *supra* note 12, at 1543. The good Senator and his co-author simply fail to notice that it is a *requirement of hard logic* quite simply that whenever the "dual" approach would make a legal difference, thus whenever it has *any* meaning, it would *always* present what they are referring to as the "two treaties" scenario, either requiring the United States to violate its treaty obligations or to be held to obligations not binding on the other treaty party and/or not bargained for. And their argument that it could not be a problem since no one can produce an example is simply incredible in view of the fact that the "dual" approach has never been the foreign relations law of the United States before, or since, this particular Senate "impulse of sudden passion," to borrow a phrase from Madison in *Federalist* 62. Surely we can understand that passion in the midst of the heated debate about proper interpretation of the ABM Treaty, without accepting its wrong-headed prescription for the treaty interpretation law of the United States.

62 *See* THE FEDERALIST NO. 64, at 14-15 (John Jay) (E. G. Bourne ed., 1937).

which the "dual" approach arises and would make a difference are inevitably settings where one of these intents cannot be realized.[63]

The "dual-unitary" debate in treaty interpretation has also brought to the fore a related issue of whether the Senate has general lawmaking power through attaching "domestic conditions" to resolutions of advice and consent to treaties. It presents this issue because the "dual" approach itself, were it to have any legal effect, creates a domestic binding meaning apart from the underlying treaty. And, it presents it as well, because the Senate has chosen to implement the "dual" approach, as a new domestically binding principle of treaty interpretation for the foreign relations law of the United States, through attaching it as a condition to resolutions of advice and consent. As with the hidden virus of the real effects of the "dual" approach, it seems likely that few members of the Senate were aware that they were raising an additional constitutional issue of significance in their push for the treaty interpretation condition.

The next two sections will address in turn these real issues of the "dual" versus "unitary" standards of treaty interpretation in the foreign relations law of the United States, and whether the Senate's advice and consent power includes a general domestic lawmaking power.

---

63 Even in settings where the other treaty party voluntarily adheres to a practice not legally binding on it, the bargain is not as anticipated, because that state is legally free to pick and choose whether it will continue its voluntary practice.

III. Disarming the Virus: "Dual" Versus "Unitary" Theories of Treaty Interpretation

A. GENERAL NOTE ON CONSTITUTIONAL INTERPRETATION

> *"[T]here are more instances of the abridgment of the freedom of the people by gradual and silent encroachments . . . than by violent and sudden usurpations."*
>
> *James Madison, Speech in the Virginia Convention, 1788*

The proper mode of treaty interpretation under the foreign relations law of the United States is an issue with substantial constitutional underpinnings. In assessing these underpinnings a range of factors are relevant.[64] First, the

64 It is not my intention at this point to definitively engage in the lively, ongoing and diverse debate about constitutional interpretation and judicial review. But it may be helpful in permitting appraisal by others to briefly set out some of the parameters and factors I would regard as useful in the treaty interpretation debate. That is the purpose of this short "General Note on Constitutional Interpretation."

With respect to the "case" for judicial review, the author would emphasize the central role of the Supreme Court in policing the basic fundaments of our constitutional democracy. These include guarantees for protection of the individual, separation of powers/checks and balances, federalism, and protection of the integrity of the electoral process. Separation of powers/checks and balances are powerfully engaged in the "dual" interpretation and its associated undefined Senate domestic lawmaking power.

For a discussion of the fundaments of the rule of law as presented by the author as Co-Chairman of the United States Delegation to the first talks between the United States and the Soviet Union on the Rule of Law, *see* John NortonMoore, *The Rule of Law: An Overview*, (Paper presented to the Seminar on the Rule of Law, Moscow and Leningrad, USSR, March 19-23, 1990) (talks Co-Chaired with the Deputy Attorney General of the United States).

For a flavor of the robust debate about theories of constitutional interpretation and judicial review, *see, e.g.*, ALEXANDER M. BICKEL, THE LEAST DANGEROUS BRANCH: THE SUPREME COURT AT THE BAR OF POLITICS (2d ed. 1986); ROBERT H. BORK, THE TEMPTING OF AMERICA: THE POLITICAL SEDUCTION OF THE LAW (1990); JOHN HART text of the Constitution, the totality of information about the intent of the language and its purposes, are important. The extreme view that would dismiss the intent of the Framers as an irrelevant, dead hand from the past, fails both to understand the political genius of the American Constitution and to understand the fundament of "constitutionalism" itself in establishing certain elemental checks and balances *against* governmental action. If constitutions were simply infinitely variable and subject to change with shifting majority opinion, then they could not serve their purpose as checks, where needed, against governmental and even majority actions. A first amendment guarantee that protected only speech deemed "correct" by a changing majority would not be much of a guarantee for human freedom.

Second, primary authority as reflected in the flow of Supreme Court and other judicial decisions of relevance to the issues should receive substantial weight. The Supreme Court is the highest judicial interpreter of the Constitution in our system and a consistent flow of decisions, also representing constitutional practice and experience over the years, is of considerable importance. A strong pattern of such practice should not be lightly set aside. This, of course, is not to suggest that change is never appropriate. *Brown v. Board of Education*[65] is a living example to the contrary.

Third, one of the great geniuses of the common law has been reliance on and learning from concrete experience. Thus, while not decisive on its own, as the *Chadha*[66] decision properly shows, constitutional experience can substantially assist in interpretation, and a strong pattern of practice should be set aside only as a result of substantial clarity to the contrary in the underlying constitutional language, purpose or policy. As Mr. Justice Frankfurter pointed out in his concurring opinion in the *Steel Seizure* case: "It is an inadmissibly narrow conception of American constitutional law to

---

ELY: DEMOCRACY AND DISTRUST: A THEORY OF JUDICIAL REVIEW (1980); LAURENCE H. TRIBE, CONSTITUTIONAL CHOICES (1985); MARK V. TUSHNET, RED, WHITE, AND BLUE: A CRITICAL ANALYSIS OF CONSTITUTIONAL LAW (1988); Thomas Grey, *The Constitution as Scripture*, 37 STAN. L. REV. 1 (1984); William H. Rehnquist, *The Notion of a Living Constitution*, 54 TEX. L. REV. 693 (1976); Antonin Scalia, *Originalism: The Lesser Evil*, 57 U. CIN. L. REV. 849 (1989); Clarence Thomas, *Toward a "Plain Reading" of the Constitution—The Declaration of Independence in Constitutional Interpretation*, 30 HOW. L.J. 983 (1987). And for an overview of a variety of issues and sub-issues in the debate, *see* MICHAEL J. GERHARDT & THOMAS D. ROWE, JR., CONSTITUTIONAL THEORY: ARGUMENTS AND PERSPECTIVES (1993).

65 Brown v. Board of Education, 347 U.S. 483 (1954) (Brown I); 349 U.S. 294 (1955) (Brown II).

66 I.N.S. v. Chadha, 462 U.S. 919 (1983). Justice Powell's concurring opinion in *Chadha* noted that "Congress has included the [legislative] veto in literally hundreds of statutes, dating back to the 1930s." 462 U.S. at 959, 959-60 (Justice Powell concurring in the judgment).

confine it to the words of the Constitution and to disregard the gloss which life has written upon them."[67] Justice Holmes was making much the same point when he said that "the life of the law has not been logic: it has been experience."[68]

Secondary authority and policy consequences may also be relevant as we trace the effects of a particular practice. In this connection, we should certainly keep in mind that constitutions are not like simple statutes or administrative regulations. A constitution is intended to serve as a fundamental charter for the relation of a people to its government. And it is intended to serve through the years. As such, a knowledge of relevant circumstances and policies sought to be effectuated in those circumstances may be of great importance. As Chief Justice Marshall noted for the Court in *McCulloch v. Maryland*,[69] "We must never forget that it is a *constitution* we are expounding."[70]

B. CONSTITUTIONAL TEXT AND THE TREATY POWER

It is possible to debate theoretically whether the power to make treaties is primarily executive or legislative, as did Hamilton and Madison in the famous "Pacificus-Helvidius" exchange.[71] Under *the Constitution of the United States,* however, there can be but one answer. For the treaty power is placed in Article II, the Executive, with a check in the Senate. It was not placed in Article I, the Legislative, with a check in the Executive.[72] The

---

67 Youngstown Sheet and Tube Co. v. Sawyer, 343 U.S. 579, 610 (1952).

68 Oliver W. Holmes, The Common Law 1 (1886).

69 17 U.S. (4 Wheat.) 316 (1819).

70 17 U.S. (4 Wheat.) at 407.

71 *See* Alexander Hamilton, First *Pacificus* Letter 29 June 1793, *reprinted in* 1 W. Goldsmith, The Growth of Presidential Power 398, 400-04 (1974); James Madison, First *Helvidius* Letter August-September 1793, *reprinted in* 1 W. Goldsmith, *supra*, at 405, 407-10. James Madison is perhaps the preeminent political theorist of all time, but he is simply arguing as an advocate in his *Helvidius* letter when he takes the position that the treaty power is primarily legislative. That is definitively not the case under his Constitution.

72 Nor was this placement in Article II an oversight of the Convention. For the August 6, 1787, draft from the Committee of detail vested the "power to make treaties," as well as the power "to appoint Ambassadors, and Judges of the supreme Court" solely in the Senate. When no agreement was reached, another Committee, sometimes referred to as the "Committee on postponed parts," proposed on September 4 language which became the present treaty clause located under the Executive and his powers. The Convention adopted this formulation on September 8. *See* 2 The Records of the Federal Convention of 1787, at 183 (M. Farrand ed., 1911) (Report of the Committee of detail); *id.* at 473 (Journal); *id.* at 495 (Committee on postponed parts); *id.* at 540-41, 547-50 (Convention adoption).

starting point for analysis under the United States Constitution, then, is that the treaty power is primarily executive in its nature.

It is also relevant in considering the text of the Constitution and the "dual-unitary" treaty interpretation debate, that the language of the Supremacy clause, art. VI, cl. 2 of the Constitution, and the Judiciary Article, art. III, § 2, both use the language: "Treaties made, or which shall be made." That is, it is the *treaty* which is the supreme law of the land, not domestic conditions attached to treaties or a separate domestic interpretation of the Senate apart from the treaty. And the judiciary power extends to cases arising under *treaties*, not domestic conditions attached to treaties or separate legally binding Senate interpretations apart from the treaty. Interestingly, the *Restatement (Third)*, despite its support for "domestic conditions," concedes that such conditions are not the Supreme Law of the Land within the Supremacy Clause. Thus, Reporters' Note 4 to § 303 says: "A condition imposed by the Senate that does not seek to modify the treaty and is solely of domestic import, is not part of the treaty and hence does not partake of its character as "supreme Law of the Land." Thus the *Restatement* view would seem to be that a "domestic condition" would not be binding on the states, a rather strange new hybrid of treaty law potentially giving rise to conflicting interpretations of treaties under the "dual" approach, as well as different legal effects for "domestic conditions," depending on the court system.

C. CONSTITUTIONAL THEORY, HISTORY AND PRACTICE

1. Separation of power theory generally

Separation of powers and checks and balances are a critical genius of the American Constitutional system. This Montesquieu mode of controlling power was chosen in the new democratic government as the preferred mode of protecting liberty and good government over the more traditional checks based on social class, as reflected in the Roman Republic, and even the now residual House of Lords in the United Kingdom.[73] One of the fundamental principles of separation of powers is that no *one* department of

---

73 Thomas Jefferson and John Adams engage in an interesting discussion about government based on merit in their famous exchange of correspondence during Jefferson's retirement. In that correspondence Jefferson powerfully makes the case for merit ("virtue and talents") rather than status ("artificial aristocracy... [of] rank and birth"). *See* 2 THE ADAMS-JEFFERSON LETTERS 387-92 (Lester J. Cappon ed., 1959) (Letter of Jefferson to Adams of Oct. 28, 1813).

For an excellent history and discussion of constitutionalism, *see* SCOTT GORDON, CONTROLLING THE STATE (1999).

government can set its own powers at the expense of the others. James Madison wrote in *The Federalist* No. 49:

> The several departments being perfectly co-ordinate by the term of their common commission, neither of them, it is evident, can pretend to an exclusive or superior right of settling the boundaries between their respective powers.[74]

Is this not precisely what the Senate (not even the full legislative department) is trying to do unilaterally with its treaty interpretation condition?

It is also relevant under general separation of powers theory that Madison, Hamilton and Jefferson all adopted the position that congressional powers which by their nature overlapped with the general grant of executive power in art. II, § 1 (which they believed included the general foreign affairs power), were to be strictly construed.[75] Further, one of the most important Supreme Court decisions in the separation of powers, *Myers v. United States*,[76] decided in 1926, explicitly adopted the Madison, Jefferson and Hamilton view that grants of authority to Congress overlapping the general grant of "the executive Power" to the President are to be strictly construed. And in dictum, the Court applied this doctrine to all of the blended powers in art. II, § 2, cl. 2, which, of course, includes the treaty power, and thus adopts the Hamilton position in his "Pacificus" letter. Chief Justice Taft wrote in his opinion of the Court:

> Our conclusion on the merits, sustained by the arguments before stated, is that Article II grants to the President the executive power of the Government, [and] . . . that the provisions of the second section of Article II, which blend action by the legislative branch, or by part of it, in the work of the executive, are limitations to be strictly construed and not to be extended by implication. . . .[77]

2. Bicameralism and the presentment clauses: *I.N.S. v. Chadha* and *Clinton v. New York City*

The Supreme Court has sought to police parts of the legislative process from assuming general legislative powers without complying with the full constitutional scheme, which includes bicameralism and presentment to the President. In so doing, the Court has emphasized both that there are certain modes for lawmaking under the Constitution, each with its precise requirements, and that this is an essential part of the separation of powers.

---

74 THE FEDERALIST No. 49, at 339 (J. Madison).

75 *See* the materials cited in JOHN NORTON MOORE, *supra* note *.

76 272 U.S. 52, 116-118, 127-28, 151-52, 163-64 (1926).

77 Myers v. United States, 272 U.S. 52, 116-118, 127-28, 151-52, 163-64 (1926).

Thus, in *Immigration and Naturalization Service v. Chadha,*[78] Mr. Justice Burger said in his opinion of the Court:

> We have recently noted that "[t]he principle of separation of powers was not simply an abstract generalization in the minds of the Framers: it was woven into the document that they drafted in Philadelphia in the summer of 1787." . . .[79] [and]
>
> The Constitution sought to divide the delegated powers of the new Federal Government into three defined categories, Legislative, Executive, and Judicial, to assure, as nearly as possible, that each branch of government would confine itself to its assigned responsibility. The hydraulic pressure inherent within each of the separate Branches to exceed the outer limits of its power, even to accomplish desirable objectives, must be resisted.[80]

In a sense, this is also exactly what the Court was doing in the *Fourteen Diamond Rings*[81] case, when it refused to permit the Senate to make law in a manner not consistent with the Constitution.

In *Chadha,* the Court emphasized the great importance of both the presentment clauses and bicameralism, and the interrelation between them, in the full constitutional scheme. Thus, it said:

> The decision to provide the President with a limited and qualified power to nullify proposed legislation by veto was based on the profound conviction of the Framers that the powers conferred on Congress were the powers to be most carefully circumscribed. It is beyond doubt that lawmaking was a power to be shared by both Houses and the President. . . .[82]
>
> The bicameral requirement of Art. I, §§ 1, 7 was of scarcely less concern to the Framers than was the Presidential veto and indeed the two concepts are interdependent. By providing that no law could take effect without the concurrence of the prescribed majority of the Members of both Houses, the Framers reemphasized their belief, already remarked upon in connection with the Presentment Clauses, that legislation should not be enacted unless it has been carefully and fully considered by the Nation's elected officials. . . .[83] [and]
>
> We see therefore that the Framers were acutely conscious that the bicameral requirement and the Presentment Clauses would serve essential constitutional functions. The President's participation in the legislative process was to protect the Executive Branch from Congress and to protect the whole people from improvident laws. The division of the Congress into two dis-

---

78 Immigration and Naturalization Service v. Chadha, 462 U.S. 917 (1983).

79 462 U.S. 946.

80 462 U.S. 951.

81 Fourteen Diamond Rings v. United States, 183 U.S. 176 (1901).

82 462 U.S. at 947.

83 462 U.S. at 948-49.

> tinctive bodies assures that the legislative power would be exercised only after opportunity for full study and debate in separate settings. . . .[84]

Most recently, in the "line item veto case" of *Clinton, President of the United States, v. City of New York,*[85] the Court demonstrated even greater sensitivity to the need for scrupulous adherence to the requirements of art. I, § 7 of the Constitution as the appropriate modality for domestic lawmaking under the United States Constitution. The Court struck down the Presidential cancellation procedure of the Line Item Veto Act. It did so despite the Act itself, including those procedures, having been duly enacted by action of both Houses of Congress and the President, and thus authorizing the challenged Presidential action in canceling certain provisions of the Balanced Budget Act of 1997. And it did so even despite what it regarded as Constitutional silence on the issue of Presidential action amending or repealing parts of duly enacted statutes, going quite beyond *Chadha*. Thus, the Court said:

> There are powerful reasons for construing constitutional silence on this profoundly important issue as equivalent to an express prohibition. The procedures governing the enactment of statutes set forth in the text of Article I were the product of the great debates and compromises that produced the Constitution itself. Familiar historical materials provide abundant support for the conclusion that the power to enact statutes may only "be exercised in accord with a single, finely wrought and exhaustively considered, procedure.". . . Our first President understood the text of the Presentment Clause as requiring that he either "approve all the parts of a Bill, or reject it in toto." What has emerged in these cases from the President's exercise of his statutory cancellation powers, however, are truncated versions of two bills that passed both Houses of Congress. They are not the product of the "finely wrought" procedure that the Framers designed.[86]

Justice Kennedy, in concurring in *Clinton,* stressed the centrality of the principle of separation of powers under the Constitution. He writes:

> Separation of powers was designed to implement a fundamental insight: Concentration of power in the hands of a single branch is a threat to liberty. The Federalist states the axiom in these explicit terms: "The accumulation of all powers, legislative, executive, and judiciary, in the same hands . . . may justly be pronounced the very definition of tyranny."[87]

Of particular relevance to the issue of domestic lawmaking by unilateral Senate domestic conditions during the advice and consent process, the

---

84 462 U.S. at 951.

85 524 U.S. 417 (1998).

86 524 U.S. 439-40 (*Chadha* citation and footnote omitted).

87 524 U.S. 450.

Clinton Court reiterates the *Chadha* language that there is but a "single . . . procedure" for the exercise of the federal legislative power.

It should be noted that in its treaty interpretation condition, the Senate not only proposes to make its new theory of treaty interpretation domestic law by simply unilaterally attaching it as a one House condition to a resolution of advice and consent, but its new theory is even far looser as it applies to individual interpretation issues. Thus, if the facts of the "broad-narrow" debate which gave rise to this Senate approach are an example of its operation, it proposes this lawmaking effect solely from an Executive Branch statement and/or expressed views of a few Senators. It is not, under the Biden Treaty Interpretation Condition, even necessary to attach the interpretation as a condition to the resolution of advice and consent, nor does it specify that the interpretation must be supported by adequate evidence suggesting that it is shared by two-thirds of a Senate quorum. Perhaps of importance in really carrying out the Senate's intent, it also does not suggest any standard that the members of the Senate intend to make domestic law, as opposed to give advice and consent to a treaty, with the knowing implication that if their interpretation is wrong and they write it into domestic law that they will either be requiring the United States to violate its treaty obligations or holding the United States to obligations not binding on the other party.

3. Treaty power theory generally

John Jay, perhaps *the* most experienced foreign policy expert among the constitutional Framers, clearly regarded a treaty as a "bargain" between nations. And he emphasized that "treaties are made, not by only one of the contracting parties, but by both. . . ." Thus, he wrote in *Federalist* 64:

> a treaty is only another name for a bargain, and . . . it would be impossible to find a nation who would make any bargain with us, which should be binding on them ABSOLUTELY, but on us only so long and so far as we may think proper to be bound by it. They who make laws may, without doubt, amend or repeal them; and it will not be disputed that they who make treaties may alter or cancel them; but still let us not forget that treaties are made, not by only one of the contracting parties, but by both; and consequently, that as the consent of both was essential to their formation at first, so must it ever afterwards be to alter or cancel them.[88]

---

88 THE FEDERALIST No. 64, *supra* note 62, at 14-15.

The Framers clearly understood the difference between the legislative process, with lawmaking by joint action of a majority of both Houses and presentment to the President, and the treaty process, an international bargain struck by the President with another Nation subject to advice and consent of two-thirds of the Senate. In sharp contrast to treatment of the legislative process by the Constitutional Convention,

There is also considerable evidence that the Senate role in the treaty power, as a check on Presidential authority parallel to the President's role as a check on legislative authority, was regarded principally as a veto. That is, with respect to the "consent" portion of the Senate role in advice and consent, there is considerable authority that the nature of the role is a "veto" or "negative," as earlier called, although it is clear that the Senate can attach to its consent, reservations, amendments or understandings *concerning the international obligation*. Thus, Thomas Jefferson wrote in the "Treaties" section of his *Manual of Parliamentary Practice for the Use of the Senate*:

> *By the Constitution of the United States, this department of legislation is confided to two branches only of the ordinary legislature; the President originating, and the Senate having a negative.*[89]

Similarly, Professor Edward S. Corwin, a giant in the field of American constitutional theory, writes in his classic treatise:

> In short, the Senate's role in treaty making is nowadays simply the power of saying whether a proposed treaty shall be ratified or not, the act of ratification being the President's. Its power is that of *veto,* which may be exercised outright, or conditionally upon the nonacceptance by the President or the other government or governments concerned of such amendments or reservations as it chooses to stipulate. . . .[90]

Even a study in 1984 done for the Senate Foreign Relations Committee on *Treaties and Other International Agreements: The Role of the United States Senate* entitles a section "The Senate's Treaty Veto," and states that "[t]he Senate has used its veto sparingly," and that "[t]he Senate's treaty power is one of the few legislative vetoes that has been recognized as permissible by the Supreme Court."[91]

It has also been stressed that the changes proposed by a Senate during the advice and consent process do not take effect until accepted internationally. This is yet another form of recognition that a treaty is a contract or compact among nations and that the advice and consent power is not a

---

proposals by James Wilson to include the House in the Treaty-making process and to eliminate the two-thirds requirement were overwhelmingly rejected by the Convention, in significant part because of concerns of the smaller states and of sectional interests. Shlomo Slonim, *Securing States' Interests at the 1787 Constitutional Convention: A Reassessment*, 14 Studies in American Political Development 1, 15-16 (Spring 2000).

89 T. Jefferson, A Manual of Parliamentary Practice for the Use of the Senate of the United States 169 (2d ed. 1812) (italics in original).

90 E. Corwin, The President: Office and Powers 1787-1957, at 211 (4th rev. ed. 1957).

91 A Study Prepared for the Senate Foreign Relations Comm. by the Congressional Research Service, Library of Congress, 98th Cong., 2d Sess. Treaties and Other International Agreements: The Role of the United States Senate 14-15 (Comm. Print June 1984).

general grant of domestic lawmaking authority. Thus, Florence Ellinwood Allen, a Judge of the United States Court of Appeals for the Sixth Circuit, writes in her 1952 monograph on the treaty power:

> [T]he framing of treaties is a wholly executive function. The treaties, so far as form is concerned, are presented to the Senate as an accomplished fact. The Senate may reject them *in toto,* make reservations, or reject separate articles; but the changes that it proposes do not become effective until they are accepted by the country with which the treaty is made.[92]

4. Treaty practice under the Constitution

There is considerable authority in the foreign affairs practice of the United States that it is the international obligation embodied in the treaty that is binding on the United States and the President. Indeed, it seems that this was overwhelmingly regarded as the rule until the Senate challenge coming out of the contentious "broad-narrow" debate in interpretation of the ABM Treaty. Examples of this practice supporting the "unitary" approach to treaty interpretation include the following:

A message of July 30, 1923, from Secretary of State Hughes to Ambassador Houghton is described in Hackworth's *Digest*:

> In a diplomatic interchange concerning the question whether the Treaty of Berlin automatically gave the United States rights accorded by the Treaty of Versailles, Germany referred to statements made by Senator Lodge in debate in the Senate upon the Treaty of Berlin. Concerning this Secretary Hughes wrote the Ambassador to Germany:
>
> Should occasion arise, you may orally explain to the German Foreign Office that expressions of opinion as to the meaning of the treaty of August 25, 1921, such as those to which the Foreign Office refers, occurring in general debate, cannot be regarded as affecting the interpretation of that treaty.[93]

In 1929, Secretary of State Kellogg expressed in telegrams to the Ambassadors to Great Britain and France that an interpretative report filed by the Senate Foreign Relations Committee during Senate consideration of the Kellogg-Briand pact "had no legal effect whatsoever upon the treaty." As described by Green Hackworth, the Legal Adviser of the Department of State, in 1943:

> When the Senate gave its advice and consent to the ratification of the Kellogg-Briand peace pact signed at Paris, August 27, 1928, the Foreign Relations Committee filed a report containing its interpretations of the treaty. The report was not put before the Senate for vote and was not included or

---

92 F. Allen, The Treaty as an Instrument of Legislation 6 (1952).

93 5 G. Hackworth, Digest of International Law 262 (U.S. Dep't of State Pub. No. 1927, 1943).

mentioned in the resolution of ratification. It concluded with the following statement:

> This report is made solely for the purpose of putting upon record what your committee understands to be the true interpretation of the treaty, and not in any sense for the purpose or with the design of modifying or changing the treaty in any way or effectuating a reservation or reservations to the same.
>
> ....

For a statement that the report of the Senate Committee had no legal effect whatsoever upon the treaty, see Secretary Kellogg to the Ambassador to Great Britain, telegram 12, Jan. 17, 1929, MS Department of State, file 711.0012 Anti-War/622; Mr. Kellogg to the Ambassador to France, telegram 25, Jan. 18, 1929, *ibid.* /623. . . .[94]

These instances in which foreign governments sought to rely on Senate materials, statements or interpretations should remind us that adopting a "dual" approach would also empower *foreign governments* with an additional source of argument against Presidential determinations concerning treaty interpretations, when they did become aware of such materials.

More recent examples in the form of Executive Branch foreign affairs expert testimony to the Senate include the following:

On September 25, 1979, during a Senate Foreign Relations Committee hearing on SALT I compliance, Sidney Graybeal, a principal ABM negotiator, commented on the effect of Executive Branch presentations to the Congress in the following terms:

> What about Soviet compliance with the agreement "as presented to Congress"?
>
> The language of the agreement, the agreed statements and the common understandings reflect what could be negotiated and what is binding on the two parties.
>
> Presentations to Congress can help explain the language and how it was derived, but they should not change the meaning of the language or the scope of the provisions of the agreement.[95]

---

94 5 G. Hackworth, *supra* note 93, at 152-53 (citations omitted). A copy of the actual telegram sent from Secretary of State Kellogg to the American Embassy in Paris, as cited by Hackworth, was declassified by the Department of State on April 28, 1989, at the request of the author of this article, and appears in my 607 page study for the Arms Control and Disarmament Agency. *See* John Norton Moore, *supra* note*.

95 *Briefing on SALT I Compliance: Hearing Before the Senate Comm. on Foreign Relations*, 96th Cong., 1st Sess. 13 (1979) (statement of Sidney Graybeal).

And a series of "Answers to Questions for the Record on the Legal Status of the SALT II Documents Transmitted to the Senate" prepared by the State Department Legal Adviser Herbert J. Hansell provided:

> Q. If . . .[a separate resolution not part of the resolution of ratification] were adopted which set forth the Senate's understanding or interpretation concerning various Treaty provisions, what would be its legal force and effect?
>
> A. Statements of understanding or interpretation not included in the Senate's resolution of ratification and the U.S. instrument of ratification accepted by the Soviet Union would not be legally binding *per se*. However, if provided to the Soviet Union prior to the exchange of instruments of ratification, and not contradicted by the Soviets, they would constitute persuasive evidence of the manner in which the Parties interpret the Treaty.[96]

D. PRIMARY AUTHORITY

Primary authority overwhelmingly supports the "unitary" approach to treaty interpretation. There is a long line of Supreme Court decisions referring to treaties as contracts or compacts among nations. This line runs from *United States v. Schooner Peggy*[97] in 1801 to *Trans World Airlines, Inc. v. Franklin Mint Corp.* in 1984.[98] Illustrative is *Foster v. Neilson*,[99] decided in 1829, where the Court said: "[a] treaty is, in its nature, a contract between two nations, not a legislative act."[100] Or *Worcester v. Georgia*,[101] decided in 1832, where Chief Justice Marshall wrote: "What is a treaty? The answer is, it is a compact formed between two nations or communities, having the right of self-government."[102] And in the more contemporary *Trans World Airlines* case, the opinion of the Court and the dissenting opinion of Mr. Justice Stevens both clearly indicated that a treaty was in the nature of a contract between nations. Thus, the opinion of the Court, delivered by Justice O'Connor, said: "A treaty is in the nature of a contract between nations."[103] And in dissenting, Justice Stevens said: "A treaty is essentially a contract between or among sovereign nations."[104]

---

96 *Answers to Questions for the Record on the Legal Status of the SALT II Documents Transmitted to the Senate, reprinted in* M. NASH, DIGEST OF UNITED STATES PRACTICE IN INTERNATIONAL LAW, 1979, at 697, 710, 713-14 (U.S. Dep't of State Pub. No. 9374, 1983).

97 5 U.S. (1 Cranch) 104 (1801).

98 466 U.S. 243 (1984). For a fuller listing and discussion of the cases, *see* JOHN NORTON MOORE, *supra* note *.

99 27 U.S. (2 Pet.) 253 (1829).

100 27 U.S. (2 Pet.) 253, 314.

101 Worcester v. Georgia, 31 U.S. (6 Pet.) 515 (1832).

102 *Id.* at 581

103 466 U.S. 243, 253.

104 466 U.S. 243, 262.

There are also several lines of Supreme Court cases suggesting that treaties are to be interpreted according to the intention of the parties or the principles of public international law, and that the scope of the treaty power is related to agreement among nations. This line of cases runs at least from *The Pizarro*[105] in 1817. Examples include the 1890 decision in *Geofroy v. Riggs*,[106] where Justice Field wrote for the Court:

> It is a general principle of construction with respect to treaties that they shall be liberally construed, so as to carry out the apparent intention of the parties to secure equality and reciprocity between them. As they are contracts between independent nations, in their construction words are to be taken in their ordinary meaning, as understood in the public law of nations, and not in any artificial or special sense impressed upon them by local law, unless such restricted sense is clearly intended. . . . [107]

In *Santovicenzo v. Egan*,[108] decided in 1931, Chief Justice Hughes said for the Court:

> as treaties are contracts between independent nations, their words are to be taken in their ordinary meaning "as understood in the public law of nations."[109]

---

105 The Pizarro, 15 U.S. (2 Wheat.) 227 (1817). *See also* the statement of Mr. Justice Story in 1821 in The Amiable Isabella, 19 U.S. (6 Wheat.) 1, 71, 72-73 (1821) ("We are to find out the intention of the parties by just rules of interpretation applied to the subject matter; and having found that, our duty is to follow it. . . ." "this Court is bound to give effect to the stipulations of the treaty in the manner and to the extent which the parties have declared, and not otherwise. We are not at liberty to dispense with any of the conditions or requirements of the treaty, or to take away any qualification or integral part of any stipulation, upon any notion of equity or general convenience, or substantial justice. The terms which the parties have chosen to fix, the forms which they have prescribed, and the circumstances under which they are to have operation, rest in the exclusive discretion of the contracting parties. . . . The same powers which have contracted, are alone competent to change or dispense with any formality.").

106 Geofroy v. Riggs, 133 U.S. 258 (1890).

107 *Id.* at 271-72.

108 Santovicenzo v. Egan, 284 U.S. 30 (1931).

109 284 U.S. at 40. For other Supreme Court decisions using materials or approaches relevant to public international law modalities of treaty interpretation, including, for example, treaty negotiating history or *travaux, see, e.g.,* Ware v. Hylton, 3 U.S. (3 Dall.) 199, at 223-28, 239 (1796) ("If the words express the meaning of the parties *plainly* . . . there ought to be no other means of interpretation; but if the words are obscure . . . recourse must be had to *other* means of interpretation. . . .") *Id.* at 239; Cameron Septic Tank Co. v. City of Knoxville, 227 U.S. 39, 50 (1913); Reid v. Covert, 354 U.S. 1, 61 (1957) (Frankfurter, J., concurring in result) (reference to I.C.J. case); Volkswagenwerk Aktiengesellschaft v. Schlunk, 486 U.S. 694, at 699-703, (1988); Eastern Airlines v. Floyd, 499 U.S. 530 (1991) (Note that this Supreme Court treaty interpretation decision is *post Stuart* and makes no reference to footnote 7 in that case).

And in *Factor v. Laubenheimer*,[110] decided in 1933, the Court said:

> Considerations which should govern the diplomatic relations between nations, and the good faith of treaties, as well, require that their obligations should be liberally construed so as to effect the apparent intention of the parties to secure equality and reciprocity between them. . . . In ascertaining the meaning of a treaty we may look beyond its written words to the negotiations and diplomatic correspondence of the contracting parties relating to the subject matter, and to their own practical construction of it. . . .[111]

We have already encountered *New York Indians v. United States*,[112] *Fourteen Diamond Rings*[113] and *Power Authority of the State of New York v. Federal Power Commission* (the *Niagara Reservation* case),[114] all of which, in a variety of ways, lend support to the "unitary" approach.

Despite a brief flurry of judicial activity arguably tilting toward the "dual" approach during the contentious public debate over the ABM interpretation issue, primary authority continues over-whelmingly to support the "unitary" approach. As we have seen, the issue arose peripherally in two cases in 1988 and 1989, in neither of which it was fully briefed or argued by counsel, and in which quite likely its consideration was at least indirectly generated by the then highly visible ongoing public debate between Senator Sam Nunn and Judge Abraham Sofaer.

The first of these cases was the *Rainbow Navigation*[115] case in 1988, in which Judge Harold H. Greene seemed to uphold a Senate domestic lawmaking authority to formally and *even informally* adopt "domestic conditions" incident to advice and consent to a treaty and also seemed to regard Executive Branch representations made in such a setting as obligatory. That it is likely that Judge Greene's opinion was influenced by the position of Senator Nunn in the "broad-narrow" debate is suggested by the context in which an initial Judge Greene opinion in the same case had been featured in the ongoing "treaty interpretation" debate spawned by this issue, and a foot-

---

110 Factor v. Laubenheimer, 290 U.S. 276 (1933). *Accord* Tucker v. Alexandroff, 183 U.S. 424, 437 (1902), Nielsen v. Johnson, 279 U.S. 47, 51 (1929).

111 290 U.S. at 293, 295. *Accord* Air France v. Saks, 470 U.S. 392, 396 (1985).

112 170 U.S. 1 (1898). It may be worthy of further note at this point with respect to the *New York Indians* case that the opinion of the Court delivered by Mr. Justice Brown also said: "[i]t [a treaty] cannot be considered as a legislative act, since the power to legislate is vested in the President, Senate and House of Representatives." 170 U.S. at 23.

113 Fourteen Diamond Rings v. United States, 183 U.S. 176 (1901). *See also* Jones v. Meehan, 175 U.S. 1 (1899).

114 247 F.2d 538 (D.C. Cir. 1957); *vacated as moot sub. nom.* in American Pub. Power Assn. v. Power Authority of the State of New York, 355 U.S. 64 (1957).

115 Rainbow Navigation, Inc. v. Department of the Navy, 699 F. Supp. 339 (D.D.C. 1988), *rev'd and vacated* 911 F.2d. 797 (D.C. Cir. 1990), *cert. denied* 499 U.S. 906 (1991).

note by Judge Greene in his opinion specifically quoting Senate statements in "the debate over the ABM treaty." Not only was the issue not fully briefed or argued by council in the case, however, but Judge Greene was apparently also unaware that the only case then decided on the legality of domestic conditions, the *Niagara Reservation* case, had been decided by the Court of Appeals in his own Circuit and had decided against the legality of such conditions. Indeed, even the dissent in that case would not have supported the broad "domestic condition" authority, going beyond a non-self-executing condition, asserted by Judge Green. Judge Greene's decision was reversed on Appeal in a unanimous opinion by the United States Court of Appeals for the District of Columbia Circuit in 1990.[116] In an opinion for the Court filed by Circuit Judge D. H. Ginsburg, and joined by Circuit Judge Ruth B. Ginsburg, now Justice Ginsburg of the Supreme Court, Judge Ginsburg said in response to the Senate consideration materials relied on by Judge Greene at the District Court level that: "Ambiguous ratification history cannot be allowed to obscure the meaning of clear Treaty language."[117] Further, the Court of Appeals decision, although itself not squarely facing the complex issues in the "dual-unitary" treaty interpretation debate, favorably quotes the Supreme Court decision in *Sumitomo Shoji America, Inc. v. Avagliano*,[118] indicating that the referent for decision in treaty interpretation is the language of the treaty and the intent of the parties. Thus, the opinion for the Court quotes *Sumitomo* as saying:

> Our analysis "must, of course, begin with the language of the Treaty itself."...
>
> The clear import of treaty language controls unless "application of the words of the treaty according to their obvious meaning effects a result inconsistent with the intent or expectations of its signatories."[119]

Rainbow Navigation will be visited in greater depth later in Part VI (B) of this article.

The second case in which the issue arose, at least peripherally, in the climate of the same highly visible public debate about the proper interpretation of the ABM Treaty, is *United States v. Stuart*,[120] decided by the Supreme Court in 1989. I will focus on this case in greater depth later in Part VI (C) of this article because of an ambiguous dictum in footnote 7 in the majority opinion and a concurring opinion by Mr. Justice Scalia in which he ad-

---

116 Rainbow Navigation, Inc. v. Department of the Navy, 911 F.2d 797 (D.C. Cir. 1990).

117 911 F.2d 802.

118 457 U.S. 176 (1982).

119 457 U.S. 176, 180 (1982). The second paragraph of this quote from *Sumitomo* is apparently quoting Maximov v. United States, 373 U.S. 49, 54 (1963).

120 United States v. Stuart, 489 U.S. 353 (1989).

dresses the real issue of the point of reference for treaty interpretation as the agreement between the parties. It should be noted at this point, however, that the issue of "dual" versus "unitary" standards of treaty interpretation was not fully, if at all, briefed or argued to the Court in this case, that is, the issue, though now stirring apparently as a result of the public debate, was still, for all practical purposes, a hidden virus. Most importantly, the majority opinion in at least two places itself adopts the traditional referent for decision, of the intent of the treaty parties, and it explicitly endorses reliance on subsequent practice of the parties which, by definition, could not be before a Senate during consideration for advice and consent. As such, even with the ambiguous footnote 7 dictum, the case seems to support the traditional "unitary" approach more than it does a "dual" approach.[121]

E. SECONDARY AUTHORITY

Many secondary authorities lend support to the treaty power as an agreement between nations, not a legislative act.[122] For example, Professor Norman J. Singer writes in Sands Fourth Edition of *Sutherland Statutory Construction*: "[a] treaty is in its nature a contract between two nations, not a Legislative act."[123] Perhaps the most detailed relevant analysis in the secondary authority, however, is the detailed ninety-six page analysis by Professors Philip C. Jessup and Oliver J. Lissitzyn prepared as an opinion in support of the position of the Power Authority of the State of New York in the *Niagara Reservation* case.[124] While not directly confronting the "dual" versus "unitary" issue in all its dimensions, since at the time it had not been heard of, this opinion did squarely relate to one such dimension, whether the Senate can attach a treaty condition operative only under domestic law, and it did address at length and adopt the most important theoretical consideration underlying the "unitary" approach; that is, the conclusion that the treaty power by its nature is a compact or contract between nations and

---

121 Treaties, of course, are subject to the restraints of the Constitution. In the classic case of Reid v. Covert, 354 U.S. 1 (1957), Mr. Justice Black said for the Court:

> no agreement with a foreign nation can confer power on the Congress, or on any other branch of Government, which is free from the restraints of the Constitution.
>
> . . . The prohibitions of the Constitution were designed to apply to all branches of the National Government and they cannot be nullified by the Executive or by the Executive and the Senate combined.

354 U.S. 16-17.

122 *See* the authorities collected in JOHN NORTON MOORE, *supra* note *.

123 1A SUTHERLAND STATUTORY CONSTRUCTION § 32.01, at 539 (Sands 4th ed., N. Singer ed. 1985 rev.).

124 OPINION OF PHILIP C. JESSUP & OLIVER J. LISSITZYN, *supra* note 25.

not a legislative power going beyond the underlying agreement. Professors Jessup and Lissitzyn concluded:

> A "treaty," as that term is used in the Constitution, is an international contract which either creates rights and duties as between two or more nations, or modifies or abrogates pre-existing rights and duties in the relations of nations, or confirms and recognizes with binding effect an existing international legal situation;
>
> ... A declaration by one party must modify the legal effect of a treaty on the relations between the parties in order to constitute a reservation to a treaty;
>
> ... The so-called "reservation" to the 1950 Niagara Treaty does not have these requisite characteristics of a treaty or of a reservation and can not legally be considered as a treaty or part of a treaty;

and,

> ... The inclusion of the "reservation" in the ratification of the Treaty was a mere colorable use of the treaty-making power and therefore derives no legal validity from the Constitution; ...[125]

As has been seen, the Court of Appeals decision in the *Niagara Reservation* case accepted the Jessup-Lissitzyn view as set out in these distinguished lawyers' opinion, and not the contrary Henkin view, as expressed by Professor Henkin in his 1956 article, which, we know, was before the Court since cited favorably by the dissenting Justice.

Charles Cheney Hyde also points out that it is impermissible to use a standard of interpretation known only to one of the treaty parties, as, of course, would frequently be the case under the "dual" approach. Thus, he writes:

> [i]t is not inconsistent with the principles stated to require that a contracting State be not permitted to enjoy recognition of a standard of interpretation known only to itself. It is the signification which both or all the parties have, or are to be regarded as having, attached to the words of their agreement which is alone the subject of investigation.[126]

In examining secondary materials, certainly the most important debate about such materials in the context of the "dual-unitary" debate, is the *Restatement (Third) of the Foreign Relations Law of the United States.* This *Restatement* is of general high quality and is heavily relied on by United States courts. In no small part that high quality comes from the high scholarship of its Chief Reporter, Professor Louis Henkin of the Columbia Law faculty and its distinguished Associate Reporters and Advisers. It should be emphasized at the outset that the *Restatement* never squarely addresses the

---

125 OPINION OF PHILIP C. JESSUP & OLIVER J. LISSITZYN, *supra* note 25, at 96.

126 2 C. C. HYDE, *supra* note 37, at 1470-71 (footnotes omitted).

"dual-unitary" issue in treaty interpretation. This may well be because the real issues have been largely outside the visible, like the hidden virus in the e-mail. Thus, the *Restatement* never addresses what would happen should there be a discrepancy between the internationally binding meaning of a treaty, and a domestic understanding of the Senate during the advice and consent process. As such, it cannot be said to even have addressed the issue.

The *Restatement*, however, adopts at least three positions which have been interpreted as supporting the "dual" approach. Although each is somewhat ambiguous and subject to a number of meanings, at least in the form in which they lend support to the "dual" approach, they are, I believe, plain wrong under both the existing foreign relations law of the United States and what that law ought to be. These are, first the proposition that: "[t]he Senate may also give its consent on conditions that do not require change in the treaty but relate to its domestic application. . . ."[127] Second, the proposition that:

> Although the Senate's resolution of consent may contain no statement of understanding, there may be such statements in the report of the Senate Foreign Relations Committee or in the Senate debates. In that event, the President must decide whether they represent a general understanding by the Senate and, if he finds that they do, must respect them in good faith.[128]

And the third is the proposition:

> A court or agency of the United States is *required to take into account* United States materials relating to the formation of an international agreement that might not be considered by an international body such as the International Court of Justice. These may include:
>
> . . . Committee reports, debates, and other indications of meaning that the legislative branch has attached to an agreement. . . .[129]

With the possible exception, as previously noted, of the *sui generis* issue of statements concerning whether a treaty is regarded as self-executing, I believe the first proposition is flat wrong under the Constitution of the United States, as will be examined in greater detail in the next section. The second proposition is quite broad and ambiguous and in some settings or interpretations could be quite innocuous, and even helpful; for example, if the President determines a clear Senate intent on a particular issue and insists on attaching it as an understanding to be conveyed to the other

---

127 *See, e.g.*, cmt. d to § 303, at 160.

128 *See, e.g.*, cmt. d to § 314 at 188.

129 Reporters' Note 5 to § 325, at 201 (emphasis added).

party. But if this proposition is intended to support the "dual" approach, with all of its hidden meaning, then I think it, too, is wrong. And the third proposition also is quite broad and ambiguous. In many settings, of course, it would be quite appropriate. Thus, the official Department of State article-by-article legal analysis frequently submitted with a treaty at the time it is transmitted by the President for advice and consent is a classic example of such "United States materials" appropriate for consideration. Indications of negotiated understandings, as reflected in State Department cable traffic and embodied in a Committee report might be a further example. Moreover, the phrase "required to take into account" is quite general and vague and itself conveys many possibilities of legal effect. As has already been seen, courts sometimes do consult Senate materials in the interpretative process. If they do so simply as a source of information, as they would a law review or treatise, or for evidence of the Executive view of the correct international meaning of the treaty, a view itself entitled to "great weight," as seems to be the principal reason such materials are examined by the courts, then fine. If the statement seeks to convey no more than this, perhaps along with the proposition that the American approach to treaty interpretation is more contextual, and thus will take into account a broader range of materials in the search for the intent of the parties, then fine. But if this proposition is taken as requiring the "dual" approach, that is, as mandating a referent for decision other than the intent of the parties, then, again, I believe that it is flat wrong.

All three of these propositions share a dubious distinction. None is supported in the *Restatement* by a single case or other authority, other than a citation to Professor Henkins' article on the *Niagara Reservation* case, which, we have seen, did not accept the Henkin thesis in that article on domestic conditions. And the *Restatement* effort to explain away the *Niagara Reservation* case simply sets out the Henkin thesis and makes no reference to the lengthy opinion by Professors Philip C. Jessup and Oliver C. Lissitzyn, which seemed to be accepted by the majority of the Court of Appeals in that case. Perhaps if the Henkin view had been clearly supported by copious authority, or if one of the authors of the contradictory opinion had not been Philip C. Jessup, one of the top international lawyers this Nation has ever produced, it might have been understandable to omit this opinion. As it is, however, I find this *Restatement* note less than candid or persuasive. Thus, Reporters' Note 4 to Section 303 says:

> *Senate conditions of domestic import.* A condition imposed by the Senate that does not seek to modify the treaty and is solely of domestic import, is not part of the treaty and hence does not partake of its character as "supreme Law of the Land." See Sec 111(1) and Comment *d.* It was once assumed, therefore, that a Senate proviso that a treaty shall not take effect for the United States until Congress adopts implementing legislation could not

> have the force of law necessary to prevent the agreement from automatically taking effect as law in the United States. See Power Authority of New York v. Federal Power Commission, 247 F.2d 538 (D.C.Cir. 1957), *vacated and remanded with instructions to dismiss as moot*, 355 U.S. 64 . . . (1957). The effectiveness of such a Senate proviso, however, does not depend on its becoming law of the land as part of the treaty. Such a proviso is an expression of the Senate's constitutional authority to grant or withhold consent to a treaty, which includes authority to grant consent subject to a condition. The authority to impose the condition implies that it must be given effect in the constitutional system. See Henkin, "The Treaty Makers and the Law Makers: The Niagara Power Reservation," 56 Colum. L. Rev. 1151 (1956). . . .[130]

The *Restatement* concedes in this note that such "domestic conditions" are "not part of the treaty" and are thus not "supreme Law of the Land." These statements, coupled with the hedged additional caveats set out in the footnote quotation of the remainder of Reporters' Note 4, suggest some uneasiness about both the legal basis for such "domestic conditions," and their potential breadth as a general domestic lawmaking power binding at least on the federal courts and the President. As required to be "given effect" but not "supreme Law of the Land" they would be a rather cabined form of law of the United States.

In the wake of the "Biden Treaty Condition" a few international law scholars and treaty experts have spotted the virus and understood its potentially serious consequences. Thus, in an article published in 1989 on "Treaty Interpretation after the Biden Condition,"[131] Professor Kenneth S. Gallant, while apparently accepting, without analysis, the *Restatement (Third)* "conditionality" argument, presented a strong exposition as to why the Biden Treaty Interpretation Condition was rife with ambiguity and contradiction, was harmful to the foreign relations of the United States, and even to the

---

130 Reporters' Note 4 to § 303 at 164. This note concludes:

> The Senate has not made a practice of attaching conditions unrelated to the treaty before it. If the Senate were to do so, or were to attach a condition invading the President's constitutional powers–for example, his power of appointment–the condition would be ineffective. The President would then have to decide whether he could assume that the Senate would have given its consent without the condition

Ibid. The cross reference to § 111(1) and cmt. d in Reporters' Note 4 adds nothing but a cross reference to the proposition that international law and international agreements are law of the United States and supreme over the law of the States. *See* § 111(1) and cmt. d to § 111 at 42 and 44-45 respectively. This is yet further evidence that the *Restatement* does not regard "domestic conditions" as treaties, or even the broader phrase, international agreements.

131 Kenneth S. Gallant, *American Treaties, International Law: Treaty Interpretation after the Biden Condition*, 21 ARIZ. STATE L. J. 1067 (1989).

role of the Senate itself, and "should be rejected as a constitutional principle."[132] Thus, he writes:

> The Biden Condition attempts to create a new category of circumstance under which United States officials cannot carry out the nation's obligations under international law. It requires the United States to interpret treaties using methods different from those used in the treaties' interpretation and application in international tribunals and general international law. Using different interpretive methods may place American officials under contradictory obligations in domestic and international law.[133]
>
> . . . .
>
> . . . . very little in American constitutional history supports the rule of the Biden Condition, and much constitutional doctrine opposes it.[134]
>
> . . . .
>
> . . . . the constitutional conception that has developed in the American tradition is that the treaty made by the United States is an agreement between the United States and a foreign nation or nations. A treaty binds the United States under international law, and its meaning is drawn from sources used in international interpretive practice. Therefore, the Senate, when it considers whether to give its advice and consent to a treaty, must determine what the treaty means, not merely in its own opinion, but in the law of nations.

---

132 *Id.* at 1114. *See also* for a mixed discussion of Justice Scalia's concerns in the *Stuart* case, D. Bederman, *supra* note 34, at 998-1002. Professor Bederman writes:

> Justice Scalia was persuasive in his concern over the unilateral character of Senate materials and the constitutional allocation of authority in the making and interpreting of treaties. But his remaining criticisms of the practice of consulting legislative history turned on its probative weight, and these concerns rang hollow.

D. Bederman, *supra* note 34, at 1001. Professor Bederman also referred to Professor Vagts's critique of a single sentence from Justice Scalia's opinion in *Stuart* as: "a devastating critique of Justice Scalia's claim." *See* the discussion of Professor Vagts's critique in Part VI of this article. But in recommending rules for treaty interpretation, Professor Bederman urges as a first rule: "Begin interpretation with the treaty's text" and as a second rule:

> When an interpreter is permitted to break from a treaty's text and search for extrinsic sources of meaning, it should remember that negotiating history and evidence of subsequent practice by a relevant number of treaty parties are to be vastly preferred over the legislative history of the advice and consent process or subsequent, unilateral interpretations by the executive branch.

Id. at 1031. This second rule proposed by Bederman is a clear rejection of the upside down final sentence in footnote 7 in the opinion of the Court in *Stuart*. And his first rule seems quite consistent with both the general international approach to treaty interpretation as embodied in Article 31 of the Vienna Convention, and the approach of Justice Scalia.

133 *Id.* at 1074-75 (footnotes omitted).

134 *Id.* at 1090.

The Senate must consider the acceptability of the uncertainties in the text, and of their possible resolution through international law and procedure.[135]

. . . .

The United States cannot reasonably expect other governments to allow the meaning of their treaty commitments to depend upon the President's statements to the Senate. To the extent that the Biden Condition actually contains the controlling principle upon which the American government practices international law, other governments will be reluctant to deal with the United States.[136]

. . . .

The Biden Condition poses a particular threat to multilateralism and to American participation in international organizations. Institutions such as the General Agreement on Tariffs and Trade (GATT) presuppose a developing system of international trade law and provide a general structure within which it can occur. Similar developing legal systems of law are presupposed by the ongoing efforts of many nations, including, since 1964, the United States, to promote international unification of private law. Freezing the meaning of documents giving structure to such multilateral agreements at the time of Senate consent would largely defeat the purpose of such agreements.

Further, when there are several parties to an agreement, it is more likely that some disagreement will arise over the meaning of the agreement's terms. Good faith attempts to adjust such differences may result in understandings that are different from those honestly held by certain governments when the agreement came into force. The United States should not preclude itself from participating in those adjustments. . . .[137]

. . . .

A strict reading of the Biden Condition would prevent the United States from participating fully in the development of international law through resort to the International Court of Justice and other international judicial or arbitral fora. If the United States cannot "agree to" a treaty interpretation at variance with the interpretation that the Executive presented to the Senate during ratification proceedings, then, arguably, it could not accept an adverse judgment requiring acceptance of such a treaty interpretation. The rejection of international judicial interpretation might be required even if the United States forcefully argued to the tribunal the position that the President had presented to the Senate, and the tribunal ruled against that position. American commitment to the rule of international law could rightfully be questioned if the Executive was without power to accede to an adverse court judgment.[138]

---

135 *Id.* at 1102 (footnotes omitted).

136 *Id.* at 1107.

137 *Id.* at 1107 (footnotes omitted).

138 *Id.* at 1108 (footnote omitted).

> . . . .
>
> Ironically, the Biden Condition would derogate the rightful prerogative of the United States Senate to shape foreign policy. The Condition would allow the Executive, through the device of "authoritative statements," to usurp the Senate's appropriate role in the formulation of the meaning of treaties. . . .
>
> Because treaties bind the United States as international law, and international law may not interpret treaties exactly as the President presented them to the Senate, the Senate's task is more complicated than mere receipt of authoritative representations from the Executive. Senators should not ignore real ambiguities or vagaries in a treaty's text by extorting a "representation" from the Executive, as the Biden Condition encourages. Rather, senators should acknowledge the potential lack of clarity in the international obligations of the United States. This means the Senate must either accept the existence of the ambiguity or use its power to resolve the ambiguity. The Senate may do the latter either by attaching a reservation or an understanding to the resolution of ratification of the treaty, which will be communicated to this nation's negotiating partner or partners, or by requiring that the compacting nations clarify the ambiguity before the treaty is ratified. The Senate should understand that unless a reservation or understanding is communicated to the United States' treaty partners, any binding effect on the Executive may eventually put the United States in a position in which it cannot meet its international obligations.
>
> Statements that the Biden Condition preserves the Senate's ability to participate in treaty-making only encourage senatorial laziness. To the extent that the Condition aims to limit the number of understandings, conditions, or reservations that the Senate explicitly adds to treaties, America's treaty partners will not be informed of how the United States interprets its obligations. Nothing in the text of the Constitution or the history of its interpretation requires this result.[139]

Similarly, in an article published in 1991 on the "Dual Treaty Approach,"[140] Professor Malvina Halberstam, a former Counselor on International Law to the Department of State, says:

> Whatever one's views on the use of legislative history to interpret statutes, it seems clear that Justice Scalia is correct in rejecting the use of legislative his-

---

139 *Id.* at 1111-12 (footnotes omitted).

140 Malvina Halberstam, *The Use of Legislative History in Treaty Interpretation: The Dual Treaty Approach*, 12 CARDOZO L. REV. 1645 (1991). For opposition to the "dual" approach by another superb international legal scholar, *see* E. Rostow, *supra* note 12. W. Michael Reisman, Hohfeld Professor of Jurisprudence at Yale Law School and currently Co-Editor in Chief of the *American Journal of International Law*, has also opposed the Biden Condition, as well as the associated coerced Executive Branch responses to the "dual" approach, such as the revised statements of Judge Sofaer or the Culvahouse letter of March 1988, as proposals which would "render the United States ineffective." *See* W. Michael Reisman, *supra* note 32, at 330.

> tory to interpret treaties, at least when such use will result in an interpretation of the treaty domestically that is different from its interpretation internationally. If the interpretation based on legislative history is narrower, i.e., imposes lesser restrictions on what the parties may do, the United States would be in breach of its obligations internationally. . . .
>
> If an interpretation based on legislative history is broader than the international interpretation, i.e., imposes greater obligations on the parties, then the United States would be subjecting itself to restrictions on its conduct for which it would receive no reciprocal benefits. Moreover, the use of a legislative history to impose obligations domestically that the United States does not have internationally would also violate the United States Supreme Court's decision in *INS v. Chadha.* Since a treaty is an agreement between two or more states, an obligation that is, by hypothesis, not part of the United States' obligations internationally, cannot be United States law as part of the treaty. . . .[141]

And Professor Halberstam concludes: "legislative history should not be used to interpret a treaty so as to impose different obligations on the United States domestically and internationally."[142]

Revisiting this issue in 1992 with even greater force, Professor Halberstam says in examining the treaty interpretation issues raised in the ABM dispute:

> a treaty cannot have different meanings domestically and internationally. A treaty is law domestically only because and to the extent that it is law internationally; it has no domestic legal effect apart from that. The treaty process is not an alternate route for domestic legislation in the absence of an international obligation. The dual treaty approach is invalid as a constitutional matter and unsound as a policy matter.[143]

She also notes what she regards as a logical flaw in the principal argument used to support the "dual" approach. Thus she writes:

> There is another flaw in the argument that since the President cannot ratify a treaty without the Senate's advice and consent, the treaty he ratifies must be the treaty as the Senate understood it. It can be argued with equal logic that since the President ratifies treaties on behalf of the United States—and need not ratify a treaty even if the Senate has given its advice and consent—the treaty he ratified is the treaty as the President understood it. Since the treaty cannot come into effect for the United States unless the Senate gives its advice and consent to ratification *and* unless the President decides to ratify, it is no more logical to argue that it means what the Senate understood it to mean when it gave its advice and consent than to argue that it

---

141 Malvina Halberstam, *supra* note 140, at 1647-48 (footnotes omitted).

142 Malvina Halberstam, *supra* note 140, at 1651.

143 Malvina Halberstam, *A Treaty Is a Treaty Is a Treaty*, 33 VA. J. INT'L L. 51, 53-54 (1992) (footnotes omitted).

> means what the President understood it to mean when he ratified it. When the concurrence of two branches of government is necessary to bring a law into effect there is no logical basis for saying that the understanding of one or the other is controlling in case of an ambiguity.[144]

Similarly, in a 1991 article on "The Scope of U.S. Senate Control Over the Conclusion and Operation of Treaties"[145] and the foreword to a symposium on "Parliamentary Participation in the Making and Operation of Treaties,"[146] Professors Stefan A. Riesenfeld and Frederick M. Abbott adverted to the new Senate treaty interpretation doctrine and rejected it as inconsistent with international law and the United States Constitution, *even in the strongest case for such "domestic conditions," that is, the determination that a treaty is not self-executing*. Thus, after a careful seventy-two page analysis of United States treaty practice, reminiscent of the work of Professors Jessup and Lissitzyn in the *Niagara Reservation* case, and consistent with the majority opinion in that case in the Court of Appeals, they conclude broadly:

> the power of the Senate to give effect to conditions to treaties is constrained by international law and the Constitution. Only a condition which is valid and effective under international law may become part of the law of the land because a condition does not have a legal identity outside the context of the treaty. The Senate does not have an ancillary constitutional power to enact domestic legislation under the guise of the treaty power.[147]

And in their foreword to the symposium, which they had organized, they write:

> We believe that the Senate lacks the constitutional authority to declare the non-self-executing character of a treaty with binding effect on U.S. courts. The Senate has the unicameral power only to consent to the ratification of

144 *Id.* at 65. Given the Biden Treaty Interpretation Condition's reliance even on informal preratification materials, it is quite plausible that the Senate and the President could have different interpretations about meaning at the time of advice and consent and subsequent ratification or accession. In such a case, Professor Halberstam's point is quite relevant. Why, constitutionally, would the Senate view prevail over the President's view? Note also that it is possible that a Senate will not have addressed an issue at all or that a setting may arise in which there is no evidence of Senate intent even in informal preratification materials yet there is evidence of a Presidential intent. Would the common practice in most legal interpretation of "supplementing" in settings where the parties intended an instrument to remain in force but did not advert to the particular issue, be permissible under the "dual" approach? Would the setting of a sole Presidential intent be advanced as binding on the courts, not just entitled to "great weight" as under present law, consistent with the logic of the "dual" approach?

145 Stefan A. Riesenfeld & Frederick M. Abbott, *The Scope of U.S. Senate Control Over the Conclusion and Operation of Treaties*, 67 CHI.-KENT L. REV. 571 (1991).

146 Stefan A. Riesenfeld & Frederick M. Abbott, *Foreword: Symposium on Parliamentary Participation in the Making and Operation of Treaties*, 67 CHI.-KENT L. REV. 293 (1991).

147 Stefan A. Riesenfeld & Frederick M. Abbott, *supra* note 145, at 643.

> treaties, not to pass domestic legislation. A declaration is not part of a treaty in the sense of modifying the legal obligations created by it. A declaration is merely an expression of an interpretation or of a policy or position. U.S. courts are bound by the Constitution to apply treaties as the law of the land. They are not bound to apply expressions of opinion adopted by the Senate (and concurred in by the President). The courts must undertake their own examination of the terms and context of each provision in a treaty to which the United States is a party and decide whether it is self-executing. The treaty is law. The Senate's declaration is not law. The Senate does not have the power to make law outside the treaty instrument.[148]

Professors Riesenfeld and Abbott go on to point out that the dicta in footnote 7 of the *Stuart* case is inconsistent with the Court's own long and excellent record in treaty interpretation cases. They note:

> We are particularly troubled by the dicta in *United States v. Stuart* regarding the supremacy of the legislative record for interpretative purposes and point in our paper to the myriad cases in which the Supreme Court has otherwise properly stated rules of treaty interpretation consistent with international law. We suggest that when the court has occasion to reconsider the issue raised in *Stuart* that it focus on its own otherwise strikingly consistent record.[149]

In a conversation on the occasion of his lecturing to the National Security Law Summer Workshop at the University of Virginia School of Law in 1995, Robert Dalton, the Assistant Legal Adviser for Treaty Affairs in the Department of State, indicated that he also took the view that the "dual" approach to treaty interpretation is incorrect and that the Senate has no general lawmaking power to attach "domestic conditions" to treaties during the process of advice and consent.[150] Mr. Dalton's position is particularly important since, as the principal official charged with treaty matters on a day-to-day basis in the Department of State, he is probably more aware of the realities of the treaty practice of the United States than any other person.

F. FURTHER INCONSISTENCIES WITH THE FOREIGN RELATIONS LAW AND PRACTICE OF THE UNITED STATES

In the *Chinese Exclusion Case*[151] in 1899 the Supreme Court established the principle that a later act of Congress, passed within the constitutional legislative authority of the Congress, and clearly inconsistent with a prior

---

148 Stefan A. Riesenfeld & Frederick M. Abbott, *supra* note 146, at 296-97.

149 Stefan A. Riesenfeld & Frederick M. Abbott, *supra* note 146, at 301.

150 Conversation between the author and Assistant Legal Adviser for Treaty Affairs, Robert Dalton, June 1995, in Charlottesville, Virginia.

151 130 U.S. 581 (1899).

treaty, will take precedence over the treaty obligation as a matter of United States domestic law as opposed to our international obligation, which would remain unmodified. The Court understood the difficult choice that it was making when confronted with a later inconsistent act of Congress, and it emphasized that this principle of United States domestic law could not have the effect of removing the Nation's international obligation. The Court also noted that it made this decision in the face of a "constitutional exercise of legislative power."[152] Since, without more, a Senate "view" as to an issue of treaty interpretation, whatever it is, is not a "constitutional exercise of legislative power" (nor, for that matter, a constitutional exercise of Executive power), it would not seem consistent with the underpinnings of this case for the "dual" approach to override a binding international treaty obligation as a matter of domestic law, which is precisely what the "dual" approach purports to do. Consider also that the "dual" approach, as it was originated, and presumably will be sought to be applied in the future, can be triggered simply by a statement of an Executive Branch witness during hearings, or the views of a few Senators, or perhaps a committee report. While it can, of course, be argued that the Senate treaty interpretation condition has a different standard, it is itself uncertain and ambiguous. Should the principle of the *Chinese Exclusion Case*, which has been criticized by many in our profession including Professor Henkin, be extended to override our binding international treaty obligations even by informal actions within the advice and consent process? This would seem neither consistent with, nor desirable under, the foreign relations law of the United States.[153]

---

152 130 U.S. 581, 581 (1899).

153 In this connection, it should be recalled that John Jay and Thomas Jefferson, perhaps *the* most experienced foreign affairs experts among the Framers, both had the view that a treaty of the United States could not be overridden even by full legislative acts. Thus, John Jay said in *Federalist* 64:

> The proposed Constitution . . . has not in the least extended the obligation of treaties. They are just as binding, and just as far beyond the lawful reach of legislative acts now, as they will be at any future period, or under any form of government.

THE FEDERALIST NO. 64 , at 437 (John Jay) (Jacob E. Cooke ed., 1961). And Thomas Jefferson, as our first Secretary of State, wrote in 1790 in a memorandum to President Washington:

> A treaty made by the President, with the concurrence of two-thirds of the Senate, is a law of the land, and a law of superior order, because it not only repeals past laws, but cannot itself be repealed by future ones.

THE JEFFERSONIAN CYCLOPEDIA 880 (New York: Funk & Wagnalls Company, John P. Foley ed., 1900). It does not seem likely that these influential Framers would have even conceived of unilaterally imposed Senate "domestic conditions" as overriding the Nation's treaty obligations.

The "dual" approach is even more clearly in violation of the important principle of United States foreign relations law embodied in the classic *Charming Betsy*[154] case. This principle, announced by Chief Justice Marshall in the early days of the Republic, is intended to minimize areas in which legislative actions would be found to be in conflict with the international legal obligations of the United States. Indeed, in a post *Chinese Exclusion Case* world, it is one of the most critical provisions of United States foreign relations law designed to promote our compliance with international law. As Chief Justice Marshall stated: "an Act of Congress ought never to be construed to violate the law of nations if any other possible construction remains. . . ."[155] This principle generally has been applied particularly rigorously by United States domestic courts. They want to be certain that the legislature knew of, and intended to override for domestic purposes, the particular international legal obligation of the United States in question, before they will do so. This principle is embodied in Section 114 of the *Restatement* which provides:

> Where fairly possible, a United States statute is to be construed so as not to conflict with international law or with an international agreement of the United States.[156]

---

154 Murray v. Schooner Charming Betsy, 6 U.S. (2 Cranch) 64 (1804). As an example of the contemporary power of this principle, *see* United States v. Palestine Liberation Organization, 695 F. Supp. 1456 (S.D. N.Y. 1988).

> Only where a treaty is irreconcilable with a later enacted statute and Congress has clearly evinced an intent to supersede a treaty by enacting a statute does the later enacted statute take precedence. . . .
>
> The long standing and well-established position of the Mission at the United Nations, sustained by international agreement, when considered along with the text of the ATA and its legislative history, fails to disclose any clear legislative intent that Congress was directing the Attorney General, the State Department or this Court to act in contravention of the Headquarters Agreement. This court acknowledges the validity of the government's position that Congress *has the power* to enact statutes abrogating prior treaties or international obligations entered into by the United States. . . . However, unless this power is clearly and unequivocally exercised, this court is under a duty to interpret statutes in a manner consonant with existing treaty obligations. This is a rule of statutory construction sustained by an unbroken line of authority for over a century and a half. Recently, the Supreme Court articulated it in *Weinberger v. Rossi, supra,* 456 U.S. at 32, 102 S.Ct. at 1516:
>
>> It has been a maxim of statutory construction since the decision in *Murray v. The Charming Betsy*, 6 U.S. (2 Cranch) 64, 118 [2 L.Ed. 208] (1804), that "an act of Congress ought never to be construed to violate the law of nations, if any other possible construction remains. . . ."
>
> F. Supp. at 1464-65.

155 6 U.S. (2 Cranch) 64, at 118.

156 RESTATEMENT (THIRD) OF THE FOREIGN RELATIONS LAW OF THE UNITED STATES § 114 (1987).

The "dual" approach, however, would domestically override our most solemn international treaty obligations without any legislation (or Executive Branch constitutional action), and would seek to do so even on vague and ambiguous "advice and consent process history," which might simply take the form of testimony by an Executive Branch official or expressed views of members of the Senate. Note that it does not even require recognition and inclusion of the interpretive issue in the Senate resolution of advice and consent or a vote by the Senate. Most seriously, however, in relation to this important principle of our foreign relations law, the "dual" approach would apply even in complete absence of any evidence that the members of the Senate were intent, not just on a particular interpretation, but to have that interpretation override the treaty obligations of the Nation if the interpretation proved to be inconsistent with the internationally correct meaning between the parties. That is, the Senate intent in giving advice and consent to a treaty is always a double intent, relating both to *meaning* and *bargain*. They believe that the meaning is X *and* that the meaning X is the internationally correct meaning bargained for and binding on all treaty parties alike. Later, in a mistake setting, just to focus on the Senate's intent that the meaning was X tells you nothing about what the Senate would have wanted to do if the internationally correct meaning turned out to be Y. In most cases, the "dual" approach to the contrary, I believe, more often than not, the Senate would not want a result either requiring the United States to shoulder higher unilateral obligations or to violate our treaty obligations, one or the other of which is the result always required by the "dual" approach. The "dual" approach, then, would seem particularly inconsistent with the modern *Charming Betsy* principle, both on the nature of the domestic acts necessary to override our treaty obligations, and on the lack of evidence that the members of the Senate really would have wanted to do so, despite the interpretation being different than they had thought.

Finally, the "dual" approach would seem inconsistent with a general effort in United States foreign policy practice to promote effective third party international adjudication of our treaty disputes[157] and to participate effec-

---

157 Even Professor David Koplow, a principal proponent of the "dual" approach, and one broadly sympathetic with the Biden Treaty Interpretation condition, has his doubts about the effects of these doctrines on the ability of the United States to effectively participate in international adjudication. Thus, he writes:

> [The Biden Condition] . . . provides that "the United States shall not agree to or adopt an interpretation different from [the current executive-legislative understanding of the treaty] except pursuant to Senate advice and consent to a subsequent treaty or protocol, or the enactment of a statute." Under this language, could the United States reliably submit disputes to binding international adjudication? Does the language require that, whenever the United States's interpretation is

tively in multilateral treaty regimes. Despite current non-acceptance of the optional clause general compulsory jurisdiction of the International Court of Justice, the United States is a party to many international treaties and agreements which contain dispute resolution clauses. Indeed, seeking such clauses in our international agreements has been, and remains, a mainstay of United States foreign policy. The "dual" approach, however, by adding another domestic legal rule that would potentially require the President to violate United States treaty obligations, would certainly not seem consistent with this thrust toward a more effective rule of law in international life. Any lawyer, domestic or international, understands that the correct meaning of language, whether embodied in a statute, a treaty or even a valentine, is not always evident. It is commonplace for contentious cases to present reasonable arguments on all sides, for mistakes to be made, and for courts to sometimes surprise in interpretation. Further, any reasonably sophisticated jurisprudence understands that complex framework agreements such as constitutions or many basic multilateral treaties, such as the UN Charter, The European Convention on Human Rights, or the General Agreement on Tariff and Trade evolve through time and are not simply frozen at the moment of conception.[158] Losing unilateral control is a price we pay for third party adjudication and the rule of law. Sadly, the "dual" approach would seem the worst kind of "old thinking" in not understanding the national interest shared by the United States and all nations in a more effective rule of law.

> rejected, this country will resist the authoritative international interpretation, unless the other party agrees to renegotiate the treaty (and give up in diplomacy a victory it just won in litigation) or new domestic United States law is created to effectuate the new ruling?
>
> This type of unilateralism in foreign affairs is not a sound device for aiding the establishment of a viable network of international law and order.

D. Koplow, *supra* note 12, at 1433-34 (footnote omitted).

158 *See, e.g.*, on this point, Rudolf Bernhardt, *Evolutive Treaty Interpretation, Especially of the European Convention on Human Rights*, 42 GERMAN YEARBOOK INT'L L. 11 (1999). Rudolf Bernhardt, of Heidelberg, writes in this recent article:

> In general, it cannot be denied that there is a certain dynamism that is relevant in treaty interpretation because later statements and practices of the parties to a treaty and of the organs of an international organization are relevant elements of interpretation. Even if one can hardly find express statements that every treaty is a living instrument and has to be interpreted accordingly, it is also obvious that in substance this is and must be accepted. Not the existence, but the extent of the evolutive or dynamic element in any treaty interpretation is the real problem.

Id. at 16. *See also* on this point, specifically with reference to the Free Trade Agreement with Canada, the North American Free Trade Agreement with Canada and Mexico, and the GATT/WTO arrangement, Detlev Vagts, *supra* note 50, at 42.

G. POLICY CONCERNS

> ***"Great nations, like great men, should keep their word."***[159]
>
> *Mr. Justice Black, dissenting in* Tuscarora Indian Nation, *1960.*

The most serious policy concern with respect to the proposed "dual" approach to treaty interpretation is that in a variety of ways it harms the rule of law and United States efforts to promote the rule of law internationally. Were other nations to adopt such an approach, following the example of the Senate condition in the United States, there would be a truck hole through efforts at treaty compliance.[160] Other nations would now feel justified in saying they would adhere to the interpretation of their Duma or other constitutional body, rather than the meaning as agreed with the United States. And even if they did not, *we* would be short changing our own treaty partners, with all the associated costs through time in doing so. The provision set out in Article 46 of the Vienna Convention on the Law of Treaties is about as far as one would want to go in recognizing internal rules consistent with a rule of law internationally. That, of course, permits a state to invoke a provision of its internal law regarding competence to conclude treaties when a "violation was manifest and concerned a rule of its internal law of fundamental importance." It seems likely that the Framers, who were so concerned that we adhere to our treaty obligations that they built into the Supremacy Clause language to ensure that past treaties "made . . . under the Authority of the United States. . . ."[161] would be "the supreme Law of the Land," even though none of these past treaties could be presented to the Senate, would have not looked favorably on the proposed "dual" approach.

A second serious policy concern of a proposal that would shift the referent in treaty interpretation from the meaning as agreed between the parties to the meaning as agreed with the Senate, is a staggering cost in United States foreign relations that has largely remained hidden in the debate. Thus, whenever it is applicable, the "dual" approach would inevitably mean either that the United States is required to violate its treaty obligations or to unilaterally comply with obligations not bargained for or binding on the other treaty party or parties. Now the first of these really undermines our

---

159 Federal Power Commission v. Tuscarora Indian Nation, 362 U.S. 99, 142 (1960). (Black, J., dissenting with the concurrence of the Chief Justice and Mr. Justice Douglas).

160 Concerning efforts to enhance compliance with treaties generally, *see* John Norton Moore, *Enhancing Compliance with International Law: A Neglected Remedy*, 39 VA. J. INT'L L. 881 (1999).

161 U.S. CONST. art. VI.

long term milieu interests in the rule of law, as well as our reputation as a dependable treaty partner with all of its associated costs, as discussed above. The second setting, however, could also be of great concern in our treaty relationships. While there are exceptions, treaty relationships are generally rooted in mutuality and shared benefit. It could be of the most serious nature in arms control, trade or other matters to be held domestically to a standard not binding on the other treaty party, and thus to set aside mutuality of obligation in a setting where we had assumed it was applicable and had bargained for it. Professor David Koplow, in his defense of the "dual" approach, argues that "[s]trict mutuality of treaty obligations is unlikely and legally unnecessary."[162] While, in making this argument against the importance of mutuality of obligation, he shows that treaties may intentionally impose *different* obligations on the treaty parties and that their domestic processes may pose *different routes or challenges to implementation,*[163] this argument shockingly misses the point. For mutuality of obligation no more requires *identical* obligations on the parties than does a contract for sale. Rather, the point is for the United States and other nations to be able to rely upon the *bargain* struck. *That* is the core meaning of *mutuality* and the core mechanism of *shared benefit through agreement*. The "dual" approach would impose a severe cost to the United States precisely where it held the Nation to a higher cost than bargained for. And this would *inevitably* be one of the logical consequences of the "dual" approach whenever it made a legal difference.

A third concern is that, although ostensibly designed to protect the intent of a consenting Senate, the "dual" approach could *never* fully effectuate that intent. Moreover, it is open to question whether more often than not this approach would undermine the Senate intent in settings in which the issue would actually arise. This paradox occurs because, as seen above, the Senate intent in approving a treaty is always a *double* intent; that is, an intent as to treaty *meaning* and an intent as to the treaty *bargain*. The Senate believes that the meaning is X *and it believes* that the meaning X is the internationally correct meaning bargained for or binding on both parties. The "dual" approach makes a difference *only* where these two differ and, thus, inevitably only one of these "intents" can be implemented. The important other "bargain" intent concerning legal obligation and mutuality of obligation will simply always be violated as the approach focuses on the intent concerning the meaning X. Basically the "dual" approach occurs in settings of mistake, or settings comparable in their effect to that of mistake. In these settings, the "dual" approach, by always favoring the meaning X over the

---

162 D. Koplow, *supra* note 12, at 1408.

163 *See generally* section II (B) (5) of the article by Professor D. Koplow, *supra* note 12, at 1408-12.

issues of legal obligation and mutuality of obligation, may actually insist on a "remedy," which is, more often than not, less congruent with the choices members of the Senate would actually have made if faced with the dilemma which triggered the approach. Although speculative, I suspect that few Senators would choose to follow a particular meaning if they knew it would, in a specific case, impose a higher burden on the United States than on the other treaty party. And I hope a considerable number would choose the good faith and credit of the United States in following its legal obligations over insistence on a particular meaning. Adding these important "intents" together, it is quite possible, if not probable, that the "dual" approach as a way of handling mistakes in treaty interpretation would actually less satisfactorily carry out the intent of most Senates through time. It certainly would in some settings.[164]

Yet another concern is that the "dual" approach would add a substantial burden in day-to-day conduct of United States foreign policy as the record of Senate advice and consent were now routinely consulted, as opposed to the usual sources for treaty interpretation. As my fellow former Counselor on International Law to the Department of State, Malvina Halberstam, notes, the "dual approach would mean:

> the President would have to review the whole pre-ratification record—testimony, correspondence, reports, statements made in the Senate—every time a question of treaty interpretation arose, to see whether he could decipher any Senate understanding—explicit or implicit—that would require him to take a particular position on the question.[165]

Translating this burdensome task into its precise human and economic costs may be difficult, but as another former Counselor on International Law to the Department, my sense is that these costs would be quite real for the Executive Branch. Indeed, these costs may be difficult to fully appreciate unless one has spent time in the Legal Adviser's Office at State or has

---

164 In jurisprudential terms, a problem in thinking clearly about this issue is that the concept of "Senate meaning" has multiple referents. That is, it not only means "Senate intent" as to the scope of the treaty right, privilege, power or immunity in question, but also "Senate intent" as to that jural relation being reciprocally binding on, or bargained with, the other treaty party. And, most centrally, whenever the "dual" approach presents itself, and there is a conflict between these "Senate intents," it presents the dual question of meaning concerning "Senate intent" as to which of these "intents" the Senate would prefer to have prevail if only one could be realized, *and* "Senate intent" as to whether this preference was intended to create a legally binding "domestic condition" apart from the treaty. *See generally* the classic discussion of ambiguity in legal terms in Wesley Newcomb Hohfeld, Fundamental Legal Conceptions (Walter Wheeler Cook ed., Foreword by Arthur L. Corbin, 1964) And for a classic representative sample of the rich philosophical literature concerning ambiguity in language, *see* Ordinary Language (V. C. Chappell ed., 1965).

165 Malvina Halberstam, *supra* note 143, at 63.

sought to decipher "Senate intent" from a complex record such as that in the ABM "broad-narrow" debate.[166] Eugene Rostow, a former Under Secretary of State, provides a flavor of the pervasiveness and inevitability of the process of interpretation in the day-to-day conduct of United States foreign policy when he writes:

> The phenomenon of presidential interpretation and reinterpretation of treaties is not "previously unknown,". . . . It occurs daily in every nook and cranny of the law. When the President sends instructions to representatives of the United States at the United Nations Security Council and at international conferences on dozens if not hundreds of subjects ranging from telecommunication and aviation to fisheries and the law of war, he is interpreting and reinterpreting treaties as he "faithfully executes" the law. . . . This process of change and development is inherent in the growth of the law. Sometimes the changes are incremental and interstitial. Sometimes they are considerable. They are in fact inevitable as law confronts life every day of the week. Laws evolve around the broad policy purposes sought by their progenitors. But the progenitors can never freeze the law into a static pattern, nor anticipate exactly how it should be applied in all future circumstances. Nor can it be assumed that every lawmaker voted for the reasons advanced by one or a number of his or her colleagues in debate, or by representatives of the Executive Branch in testimony before committees.[167]

Must the Executive Branch now review the informal preratification record for each interpretation in this multiplicity of interpretations? And how deeply must they dig into the record?

Of related jurisprudential concern is the *tilt* of the "dual" approach toward a wishful belief in a treaty so clear as to cabin all subsequent interpretation. Is such an objective for a treaty, or any other form of legal prescription, anything but fantasy? Professor W. Michael Reisman, Hohfeld Professor of Jurisprudence at Yale, points out in this connection:

> [O]ne reads with . . . disbelief, in the 1987 Senate Foreign Relations Report that
>
> > [t]he committee is aware of *no* instance in which a treaty was reasonably supposed by the Senate, when it consented to ratification, to mean one thing, and it was argued later by the Executive to mean something altogether different.

---

166 My own experience in carefully examining the full treaty advice and consent process in the ABM "broad-narrow" debate provides an appreciation of the monumental task this review may entail in a contentious treaty interpretation case.

167 E. Rostow, *supra* note 12, at 1457. Professor Rostow also writes: "Since the President necessarily interprets and reinterprets every statute and treaty each time he applies them to new fact situations, the constitutional authority . . . [to do so] is an essential part of the executive power entrusted to the President under Article II of the Constitution." E. Rostow, *supra* note 12, at 1455.

> Can one find any enduring treaties, or laws for that matter, that have not undergone interpretive transformations? Is there any lawmaker with the omniscience or prescience to anticipate every eventuality and to provide explicitly for it and then prohibit all applicative initiative? And if there were such an entity with such objectives, is language capable of this task?[168]

Surely the legal realists and every other modern approach to jurisprudence and communication have alerted us to the inherent interpretive difficulties in law and language.[169] Nor is this even to consider the desirability of complete rigidity in legal prescription.

Further, and again paradoxically, the "dual" approach may actually reduce rather than enhance the Senate role in advice and consent to treaties. For that role relates not solely to the *domestically* binding meaning of a treaty but rather to its real meaning as binding the United States *internationally*. It is the job of the Senate to carefully consider and assess the meaning of the treaty in *both* dimensions. Simply to rely on the "dual" approach to protect the Senate, as has been seen, cannot protect the Senate intent or its role in relation to the international meaning. Most importantly, it cannot protect the *United States*, which one assumes is the principal purpose of the Senate check. The "dual" approach may encourage some to take false comfort in believing they are now "protected," but there is really no substitute for careful Senate consideration of all the issues it believes important. And those issues viewed as of particular importance should be treated in amendments, understandings or reservations fully attached to the resolution of advice and consent and conveyed to the other treaty party. Only in this way, in effectuating a correct international legal meaning on important points, can the interests of the Country be truly protected. Sadly, this concern that the "dual" approach may even discourage an active Senate role, is not an imaginary concern. When I was conducting interviews on the Hill for ACDA in relation to the "broad-narrow" issue, I was presented with an argument that the President had better accept the approach that Executive Branch statements are "authoritative" or the Senate will really have to closely examine future treaties sent up. That, however, *is* the job of the Senate and there is no magic bullet to avoid doing that job in a way which will

---

168 *See* W. Michael Reisman, *supra* note 32, at 327.

169 *See, e.g.*, such classics as Oliver Wendell Holmes, *The Path of the Law*, 10 HARV. L. REV. 457 (1897); BENJAMIN N. CARDOZO, THE NATURE OF THE JUDICIAL PROCESS (1921); KARL N. LLEWELLYN, THE COMMON LAW TRADITION (1960); LUDWIG WITTGENSTEIN, PHILOSOPHICAL INVESTIGATIONS (1953); G. E. MOORE, PHILOSOPHICAL Papers (1959).

This jurisprudential concern, however, should not be taken to the point of nihilism. Language does convey meaning in context. And it is certainly understandable that the Senate would wish to pin down important issues. Even so, the "dual" approach is not the best way to achieve this objective and even its tilt seems to underestimate the fluidity of legal prescription and the interpretive process.

be effective internationally as well as domestically. Professor Malvina Halberstam nails this point precisely when she says:

> It is argued in support of the dual treaty approach that the legislative history rather than the negotiating history—which may be considered in interpreting the treaty under international law—should be controlling domestically because it would be too burdensome for the Senate to keep informed of the negotiating history, and that an understanding on every point the Senate considers important would make the treaty unmanageable. But surely, the purpose of the constitutional requirement that the Senate give its advice and consent to treaties was not to ensure that domestic law comports with the Senate's understanding but, rather, to ensure that the United States does not bind itself *internationally* to that which the Senate considers objectionable. The justification for the dual treaty approach relieves the Senate of that responsibility. Thus, under the dual treaty approach, the Senate would abdicate the very function that the advice and consent requirement was designed to serve.[170]

Finally, one of the important policy points to note in relation to the choice between the proposed new "dual" approach to treaty interpretation and the traditional "unitary" approach is that there seems to be no problem in need of a remedy. The "dual" approach is promoted, it is said, to keep the Executive Branch honest in presenting treaties to the Senate. Yet despite the contentious public debate in the "broad-narrow" setting about a contemporary interpretation of the ABM Treaty, apparently no one has been able to find a single example in American constitutional history where a President has sought to mislead a Senate in presenting a treaty for advice and consent. It is, at least to the present, simply a non-problem. Moreover, in settings where there were an intent to mislead the Senate, there is a host of available remedies. These range from enacting legislation, holding hearings, withholding cooperation, criminal sanctions, and, in the most extreme cases, even impeachment.

---

170 Malvina Halberstam, *supra* note 140, at 1649 (footnotes omitted). Professor Halberstam cites an article by Michael J. Glennon for the proposition she is refuting in this passage. The article is Michael J. Glennon, *Interpreting "Interpretation": The President, The Senate, and When Treaty Interpretation Becomes Treaty Meaning*, 20 U.C. DAVIS L. REV. 913, 919-20 (1987). Not surprisingly, this article by Professor Glennon was reprinted in the hearings on the ABM Treaty "broad-narrow" debate. *See* Malvina Halberstam, *supra* note 140, at 1649 n.19.

Of relevance to efficient performance of the Senate's role in advice and consent, as well as the interpretive roles of the Executive Branch and the courts, practice under the "dual" approach would add an additional layer of concern for all three branches as to whether Administration witnesses had spoken "authoritatively" on a treaty or were merely expressing their personal views or had exceeded their authorized scope of testimony. For a discussion of these issues as they arose in the process of Senate advice and consent to the INF Treaty, *see* Gary Michael Buechler, *supra* note 12, at 1992-94.

H. A BRIEF COMPARATIVE NOTE

To my knowledge, there has been no comprehensive comparative study systematically reviewing the law of every country in the world for signs of a "dual" approach to treaty interpretation. In the early 1990s, however, Professor Stefan A. Riesenfeld, a distinguished American international lawyer, organized a symposium of international scholars which met both in the United States and Switzerland, on the subject "Parliamentary Participation in the Making and Operation of Treaties."[171] The symposium included legal experts from Brazil, France, Germany, Italy, the Netherlands, Switzerland, and the United Kingdom, as well as the United States. This international symposium was motivated in substantial part by the organizers' concern about the new "dual" approach to treaty interpretation reflected in the Biden Condition and the application of the doctrine of "domestic conditions" even to the issue of whether a treaty is self-executing under national law. Thus, they write in the foreword to the symposium as their initial reason for the Symposium:

> We were motivated to convene this symposium by a problem that affects particularly the U.S. constitutional system, that is the attachment by the U.S. Senate of qualifications to its consent to the ratification of treaties that purport to control their domestic effect. In our opinion, the Senate threatens to undermine the credibility of U.S. participation in the international legal process and to deprive U.S. citizens of their constitutional rights. It ultimately threatens the creation of a more democratic international legal system. We are not especially concerned that the legislative branch in the United States is able by the passage of legislation to modify the internal effect of treaties under the last in time doctrine. Rather we are concerned with unicameral efforts by the Senate to appropriate the legislative power to itself. We are similarly alarmed by the Senate's recent attempts to assert post-ratification control over the interpretation of treaties, an activity that also threatens to undermine the integrity of the international legal system and that is not supported by the Constitution. We hoped that the foreign participants in this enterprise would help to illuminate for American legislators, courts and scholars the uniqueness of the Senate's perspective on its role in the international legal system and the potential for harm inherent in that perspective.[172]

The organizers also suggest, based on the collective comparative knowledge of the participants at the symposium, that:

> If the position asserted by the U.S. Senate is adopted by the courts—and we stress that this position has never been adopted by a U.S. court—the United States would be unique in permitting a single legislative chamber of a bi-

---

171 *See*, for the published proceedings of this symposium, *Symposium on Parliamentary Participation in the Making and Operation of Treaties*, 67 CHI.-KENT L. REV. 293 (1991).

172 Stefan A. Riesenfeld & Frederick M. Abbott, *supra* note 146.

> cameral legislature to override the terms of a treaty by the mechanism of a unicameral act.[173]

Non-U.S. participants also expressed strong concern about any "dual" approach to treaty interpretation, and some viewed the issue also as one of the independence of the judiciary in treaty interpretation. The organizers summarize these views:

> The non-U.S. participants in our symposium, particularly Professors Frowein and Wildhaber, expressed strong dissatisfaction with the idea that a treaty may have separate meanings for international and domestic law purposes. In Germany and Switzerland, as examples, the courts would not be bound by representations made by the executive to the parliament. Professors Frowein and Wildhaber each expressed grave concern that acceptance of the idea that a treaty may have independent meanings under domestic and international law would undermine the integrity of the international legal system. . . .
>
> None of the non-U.S. participants in the symposium believe that their parliament has the power to control the national courts' interpretation of a treaty. In France, both the ordinary and the administrative courts have ceased applying authoritative executive treaty interpretations to bring the judiciary into compliance with France's international treaty-based commitment to an independent judiciary. In the United Kingdom the courts do not look at the record of parliamentary debate with respect to any question of statutory interpretation, including statutes implementing treaties, but rely strictly on the text of the statute. This is not to suggest that courts in the United States may not consult the record of legislative approval of a treaty. It is rather to suggest that this record does not control the meaning of the treaty, which meaning must rather be determined in accordance with applicable rules of international law.[174]

The symposium organizers also quote Professor Frowein in strong opposition to the "dual" approach now incorporated in the Biden Condition. They quote him as saying:

> seen from the German perspective, you would always start from the idea that every treaty, as an international legal instrument binding upon the states which have become members, is a legal rule which has one correct interpretation only. . . . We must also agree that the interpretation may change . . . with a certain time period elapsed. But; from a German perspective, although you would be faced with the fact that, for instance, the federal government will have explained in very great detail the terms of the treaty in the internal ratification procedure, you would never say that this in itself becomes binding on either administrative authorities, governmental authorities or the courts. Because there is, under German law, no possibility to

---

173 Stefan A. Riesenfeld & Frederick M. Abbott, *supra* note 146, at 299.

174 Stefan A. Riesenfeld & Frederick M. Abbott, *supra* note 146, at 301-02.

> make binding commands by explaining the text of a treaty. That is, of course, quite impossible.[175]

It is also worth noting with respect to Professor Tribe's view of only materials before the Senate at the time of initial Senate consideration may be taken into account in treaty interpretation, that even in the United Kingdom, which does not generally permit an examination of legislative history in statutory interpretation *and* which only incorporates treaties into domestic law by legislation, House of Lords decisions have looked to background treaty history, including foreign language texts and *travaux préparatoires*.[176] And Lord Diplock, in doing so in a 1980 case, also raised the question of whether United Kingdom courts were even legally bound by the interpretive provisions of the Vienna Convention on the Law of Treaties, which, of course, permit consultation of non-textual materials in certain settings and, even more fundamentally, look to the intent of the treaty parties, not that of the legislature of an implementing state. Thus, he says:

> in exercising its interpretative function of ascertaining what it was that the delegates to an international conference agreed on by their majority vote in favour of the text of an international convention where that text itself is ambiguous or obscure, an English court should have regard to any material which those delegates themselves had thought would be available to clear up any possible ambiguities or obscurities. Indeed, in the case of Acts of Parliament giving effect to international conventions concluded after the coming into force of the Vienna Convention on the Law of Treaties, I think an English court might well be under a constitutional obligation to do so. By ratifying that convention, Her Majesty's government has undertaken an international obligation on behalf of the United Kingdom to interpret future treaties in this manner and, since under our constitution the function of interpreting the written law is an exercise of judicial power and rests with the courts of justice, that obligation assumed by the United Kingdom falls to be performed by those courts.[177]

The available evidence suggests that the proposed "dual" interpretation doctrine, embodied in the Biden Treaty Interpretation Condition, is a highly unusual proposal without counterpart in the foreign relations law of

---

175 Stefan A. Riesenfeld & Frederick M. Abbott, *supra* note 146, at 301, n.22.

176 *See*, for example, James Buchanan & Co Ltd v. Babco Forwarding and Shipping, [1977] 3 All E.R. 1040 (Nov. 9, 1977) (French language text); Fothergill v. Monarch Airlines Ltd, [1980] 2 All E.R. 696 (July 10, 1980) (French language text and *travaux*). One recurring concern in these cases, suggesting broader use of these non-textual materials rooted in the negotiations and intent between the parties, is the need to promote international uniformity in interpretation of treaties, a concern which cuts to the core of the problem with the "dual" approach.

177 Fothergill v. Monarch Airlines Ltd, [1980] 2 All E.R. 696, 707 (July 10, 1980) (opinion of Lord Diplock). The substantive provisions of the Vienna Convention on the Law of Treaties, including Section 3 on "Interpretation of Treaties," are generally regarded as customary international law, and, as such, are binding on the United States.

other countries. Most importantly, it would seem highly likely to be viewed by other countries as cause for real concern in its effect on the international legal system and their treaty relations with the United States.

I. THE RIGHT STUFF

> ***"There is no error so monstrous that it fails to find defenders among the ablest men."***
>
> *Lord Acton, 1881*

It is common sense and fair play. It is "do unto others as you would have them do unto you." It is international law. And it is the foreign relations law of the United States as repeatedly declared by the Supreme Court. Treaties should be interpreted by reference to the shared intentions of the parties, not by reference to the shared intent of the President and the Senate. A treaty is not an agreement between the President and the Senate, it is an agreement between nations.

Equally obviously, the President and the Senate should work together in good faith to ensure that shared intentions of the President and the Senate are conveyed to the other party for agreement or renegotiation. That is a difficult job, but it will not be helped by the false comfort, and enormous costs, of the "dual" approach.

IV.
"Domestic Conditions": The Invisible Issue and the Trail of Invisible Authority

If the complexities and costs of the "dual" approach have been a hidden virus in the debate about treaty interpretation, the role of "domestic conditions" has been all but invisible. Thus, it is unlikely that the Senate even understood that it was implicitly, at least, dealing with the scope of its own authority under the Constitution to attach "domestic conditions" to treaties during the advice and consent process, when it embarked on a campaign for what became the "dual" approach and the Biden Senate Treaty Condition now routinely attached to treaties.

"Domestic conditions" are those which take effect, if at all, solely under national law, and not as part of the international agreement or even a broader international bargain. Since the effect of the "dual" approach is solely to alter domestic law, as opposed to the internationally correct legal meaning of the treaty, all such interpretations are inevitably a form of "domestic condition." If "domestic conditions," then, are not within Senate authority the "dual" approach should fall on that ground alone. Even if, however, "domestic conditions" are within Senate authority, the "dual" approach and/or the generic Biden Condition may still be unconstitutional.

This section will examine these issues.

A. DOES THE SENATE HAVE AUTHORITY TO ATTACH "DOMESTIC CONDITIONS" TO TREATY ADVICE AND CONSENT?

The issue to be considered here is whether the Senate has general lawmaking authority over domestic law which it can exercise by attaching "domestic conditions" to its treaty advice and consent, and, if it does have any such authority, what are its limitations? There are three theoretical possibilities on which to assess any such Senate "domestic conditions" lawmaking authority.

The first possibility is that such an exercise might be within the legislative powers of the Senate. That possibility is quickly and definitively eliminated, however, by art. I, § 1 of the United States Constitution. It provides: "All legislative Powers herein granted shall be vested in a Congress of the United States, which shall consist of a Senate and House of Representatives."[178] The Senate, acting alone, is plainly not the "Congress" under this definition and thus, quite simply, it possesses no unilateral legislative power.

The second possibility is that "domestic conditions" attached to a treaty are part of the treaty and take their legal effect from the treaty. If a treaty is a contract or compact between nations as the Supreme Court has repeatedly held, however, then "domestic conditions," whether or not attached to the treaty, are plainly not part of the treaty. This is sufficiently clear that even the *Restatement*, which supports at least limited authority for such "domestic conditions," says: "A condition imposed by the Senate that does not seek to modify the treaty and is solely of domestic import, is not part of the treaty. . . ."[179] As has been seen, this seems also to be the import of the only case in the United States which has squarely addressed this issue after full briefing and argumentation, that is, the 1957 decision of the Court of Appeals for the District of Columbia Circuit in the *Niagara Reservation* case.

The final possibility is simply to assert that the Senate's ability to grant or withhold consent carries with it the ability to impose conditions on that consent. That is the apparent view of Professor Henkin, expressed in an article he wrote as a lecturer in law, and subsequently embodied in the *Restatement* under his tenure as Chief Reporter, which we will further examine in the next section. But there are powerful arguments against this general proposition, as well as the other rejected possibilities above.

First, as has been seen, there is a long line of Supreme Court decisions that a treaty is a contract or compact among nations. There is also considerable evidence, including Jefferson's *Manual of Parliamentary Practice for the Use of the Senate*, that the role of the Senate concerning treaties is that of a "negative" or veto. There seems to be no evidence that the Senate was to be given general lawmaking power to make domestic law apart from the treaty it was considering. Given the care with which the legislative power was considered and structured in the Constitution, it is really quite an extraordinary leap to believe that the Framers intended for the advice and consent power with respect to treaties to also include a domestic lawmaking power. Moreover, the treaty advice and consent power is not the only

---

178 U.S. CONST. art. I, § 1.

179 RESTATEMENT (THIRD) OF THE FOREIGN RELATIONS LAW OF THE UNITED STATES, Reporters' Note 4 to § 303, at 164 (1987).

such in the Constitution. The language of the Senate "veto" set out in art. II, § 2, cl. 2, of "by and with the Advice and Consent of the Senate" is also the identical language used in that clause for the Senate "veto" in appointment of Ambassadors, Judges of the Supreme Court, and all other officers of the United States.[180] If, then, the Senate has the ability to attach "domestic conditions" to treaties under this theory, one would assume the Senate also would have the ability to attach "conditions" to the approval of appointments, including Supreme Court Justices.[181] Indeed, this same theory of granting or withholding consent as a basis for domestic lawmaking might also be asserted by the President under the presentment clauses of art. I, § 7 of the Constitution.[182] Further, in its broadest ramifications, this theory could even be asserted to support a power to make binding domestic law as a condition attached to the exercise of *any* one House or one branch power, such as the "sole Power of Impeachment" of the House of Representatives. Such a theory would seem of great consequence, and quite far reaching under the Constitution.

Again, however, the only treaty law case in the United States which seems to have squarely addressed this issue after full briefing and argumentation, the *Niagara Reservation* case, did not accept the validity of a Senate imposed "domestic condition" and, thus, would also seem to have rejected this "condition argument" as well. Indeed, this case refused to accept a "domestic condition" as a reservation to a treaty despite the fact that it presented *the* strongest category of domestic conditions, that of whether the treaty would directly have an effect as domestic law or whether it would only have an effect in the United States subsequent to a later Act of Congress as per the

---

180 With respect to potential interference of the "dual" approach with the Courts, as well as with the Executive, there is also a parallel in constitutional language between the art. II, § 1 general grant: "The executive Power shall be vested in a President. . . ." and the art. III, § 1 general grant: "The judicial Power of the United States, shall be vested in one supreme Court . . . [and in inferior Courts]."

181 An early opinion of the Attorney General rejects the ability of the Senate to attach conditions to vary a Presidential appointment as submitted. It says: "It's [the Senate's] constitutional action is confined to a simple affirmation or rejection of the President's nominations. . . ." 3 OPS. ATTY. GEN. 188 (1837). In this case the Attorney General gave an opinion that a particular Navy commission failed when the Senate sought to attach to it a designation of rank which would have placed the new lieutenant on the register above one hundred sixty-two other lieutenants.

182 Professor Kenneth S. Gallant writes in his article on the "Biden Condition":

> The idea that the President's understanding of legislation is relevant to statutory interpretation has been highly controversial. No one, however, is claiming that the President's understanding of legislation, even as received from members of Congress, is controlling. Yet the Senate, through the Biden Condition, is asserting that its understanding of treaties controls their interpretation.

See Kenneth S. Gallant, *supra* note 131, at 1101.

Senate reservation. Indeed, the dissenting Court of Appeals Judge, Circuit Judge Bastian, specifically pointed this out. He said:

> Before turning to petitioner's argument that the reservation in question is beyond the Senate's constitutional power it is important to carefully delineate what is *not* before the court in this case. Doing so should be an aid to a proper understanding of what is. First, the Senate has not by its reservation sought to extort as its price for ratifying the treaty that it be allowed, independently of the Congress at large, to determine the nature and status of domestic legislation or policy. It has not provided that its conditional ratification is to be regarded as withdrawn if the Federal Power Act *is ever applied* to the water in question. It has merely left the question as to whether that Act or some other should be applied open to determination of both houses of Congress and the President. It has not demanded its way. Its reservation is not self-serving, but purports to extend to the Congress and the President a voice in determining how the increased water supply will be developed. This then is a case where the Senate has not sought to limit the participation of the Congress at large and the President in decisions regarding domestic policy. It is a case in which the Senate has sought to enlarge their participation.[183]

Second, to imply a general domestic lawmaking power in the Senate alone pursuant to its advice and consent power, presumably not just in relation to treaty approval, but also all such matters including the appointment of Supreme Court Justices, as this power appears in art. II, § 2, cl. 2, would seem profoundly at odds with the decisions of the Supreme Court in the *Chadha* and *Clinton* cases and the underlying principles of separation of powers and checks and balances policed by the Court in those cases. If the one house legislative veto, with its substantial basis in legislative practice, and the line item veto, as authorized formally by the full art. I, § 7 process of both Houses of Congress and the President acting together, are not valid, it would seem quite a stretch to argue that the Senate alone should have a domestic lawmaking power of undefined scope to be exercised at its discretion on the occasion of consideration of a treaty or an appointment. Certainly this would be fundamentally at odds with the very purpose of including both houses of Congress and the President in the general federal domestic lawmaking process. Such a limited process would be expected to make it much easier for special interests to obtain their goals and thus, to subvert the real protections for the people of the United States, which underlie the separation of powers and checks and balances principles. These were, indeed, among the most fundamental principles of the United States Constitution, as expounded by Madison and other Framers. Such an undefined Senate lawmaking power would also seem to run counter to the ex-

183 Power Authority of New York v. Federal Power Com'n, 247 F.2d 538, 547 (D.C. Cir. 1957), *vacated and remanded with instructions to dismiss as moot*, 355 U.S. 64 (1957).

pectations of the House of Representatives, which has assumed based on general constitutional practice, that to the extent legislation is required to implement treaties domestically it will play a role in that process. Yet if the Senate power is based on a general authority to condition consent on acceptance of domestic conditions, why could it not attach full implementing legislation to its resolution of advice and consent and bypass the House?

Third, at least if the *Restatement* view is accepted, that the Senate does have a power to condition consent on acceptance of domestic conditions but that such conditions are not "the supreme Law of the Land" under the Article VI Supremacy Clause, then this doctrine could create further confusion in undermining uniformity in United States federal law, by creating one class of law binding only on federal officials and judges, presumably with state officials and judges potentially governed by different rules with respect to the same case. On policy grounds at least this would seem an undesirable result in matters *even relating to* United States treaties. And it would seem counter to the very purpose of the Supremacy Clause, which is to make the laws and treaties of the United States also binding on the States. That the *Restatement* is driven to this remarkable distinction between the domestic condition as binding and yet, not "the supreme Law of the Land," suggests that the origins of this doctrine lie in logic-chopping rather than full analysis of its implications.

Fourth, just as the constitutional structural issue concerning separation of powers would seem inconsistent with the doctrine that the art. II, § 2, cl. 2 "advice and consent" powers of the Senate include an incidental one House domestic lawmaking power, so too, the constitutional structural underpinnings with respect to the respective powers of the federal and state governments would seem to at least cast some additional doubt on this "domestic condition" doctrine. That is, yet another important underlying principle of our federal constitutional system is that the powers of the federal government are limited. While generations of law students reared on an expansive commerce clause may have largely forgotten this structural underpinning, it is unquestionably significant, and is now undergoing some degree of rediscovery by the courts.[184] The structure of this principle, at least as a general principle, is explicit with respect to the federal legislative power. That is, the Constitution uses the language in art. I, § 1 of "[a]ll legislative Powers herein granted. . . ." Further, the Ninth and Tenth Amendments to the Constitution respectively speak of rights retained by the people, and reserve "to the States respectively, or to the people" "powers not delegated to the United States by the Constitution, nor prohibited by it to the States. . . ." Although not free from doubt, it seems likely that

184 *See, e.g.,* United States v. Lopez, 517 U.S. 549 (1995).

the treaty power entrusted to the federal government also has restrictions rooted in this same structural underpinning of the Constitution. In the case of the treaty power, however, these are implicit in the nature of that power, rather than explicit. Thus, the official position of the Department of State today, as embodied in its *Foreign Affairs Manual, Handbook on Treaties and Other International Agreements* provides under constitutional requirements for treaties:

> The President, with the advice and consent of two-thirds of the Senators present, may enter into an international agreement on any subject *genuinely of concern in foreign relations*. . . .[185]

This makes it clear that for the Department, a prerequisite for a constitutional international agreement is that it must be on a subject "genuinely of concern in foreign relations." This requirement is assumed to be implicit in the nature of the federal treaty power and, of course, parallels the many Supreme Court decisions indicating that a treaty is a contract or compact between nations. But by definition, domestic conditions are those not part of an agreement or bargain with the other treaty partner. And as a matter of underlying constitutional structure, to read into the advice and consent power the power to make separate domestic law apart from the underlying treaty can increase the risk of an end run around this treaty law limit on federal power. At the least it would raise the question of how such limits would be defined in the treaty advice and consent context given that, definitionally, such purely domestic lawmaking was not deemed part of the international bargain. Now, in the real world, the foreign affairs concerns of the United States are so vast it would be hard to imagine a treaty invalid under this Circular 175 requirement. Nevertheless, I believe that the principle is valid, and if, for example, the Supreme Court were to strike down an act of Congress as beyond its art. I, § 8 powers, and the Senate and the President were immediately to collude to undo the Court decision by entering into a treaty without any genuine foreign affairs concern and solely for the purpose of overturning the Court decision, I believe that the Court would and should strike down the treaty. While this principle seems unlikely to be tested in real world treaty settings, it does present at least another concern with respect to an undefined Senate authority to attach

---

185 UNITED STATES DEPARTMENT OF STATE, HANDBOOK ON TREATIES AND OTHER INTERNATIONAL AGREEMENTS, FOREIGN AFFAIRS MANUAL 11 FAM 710, 721.2 (emphasis added). While serving as the Counselor on International Law to the Department of State, the author participated in an early draft of this State Department treaty procedure sub-chapter of the Foreign Affairs Manual called internally the "Circular 175 Procedure," including the quoted material.

Circular 175 is reprinted in the latest treaty study of the Senate Committee on Foreign Relations. *See* TREATIES AND OTHER INTERNATIONAL AGREEMENTS: THE ROLE OF THE UNITED STATES SENATE 301, 303, 103d Cong., 1st Sess., (Comm. Print 1993).

purely domestic conditions to its advice and consent as exercised pursuant to art. II, § 2, cl. 2.[186]

This further constitutional requirement, of relevance to the permissibility of a general Senate "domestic conditions" power in relation to treaty approval, that treaties must be on a subject "genuinely of concern in foreign relations," does not appear in the State Department Foreign Affairs Manual solely out of a deductive inference about the nature of the federal system. Rather, it is rooted in repeated statements of the Supreme Court. Thus, to quote several of the relevant cases, in the 1890 decision of the Court in *Geofroy v. Riggs*,[187] the Court used the qualifying language in describing the scope of the treaty power as "touching any matter which is properly the subject of negotiation with a foreign country."[188] And in the 1924 decision

---

186 The present *Restatement* drops the "international concern" requirement reflected in the previous *Restatement* and the current Circular 175 of the Department of State. *See* RESTATEMENT (THIRD) OF THE FOREIGN RELATIONS LAW OF THE UNITED STATES, Reporters' Note 6 to § 302, and Reporters' Note 13 to § 303 (1987). Reporters' Note 6 to § 302 says: "This section is in accord with section 117 of the previous Restatement, except that this Restatement [*Restatement (Third)*] rejects the requirement that the subject of an agreement be of international concern. . . ." *Ibid.* Reporters' Note 2 to § 302, however, does say: "A treaty or other international agreement must be a bona fide international act with one or more other nations, not a unilateral act dressed as an agreement; no agreement of the United States appears to have been challenged in the courts as not being a bona fide agreement." *Ibid.*

This issue, of course, is not that of *Missouri v. Holland,* in which the Court made it clear that the treaty power is broader in scope, and not limited by, the art. I, § 8 legislative powers of the federal government. *See* Missouri v. Holland, 252 U.S. 416 (1920). The issue, rather, is whether there is any limit on the scope of the treaty power by virtue of its nature as a power to make international agreements; that is, whether there is any limit at all on the treaty power other than violation of specific prohibitions in the Constitution. In this connection, it should be noted that the very reason the treaty power transcends the art. I, § 8 enumerated legislative powers is that it is an exercise of the federal foreign relations power, either conceived as inherent in the federal government, or in the international treaty (or more broadly agreement) power of the Nation, or as an attribute of a broader implied power in foreign affairs. An exercise *not* pursuant to that power, then could, of course, not take its authority from that power *and* would still be subject to the structural limitations both of federalism and the Article I legislative process. Thus, the "genuinely of concern in foreign relations" standard in the State Department Circular 175 would seem to be on sound theoretical ground in so limiting international agreements. And since "domestic conditions" are, by their nature, neither part of the treaty nor other than a condition solely of domestic import, it would seem that they would both be subject to the structural limits of the federal system rooted in the nature of federalism and the Article I legislative power, and unconstitutional non-exercises of the federal international agreement power. That is, in *Missouri v. Holland* terms, a "domestic condition," unlike a treaty, is simply not "made . . . under the Authority of the United States" as set out in the Supremacy Clause.

187 Geofroy v. Riggs, 133 U.S. 258 (1890).

188 133 U.S. at 267. And earlier in its opinion the Court described as "clear" the proposition: "[t]hat the treaty power of the United States extends to all proper subjects of negotiation between our government and the governments of other nations. . . ." 133 U.S. 266.

of *Asakura v. City of Seattle*,[189] the Court said that the treaty power extends "to all proper subjects of negotiation between our government and other nations."[190] Are "domestic conditions" contemplated within the thrust of these statements? Further, Circuit Judge Bazelon, writing for the majority of the United States Court of Appeals District of Columbia Circuit in the *Niagara Reservation* case, reminds us that at least two United States Secretaries of State have taken the position that the treaty power is or should be limited to matters of international concern. He points out:

> Our present Secretary of State has said that the treaty power may be exercised with respect to a matter which "reasonably and directly affects other nations in such a way that it is properly a subject for treaties which become contracts between nations as to how they should act"; and not with respect to matters "which do not essentially affect the actions of nations in relation to international affairs, but are purely internal." He had earlier said:
>
> > ". . . I do not believe that treaties should, or lawfully can, be used as a device to circumvent the constitutional procedures established in relation to what are essentially matters of domestic concern."
>
> Charles Evans Hughes, just before he became Chief Justice and after he had been Secretary of State, addressing himself to the question whether there is any constitutional limitation of the treaty power, said:
>
> > ". . . The [treaty] power is to deal with foreign nations with regard to matters of international concern. It is not a power intended to be exercised, it may be assumed, with respect to matters that have no relation to international concerns. . . . [I]f we attempted to use the treaty-making power to deal with matters which did not pertain to our external relations but to control matters which normally and appropriately were within the local jurisdictions of the States, then I again say there might be ground for implying a limitation upon the treaty-making power that it is intended for the purpose of having treaties made relating to foreign affairs and not to make laws for the people of the United States in their internal concerns through the exercise of the asserted treaty-making power."[191]

---

189 Asakura v. City of Seattle, 265 U.S. 332 (1924).

190 265 U.S. at 341. The Court also said: "[t]he treaty-making power of the United States . . . does not extend 'so far as to authorize what the Constitution forbids'. . . ." 265 U.S. at 341.

191 Power Authority of the State of New York v. Federal Power Commission, 247 F.2d 538, 543 (1957) (footnotes omitted). The Hughes quote above, also referred to in Reporters' Note 2 to § 302 of the *Restatement (Third)* on the issue of "international concern" in treaty scope can be found directly at Charles Evans Hughes, as President of the American Society of International Law, 23 PROC. AM. SOC'Y INT'L L. 194 & 196 (1929).

Given the modern understanding as to the sweep of issues of international concern, certainly including human rights treaties in an effort to promote human dignity, democracy and the rule of law worldwide, this limitation on the treaty power is unlikely to have any detrimental effect on the real-world exercise of the treaty power. But the underlying principle continues to speak directly and cogently to any Senate asserted general unilateral domestic lawmaking power in the exercise of its advice and consent power.

Similarly, Attorney General Herbert Brownell, Jr., in Administration testimony during 1953 in opposition to the Bricker Amendment stated: "[o]ur federal system did not contemplate having treaties deal with matters exclusively domestic in their nature."[192] And he further pointed out: "[t]he view of the Supreme Court has always been that, 'the treaty power of the United States extends to all proper subjects of negotiation between our government and the governments of other nations.'"[193]

Fifth, it should also be noted against any one house Senate power to attach "domestic conditions" incidental to its Article II, advice and consent powers, that the Framers certainly understood how to specify such related incidental powers if they had intended to do so. For art. I, § 8 of the Constitution concludes the enumeration of *legislative* powers with the famous "necessary and proper" clause providing:

> [t]o make all Laws which shall be necessary and proper for carrying into Execution the foregoing Powers, and all other Powers vested by this Constitution in the Government of the United States, or in any Department or Officer thereof.[194]

There is no such comparable clause accompanying the Senate "negative" in the exercise of its advice and consent power in art. II, § 2. And in a structural parallel in the Constitution, the President is also not given a power to make domestic law incidental to the exercise of the Presidencies' power to "negative" legislative initiatives under the presentment clause of art. I, § 7. Moreover, when this power incidental to other powers *is* specified, it is a *legislative* power, not a power incidental to other Departments in the exercise of their powers.

Sixth, at least with respect to "domestic conditions" said *to arise from informal Senate preratification history*, the "legislative history" analogy seems fundamentally misplaced. Whatever one's approach to the permissible scope of reliance on "legislative history" in statutory interpretation, all agree that its use is for the purpose of *interpreting a formal lawmaking prescription* adopted through normal legislative procedure and a vote. No one suggests that legislative history alone, absent an enactment to be interpreted, can

---

192 Statement by Honorable Herbert Brownell, Jr., *supra* note 29, at 5.

193 Statement by Honorable Herbert Brownell, Jr., *supra* note 29, at 35. In footnote 80, appended to this proposition, General Brownell cited a variety of Supreme Court decisions before and after the 1920 decision in *Missouri v. Holland*, and including that case. Thus, his footnote in full provided: "*Geofroy v. Riggs*, 133 U.S. 258, 266 (1890). See also *Holmes v. Jennison*, 14 Pet. 540, 569 (Opinion of Taney, C.J.)(1840); *Holden v. Joy*, 17 Wall. 211, 243 (1872); *In re Ross*, 140 U.S. 453, 463 (1891); *Missouri v. Holland*, 252 U.S. 416, 433-434 (1920); *Asakura v. Seattle*, 265 U.S. 332, 341 (1924); *Santovincenzo v. Egan*, 284 U.S. 30, 40 (1931)."

194 U.S. CONST. art. I, § 8, cl. 18.

make binding law. But that is exactly the posture of informal Senate preratification history in the absence of inclusion of a relevant provision to be interpreted in a resolution of advice and consent. Such "history" cannot be an interpretation of the resolution of advice and consent which contains no relevant provision. And it cannot be an interpretation of the treaty, in many cases as in its purported assertion in *Rainbow Navigation* simply because it is not an interpretation of the treaty at all, but rather a side agreement of domestic relevance, and in all cases simply because interpretation of the treaty refers to ascertaining the intent of the parties, not simply the intent of the domestic processes for treaty approval of one of the parties. Indeed, the "legislative history" analogy is an inapt role reversal. In legislation, where one looks to legislative history, it is the legislation, and the legislative act, from which the authority of the law arises. And the role of the President is that of a veto. In a treaty, however, the authority arises from the agreement or compact between nations and it is from the agreement that the authority arises. And the role of the Senate, absent formal reservations, understandings, amendments or international conditions, is that of a veto. The legislative history of the Senate's veto, absent a relevant provision in the resolution of advice and consent, should be no more authoritative than the legislative history of the President's veto. In both cases, history may be relevant to interpretation, but it is not of itself "authoritative" or legally binding.[195]

---

195 This point is made in an interesting manner in the note by Gary Michael Buechler, *supra* note 12, at 2016-17. Mr. Buechler writes:

> In the treaty-making context, the roles of the President and Congress are the reverse of the roles each plays during the statutory lawmaking process. Treaties are negotiated with the foreign power by the Executive, with little or no Senate involvement. Once a treaty has been drafted, it is presented by the Executive to the Senate. Through the advice and consent process, the Senate has an absolute veto power over any treaty. The Senate's only official role in the drafting of treaties is limited to its ability to explicitly condition its advice and consent. Finally, as a matter of domestic law, the Executive must consent to any explicit conditions before the Senate's language becomes a part of the treaty. Thus, if treaties are to be interpreted in the same manner as statutes, that is, by looking to the intent of the drafter, it is the intent of the Executive—not the Senate—that should be examined.
>
> Those who would approach treaty interpretation according to the rules of statutory interpretation fail to consider this role reversal. These commentators place undue significance on Senate-generated interpretations of the treaty that are not expressed as explicit conditions. The distinction between congressional drafting of statutes (with presidential review) and presidential drafting of treaties (with Senate review) is highlighted by the placement of the statute-making rules in article I—describing the legislative powers—and the treaty-making rules in article II—describing the executive powers. By placing great weight on Senate-generated interpretations of a proposed treaty these commentators allow the Senate (or even, perhaps, a few Senators) to impose its interpretation on a treaty without either formal Senate or Executive action.

Id. (footnotes omitted).

Finally, it can at least be questioned whether it is desirable to have the Senate engage in separate domestic lawmaking as it is tasked with giving advice and consent concerning a treaty. Quite apart from the easier one house mark for special interests, a concern going to separation of powers in the legislative process as discussed above, will the Senate as effectively perform its role in considering the international agreements of the United States on their merits as internationally binding the Nation if it is simultaneously engaged in domestic lawmaking? The experience, at least, in the constitutional debate incident to the "broad-narrow" debate would give pause in this, with at least one highly placed congressional staff member explaining to the author that the Senate needs the "dual" approach precisely so that it will *not* be required to review treaties as carefully as it would otherwise.

B. EVEN IF "DOMESTIC CONDITIONS" ARE WITHIN SENATE AUTHORITY, ARE THE "DUAL" APPROACH AND THE "SENATE TREATY CONDITION" CONSTITUTIONAL?

1. Constitutionality of the "dual" approach

Since, by definition, the "dual" approach is a form of "domestic condition" with a meaning separate from the underlying treaty, if for the above or other reasons domestic conditions generally are in violation of the Constitution, then, of necessity, the "dual" approach to treaty interpretation is also unconstitutional. But there are powerful additional reasons for believing that the "dual" approach is unconstitutional even if domestic conditions generally, or even certain domestic conditions, are permissible.

First, since the "dual" approach, whenever it has an effect of its own, seeks to compel the President to ignore the legally binding meaning of a treaty between the parties it would seem simultaneously in violation of the Supremacy Clause and of the President's obligation in art. II, § 3, to "take Care that the Laws be faithfully executed. . . ." For Article VI, the "Supremacy Clause" is quite clear. The Constitution, the laws of the United States, and "Treaties made" are "the supreme Law of the Land. . . ." It has already been established that a long line of Supreme Court cases establishes that a treaty is a contract or compact among nations. As such, it is the correct meaning of the treaty as an international bargain that is the "Law of the Land," unless overridden by subsequent legislation. Surely core purposes of the Supremacy Clause were to ensure uniformity of federal law throughout the United States and to ensure faithful adherence to the treaty obligations of the United States within every jurisdiction in the United States. Neither of these goals would be met if we adopted the *Restatement* view that domestic conditions must be given effect, yet are not the Supreme Law of the Land for purposes of the Supremacy Clause, and this doctrine were to be applied to the "dual" approach to treaty interpretation.[196] It is important to note in this connection that quite apart from the constitutionality of "domestic conditions" generally, the "dual" approach always directly offends the Supremacy Clause and its direction that treaties made are "the supreme Law of the Land," for unlike certain other variants of such conditions, "dual" approach domestic conditions, if of binding legal effect, would *always* contradict *the treaty itself.*

Second, the "dual" approach would seem also to interfere with the President's general foreign affairs power in a number of serious ways.[197] Thus, it would complicate United States foreign relations by compelling the President, whenever it was applicable, either to violate the solemn international legal obligations of the United States or to be held to higher requirements than had been bargained for in the international agreement. It would have important consequences for the ability of the United States to participate in international Courts and Tribunals and adhere to the decisions of those Courts. For whenever the "dual" approach mandated that the Senate had a different intent, then the President would be obligated not to follow another interpretation, even if proclaimed after careful review by an international Court in which the United States had been fully participating. The "dual" approach would also greatly complicate the job of the Executive Branch in its day-to-day interpretation of a multiplicity of treaty issues. For if such an approach were to be adopted, it would require the Executive Branch to routinely examine the record of Senate advice and consent in addition to the usual sources under the Vienna Convention and those typically heavily relied on, such as the submission statement of the President with any accompanying legal analysis of the Treaty. In important cases, examination of the record of Senate consideration may already be done, but the "dual" approach would more broadly extend this burden to routine treaty issues as well. It would also seem to diminish the important role of the Executive in commenting, where appropriate, for domestic courts and other domestic fora, on the interpretation of international agreements, a

---

196 Professor Halberstam notes on this latter point: "[w]here the legislative history results in an interpretation that is narrower, i.e., more permissive, than the interpretation internationally, the United States would be in breach of its international obligations. Thus, the dual treaty approach would also undermine the very purpose of the supremacy clause, which was to make the obligations that the United States undertakes internationally binding domestically." Malvina Halberstam, *supra* note 140, at 1649-50.

197 I agree with Thomas Jefferson that the grant of "[t]he executive Power" in Article II carries with it the general foreign affairs power and that "[e]xceptions are to be construed strictly. . . ." *See* 16 THE PAPERS OF THOMAS JEFFERSON 378-79 (Julian P. Boyd ed., 1961). For a fuller exposition of this point, *see* JOHN NORTON MOORE, *supra* note *. The modern scholar who has "rediscovered" this critical point most effectively is Robert F. Turner. *See, e.g.*, Robert F. Turner, *War and the Forgotten Executive Power Clause of the Constitution: A Review Essay of John Hart Ely's* War and Responsibility, 34 VA. J. INT'L L. 903 (1994).

role said by the *Restatement* generally to be accorded "great weight." In view of these, and no doubt other, ways in which the "dual" approach, sought to be established by implication from the advice and consent power, would interfere with the President's responsibility in the conduct of foreign relations, the conclusion of Chief Justice Taft writing for the Supreme Court in the first critical separation of powers case, *Myers v. United States*,[198] would seem most appropriate. He wrote:

> Our conclusion on the merits, sustained by the arguments before stated, is that Article II grants to the President the executive power of the Government, [and] . . . that the provisions of the second section of Article II, which blend action by the legislative branch, or by part of it, in the work of the executive, are limitations to be strictly construed and not to be extended by implication. . . . [199]

Third, the "dual" approach, by making it easy to violate the international legal obligations of the United States, would seem to violate the structural balance, with constitutional underpinnings, reflected in the foreign relations law of the United States with respect to the uneasy relationship between the international obligations of the United States and the adoption of subsequent inconsistent legislation. The uneasy truce in existing law is that the subsequent inconsistent legislation will prevail for purposes of domestic law, but we require an extraordinarily high standard as to congressional intent to violate our international legal obligations before we will construe the later act as inconsistent with our international obligations. As has been seen, this is the principle of the *Schooner Charming Betsy*[200] where Chief Justice Marshall stated that "an Act of Congress ought never to be construed to violate the law of nations if any other possible construction remains. . . ."[201] And, as has been seen, the *Restatement* adopts this as black letter foreign relations law when it says in § 114: "Where fairly possible, a United States statute is to be construed so as not to conflict with international law or with an international agreement of the United States."[202] The "dual" approach, however, would not simply set aside under domestic law the international legal obligations of the United States pursuant to a very clear mandate from both Houses of Congress, signed into law by the President, but it would purport to trump our international legal obligations simply by the actions of one house, by definition in a setting in which it is unlikely to have adverted to a consequence of its action as violating our inter-

---

198 Myers v. United States, 272 U.S. 52 (1926).

199 272 U.S. 52, 163-64 (1926).

200 Murray v. Schooner Charming Betsy, 6 U.S. (2 Cranch) 64 (1804).

201 6 U.S. (2 Cranch) 64, at 118.

202 THE AMERICAN LAW INSTITUTE, RESTATEMENT (THIRD) OF THE FOREIGN RELATIONS LAW OF THE UNITED STATES § 114 (1987).

national legal obligations, simply because it believed that the intent it had was the correct international meaning. Is it structurally sound under the Constitution of the United States to make it this easy to violate our treaty obligations? Would such a result be consistent with the Framers concern that we adhere to our treaty obligations, something done quite poorly under the Articles of Confederation? Moreover, as the final point in this part will discuss, some of the incarnations of the "dual" approach would trigger this approach and, thus, where applicable override our international legal obligations, on quite thin "evidence" as to the Senate intent, even on the primary interpretive issue.

Fourth, since the United States is bound by important principles of customary international law with respect to observance of its treaty obligations, including *pacta sunt servanda,* and that "[a] party may not invoke the provisions of its internal law as justification for its failure to perform a treaty . . . [subject to the rule we have earlier seen concerning internal law regarding competence to conclude treaties where a violation was 'manifest' and of 'fundamental importance'],"[203] the constitutional underpinnings of the foreign relations law of the United States should simply override any effect of the "dual" approach by the direct application in United States Courts of these fundamental international legal obligations of the United States. The classic case in this regard is *The Paquete Habana*[204] in which Mr. Justice Gray declared for the Court that: "[i]nternational law is part of our law, and must be ascertained and administered by the courts of justice of appropriate jurisdiction, as often as questions of right depending upon it are duly presented for their determination."[205] Most importantly for our consideration here, however, Justice Gray qualified this obligation by adding that customary law would apply "where there is no treaty, and no controlling executive or legislative act or judicial decision. . . ."[206] Note that Senate-imposed "domestic conditions" attached to treaties are *not* on his list. Note also that, as we have seen, the "dual" approach, as a form of "domestic condition," is neither a treaty nor a legislative act and, as such, there is no basis in the foreign relations law of the United States for it to trump fundamental customary international legal obligations of the United States. And finally, note that the obligation sought to be trumped by the "dual" approach is precisely the "treaty" obligation referred to by Justice Gray. If "domestic conditions" cannot trump the customary law obligations

---

203 *See* articles 26, 27 & 46 of the Vienna Convention on the Law of Treaties, May 23, 1969, U.N. Doc. A/CONF. 39/27. Although the United States is not yet a party to this Convention, it regards the substantive provisions of the treaty as customary international law.

204 175 U.S. 677 (1900).

205 175 U.S. at 700.

206 175 U.S. at 700.

of the United States how can they trump the treaty law obligations of the United States?

Fifth, the "dual" approach is not just a purported exercise in prospective lawmaking, rather it is an effort to direct, prospectively and retrospectively, the mode of decision, and weight to be given evidence to be used, in interpreting the treaty obligations of the United States, a role which belongs to the courts in justiciable cases and controversies. Further, the Senate action which triggered the "dual" approach was motivated by, and also directed at, an effort to compel a *particular* interpretation of a *particular* treaty, *after* the adoption of that treaty. Even if the full legislative process could adopt such rules, and the permissible parameters of any such action are unclear, could any such potential interference in the role of the courts as a principal interpreter of treaties, be unilaterally imposed by the Senate, indeed even by Senate informal "legislative history?" There is a sour flavor in this Senate imposed "dual" approach, of the problem presented for the Supreme Court in the classic 1871 case of *United States v. Klein*,[207] in which the Chief Justice said in the opinion of the Court striking down an effort by Congress to limit the effect of a pardon "as evidence of the rights conferred by it":[208]

> In the case before us no new circumstances have been created by legislation. But the court is forbidden to give the effect to evidence which, in its own judgment, such evidence should have, and is directed to give it an effect precisely contrary.
>
> We must think that Congress has inadvertently passed the limit which separates the legislative from the judicial power.[209]

Finally, various incarnations of the "dual" approach would seem to violate another structural component of the Constitution related to the necessity of the Senate to act with the concurrence of "two thirds of the Senators present." Thus, the insistence that the statement of any Executive Branch official to the Senate would automatically create a domestically binding legal obligation as to the meaning of the treaty, by itself bypasses the requirement of adequate evidence within the advice and consent process of an intent of "two thirds of the Senators present." Specific statements by Executive Branch officials may or may not have that effect, but the issue is the intent of "two thirds of the Senators present," and there is certainly no constitutional principle of automatic lawmaking simply by Executive Branch

---

207 United States v. Klein, 80 U.S. 128 (1871).

208 80 U.S. at 144.

209 80 U.S. at 147. *See also* Kolovrat v. Oregon, 366 U.S. 187, 194 (1961) ("courts interpret treaties for themselves . . . .").

statement during the advice and consent process (any more than during the legislative process). This same point is also relevant with respect to other variants of the "dual" approach, which seem not to clearly focus on the need for an intent shared by "two thirds of the Senators present" as the legal standard for *any effect* of Senate action during the advice and consent process.[210] The importance of the "two thirds" standard would seem consistent with the decision of the Supreme Court in the important treaty law case, *Fourteen Diamond Rings v. United States*,[211] which regarded an effort at Senate interpretation of a treaty which fell short of "two thirds of a quorum" as "absolutely without legal significance. . . ."[212]

2. Constitutionality of the "Senate Treaty Condition"

The "Biden Senate Treaty Condition," attached initially to the INF Treaty and subsequently to many other treaties, is a special form of "domestic condition" and "dual" approach. Thus, if domestic conditions are, as a general proposition, unconstitutional, then the Senate Treaty Condition is also unconstitutional. Similarly, if the "dual" approach is unconstitutional, then the Senate Treaty Condition is unconstitutional. For the reasons discussed above, I believe that the Treaty Condition is unconstitutional as within both of these unconstitutional categories without more. But there is more, and for these additional reasons also, I believe that this condition is unconstitutional and without legal effect.

The "Senate Treaty Condition" seeks to affirm, not simply a particular interpretation for one treaty under consideration by the Senate, but rather a modality of interpretation adopting the "dual" approach as applicable to the interpretation of all treaties. As such, it is a form of "domestic condition" purporting to go beyond relevance even to the treaty to which it is attached and purporting to legally mandate a modality of treaty interpretation generally, in an area which, as has been seen, certainly reflects important constitutional underpinnings. It is as though the War Powers Resolu-

---

210 Some variants of the "dual" approach, such as the principles set forth in the Byrd-Nunn letter to Secretary of State Shultz of February 5, 1988, seem not even to focus meaningfully on the *Restatement* test that the President must decide whether Senate statements "represent a general understanding by the Senate. . . ." in order to be binding on the President. *See* THE AMERICAN LAW INSTITUTE, RESTATEMENT (THIRD) OF THE FOREIGN RELATIONS LAW OF THE UNITED STATES, cmt. d to § 314 (1987). And even this *Restatement* test does not clearly focus on the real requirement of concurrence by "two thirds of the Senators present," as set out in art. II, § 2, cl. 2 of the Constitution and the *Fourteen Diamond Rings* case. *See* the Letter from Senators Robert C. Byrd and Sam Nunn to Secretary of State George P. Shultz (Feb. 5, 1988). This letter is set out and discussed in detail *in* JOHN NORTON MOORE, *supra* note*.

211 Fourteen Diamond Rings v. United States, 183 U.S. 176 (1901).

212 183 U.S. 176, at 180.

tion, adopting a congressional view of the war powers at the expense of the presidency, were sought to be enacted into law, not by both Houses over the veto of the President, but by the Senate alone, seeking to mandate its own view of treaty interpretation and an expansive "domestic conditions" power, of potential concern both to the House of Representatives and the President. And, of course, the Constitution and its principles cannot be changed, even by the modality adopted, in the now widely regarded as suspect, War Powers Resolution.[213]

Constitutionally, this "Biden Treaty Condition" presents special concerns in many respects, including assertion of a Senate "domestic conditions" power going beyond relevance to the particular treaty before the Senate, and seeking to mandate a particular general modality for the President to carry out his duty to "take Care that the Laws be faithfully executed" in the treaty interpretation area. Both would seem unconstitutional encroachments. The Senate, of course, also seeks by this condition to impose, and write large, a blanket modality of treaty (and constitutional) interpretation on the courts as well, since it is asserting a general lawmaking power affirming what it declares to be "the constitutionally based principles of treaty interpretation." This too would seem to raise constitutional issues in relation to the independence of the judiciary and, of course, cannot remove their authority to declare such actions unconstitutional.

The especially suspect nature of the Biden Condition is evident in that even the *Restatement*, which in a variety of ways has tilted toward "domestic conditions" and the "dual" approach, would not seem to countenance the condition. Thus it says:

> The Senate has not made a practice of attaching conditions unrelated to the treaty before it. If the Senate were to do so, or were to attach a condition in-

---

213 On both policy and legal grounds, the War Powers Resolution has come under strong criticism in recent years. Particularly interesting in this regard was a Senate colloquy on May 19, 1988, accompanying the introduction of legislation to amend the Resolution, in which Senate Majority Leader George Mitchell, former Majority Leader Robert Byrd, Armed Services Committee Chairman Sam Nunn, Ranking Republican John Warner, and several other Senate leaders took turns attacking the Resolution. Senator Warner, for example, said: "[T]here are provisions which are clearly unconstitutional." 134 CONG. REC. 6177 (daily ed. May 19, 1988). And Senator Mitchell asserted:

> Although portrayed as an effort "to fulfill . . . the intent of the framers of the U.S. Constitution," the War Powers Resolution actually expands Congress' authority beyond the power to declare war to the power to limit troop deployment in situations short of war. . . . The War Powers Resolution therefore threatens . . . the delicate balance of power established by the Constitution. . . .

134 CONG. REC. 6177-78 (daily ed. May 19, 1988). For a detailed discussion of the constitutional shortcomings of the War Powers Resolution, *see* ROBERT F. TURNER, REPEALING THE WAR POWERS RESOLUTION: RESTORING THE RULE OF LAW IN U.S. FOREIGN POLICY (1991) (Foreword by Gerald R. Ford).

> vading the President's constitutional powers—for example, his power of appointment—the condition would be ineffective.[214]

Similarly, Professor Louis Henkin, the Chief Reporter of the *Restatement*, and one, arguably, whose work provides the principal intellectual underpinning of at least "domestic conditions," if not the "dual" approach itself, seems to suggest that the INF Treaty Condition is not a legally binding "condition of consent but only an expression of the Senate's view of the Constitution." Thus, he writes:

> In my view the constitutional principle declared by the Senate [attached to the INF Treaty] is sound and its implications for treaty interpretation unexceptionable. But its title as a condition is dubious. The President, eager to make the treaty, accepted the Senate's consent subject to the Senate's "condition," but issued a statement declaring the condition to be "improper." Proper or not, such conditions are not very significant except as a salvo in President-Senate warfare in the conduct of their shared treaty power. Attaching a constitutional principle as a "condition" of consent to a treaty does not bind future Presidents to that principle. A future President might not agree that there is such a constitutional principle. The principle may not bind even the President who ratified that particular treaty. The principle is not really a condition of consent but only an expression of the Senate's view of the Constitution. The Senate's view may be disputed by the President and must stand or fall on its merits.
>
> Non-amending conditions sometimes reflect distrust between the United States and the other party to the treaty, or Senate mistrust of the Executive (or of later Executives). Sometimes such conditions are blows in larger battles with the President. They reflect and inevitably aggravate friction in the treaty process and beyond, another consequence of our bifurcated treaty procedure.[215]

---

214 The American Law Institute, Restatement (Third) of the Foreign Relations Law of the United States, Reporters' Note 4 to § 303 (1987). The theory of the *Restatement* as to its own limitation here, other than, of course, the specific invasion of constitutional powers part of it, is never explained. That is, it asserts in this same Reporters' Note that the basis for the Senate "domestic condition" power is the Senate's ability "to grant or withhold consent to a treaty, which includes authority to grant consent subject to a condition." Why under that theory is the power limited to conditions related to the treaty? In any event, the *Restatement* test is sufficiently broad as apparently to include implementing legislation for domestic implementation of the treaty, a subject which certainly has plausible relation to implementation of the treaty, and a power which would likely come as a surprise to the House of Representatives.

215 Louis Henkin, *Treaties in a Constitutional Democracy*, 10 Mich. J. Int'l L. 406, 417 (1989). This statement by Professor Henkin that the Senate Treaty Condition is not really a binding "condition of consent" seems not to be shared by at least one of the major author's of the Condition, who argues that it even applies retroactively to govern the interpretation of the 1972 ABM Treaty. *See* Biden & Ritch, *The End of the Sofaer Doctrine: A Victory for Arms Control and the Constitution*, 18 Arms Control Today 3, 8 (Sept. 1988). "In my judgment, the facts of the case are such that the Senate, by enacting the Biden Condition [the INF Treaty Interpretation Condition], has effectively declared the 'rein-

C. THE *RESTATEMENT* POSITION AND THE TRAIL OF INVISIBLE AUTHORITY[216]

The *Restatement* does not address the core issue in the "unitary-dual" debate as to the governing law under the foreign relations law of the United States in a setting in which a meaning of a treaty understood by the Senate at the time of advice and consent turns out not to be the internationally correct meaning of the treaty. This issue is apparently for the *Restatement* what it has been for other authorities, simply a hidden virus whose presence and implications have not been fully understood. One can only hope that the distinguished Reporters of the *Restatement,* whose commitment to the rule of law is unquestioned, would reject the "dual" approach as the issue and its implications become more fully understood. Nor has the *Restatement* adopted the most extreme views in the debate, that, for example, the normative basis for treaty interpretation is the meaning shared between the President and the Senate, as opposed to the meaning shared between the treaty parties, or that no materials can be taken into account in treaty interpretation other than those before the Senate at the time of Senate consideration for advice and consent.

Sadly, however, the *Restatement*'s views on a number of issues have given aid and comfort to the "dual" approach and to a variety of other even more extreme views about treaty interpretation under the Constitution. The first of these is the *Restatement* position in support of a broad Senate authority to attach "domestic conditions" to its approval of treaties. This position is a prerequisite for the "dual" approach and, as this article has urged, is constitutionally incorrect. As has been seen, it is reflected in the *Restatement* in a number of places, including cmt. *d* to § 303, and Reporters' Note 4 to § 303. The *Restatement* expresses the view in comment *d* that the condition must have "plausible relation to the treaty, or to its adoption or implementation," which is rather a broad standard. And in Reporters' Note 4 it uses a core test of impermissibility as to whether the Senate has "made a practice of attaching conditions unrelated to the treaty before it." Remarkably, in Reporters' Note 4 it concedes that such "domestic conditions" do "not partake of [the

---

terpretation' of the ABM Treaty to be invalid and unconstitutional." *Id.* at 8. Professor Henkin's distancing himself from the "Biden Condition" while declaring its constitutional principles "unexceptionable," would itself seem an admission of the tenuous nature of the "dual" approach, as well as of this condition, under the caveats set forth in the *Restatement* itself.

216 While the author is critical of the *Restatement of the Foreign Relations Law of the United States* with respect to the core issues discussed in this article, it should not be assumed that he is in general a critic of the *Restatement*. On most issues, I believe that the *Restatement* does its job well, and that it is a highly professional and useful source. It has also had substantial impact in the Courts, perhaps even more than any other *Restatement*. Its success in no small measure is due to its outstanding Chief Reporter, Associate Reporters and Advisers, as well as the high professionalism of the American Law Institute.

treaties] . . . character as 'supreme Law of the Land.'" It is important to note that the *Restatement* cites absolutely no authority for its position that the Senate has a "domestic condition" authority, even if not part of the law of the land. More remarkably, it does cite the *Power Authority* case in Reporters' Note 4, but does not clearly reveal to the reader that the case was counter to the just expressed *Restatement* view. Indeed, the reader is invited to read Reporters' Note 4 to marvel at the finesse with which the Reporters sought to deal with *the* critical precedent on the issue which basically went against them. One can only speculate that the concession made that such "domestic conditions" are not the "supreme Law of the Land" may have been a concession driven by the obvious existence of this case. Nor does the *Restatement* explain to the reader precisely how "domestic conditions" "must be given effect in the constitutional system" when they are not part of the "supreme Law of the Land."

The *Restatement* also takes the position, in broad general terms that could imply agreement with the "dual" approach, that Senate consent given on the basis of a particular understanding as to the meaning of a treaty must be respected if the President makes the treaty. This is reflected in § 314 (2) and in cmt. *d* to this section. Comment *d* further adopts the view that such Senate understandings must be respected, even if not part of the resolution of advice and consent but simply reflected in the informal "legislative history" in the event the President determines that such history reflects "a general understanding by the Senate. . . ."[217] As has been seen, one problem with this position is its failure to precisely identify the constitutional requirement for effective Senate action on any issue associated with treaty advice and consent, that is, the concurrence of "two thirds of the Senators present" as set out in art. II, § 2, cl. 2. Another problem is the failure to meaningfully consider on the intent issue itself the effect of failing to adopt an understanding as a condition in the Senate resolution of advice and consent and thus generally the absence even of a Senate vote on the condition. That is, might such a failure usually, or even always, carry implications for the intent of the Senate concerning whether it just held a particular meaning, or whether it intended to impose that meaning as a condition of treaty advice and consent? And if the reference were to the "dual" approach, to what language would the "legislative history" attach in the absence of a specific condition set out as part of the resolution of advice and consent? It could not attach to the treaty itself because the treaty itself has a different meaning in any case in which the "dual" approach would make a differ-

---

217 For an indication of non-agreement with the position of the *Restatement (Third)* on these issues, and its even more extreme variant embodied in the "dual" approach, *see* E. Rostow, *supra* note 12 at 1459. Professor Rostow, former Dean of the Yale Law School and Under Secretary of State, says: "I do not agree with the language on this subject put forward in the A.L.I.'s new Restatement on Foreign Relations Law." *Ibid.*

ence. Perhaps the Reporters really have in mind for this section that the President should seek to convey to the other treaty parties the Senate interpretation in some fashion to make it part of the international bargain of the treaty itself. Indeed, that seems to be the thrust of cmt. *b* to § 314 (2) as to the meaning of this *Restatement* position. If so, there is, of course, no real issue here, although this intent could have been facilitated by requiring such conditions and understandings intended by the Senate to be conveyed, to actually be identified in the resolution of advice and consent rather than simply admonishing the President to be responsible also for views expressed in floor debates and committee reports. Indeed, under the *Restatement* view, as a practical matter, how does the President decide which views in floor debates and Committee reports must be conveyed to the other treaty parties? These issues aside, perhaps the greatest shortcoming of this *Restatement* position concerning a Senate understood meaning is that it fails to address the "unitary-dual" issue and, without doing so, on its face lends itself to an interpretation supporting the "dual" approach. As with its position on "domestic conditions" generally, once again, this section of the *Restatement*, with its elaborate Comments and Reporters' Notes, fails to cite a single authority for its position on Senate understood meanings.

Finally, the *Restatement* espouses a view, which, although not a real issue or problem of itself, can without adequate understanding of the "unitary-dual" issues lend itself to the "dual" interpretation or other extreme views about treaty interpretation. Thus, Reporters' Note 5 to Section 325 on "Interpretation of International Agreement" provides:

> *Use of domestic sources.* A court or agency of the United States is required to take into account United States materials relating to the formation of an international agreement that might not be considered by an international body such as the International Court of Justice. These may include:
>
> (i) Committee reports, debates, and other indications of meaning that the legislative branch has attached to an agreement which, as a matter of internal law, requires the assent of the Senate or of Congress. . . . [218]

There is, I believe, nothing wrong with reviewing such materials for the purpose of determining the meaning between the parties or for the view of the Executive entitled to "great weight" in the courts on matters of treaty interpretation, and the courts have reviewed such materials for these purposes. But supporters of the "dual" approach can, without further explanation as to the purpose of reviewing such materials, mistake this Note as suggesting that the purpose of treaty interpretation in United States courts is a search for the shared intent of the President and the Senate, or the President and the Congress, as opposed to the shared intent of the parties. Or

---

218 The American Law Institute, Restatement (Third) of the Foreign Relations Law of the United States, Reporters' Note 5 to § 325 (1987).

this Note could be interpreted to suggest a preference in the interpretive process for such domestic "legislative history" materials as opposed to the standard international treaty interpretive sources including the negotiating record between the parties. In this case, however, I believe that in the full context of § 325 of the *Restatement*, such interpretations would be unfair to the *Restatement*, as they would be distortions of the core meaning of that Section, which quite generally adopts a view of treaty interpretation close to the international standard set out in the Vienna Convention. Moreover, § 325 is clearly inconsistent with the extreme view that only materials before the Senate can be taken into account in treaty interpretation since it expressly includes in the interpretive process subsequent agreements between the parties unlikely to be present during Senate advice and consent. And, although the introductory language in Reporters' Note 5 uses mandatory language of a court or agency "is *required* to take into account United States materials," the voluntary language "[t]hese *may* include" precedes the further description of "[c]ommittee reports, debates, and other indications of meaning . . . [from] the legislative branch. . . ."[219]

It may be instructive to examine previous *Restatements* and their drafts in relation to these issues generally. Thus, a draft of the *Restatement (Second)*, which becomes Reporters' Note 5 to § 325 in the *Restatement (Third)*, candidly noted the lack of decisional authority, concerning "Domestic criteria that are not material internationally":

> There is virtually no precise decisional authority on this matter, probably because of the domestic interpretative rule, stated in § 155, that executive interpretations of international agreements are given great weight by courts in the United States or because, as explained in Comment *a* to this Section, the courts wish to avoid if possible creating disharmony between the international and the domestic meanings of international agreements.[220]

---

219 In this connection it might be noted that footnote 7 in *United States v. Stuart*, in quoting Reporters' Note 5 to § 325 of the *Restatement*, moves directly from the "is required to take into account" language of the introduction to that Note to the language concerning "[c]ommittee reports, debates, and other indications of meaning . . . [from] the legislative branch . . . ," and omits the voluntary language of "[t]hese may include," which directly precedes the reference to these "legislative history" materials. *See* United States v. Stuart, 489 U.S. 353, 367 n.7 (1989). The fact that this material from Reporters' Note 5 appeared in footnote 7 of the *Stuart* case suggests that it may have been misinterpreted as suggesting, as that footnote later does, that such "legislative history" materials would be a better interpretive guide than a treaty's negotiating history. That certainly would not seem the thrust of § 325.

220 American Law Institute, Restatement of the Foreign Relations Law of the United States § 154, cmt. b, at 555 (Prop. Off. Draft 1962). Further, the first paragraph to this cmt. b to § 154, which becomes Reporters' Note 5 to § 325, uses the qualifying language "to some extent" to modify the "are required to take into account" of Reporters' Note 5, as well as the word "interpretative" before the word account. *Id.* at 554. Reporters' Note 2 on "History of Negotiations" in this draft also includes a long line of Supreme Court decisions which used *travaux* and diplomatic correspondence in interpretation. *Id.* at 557.

Similarly, this 1962 *Restatement Draft* also says in cmt. *b* to § 138:

> If the Senate does not insert its understanding in its resolution of advice and consent . . . it should never have more than an interpretative significance. Where Senate action in giving its consent is thus ambiguous, the courts should be left free to interpret the Senate's intent with respect to the internal effect of the "understanding." Even as so restricted, the situation is one that creates possibilities for serious variance between domestic effect and international effect. Hence, considerations of policy support a limited, interpretative effect to this manifestation of Senate intent.[221]

One wonders why the present *Restatement* has not used the candid acknowledgment as to the lack of decisional authority for its position (much less candidly admitting that its view on "domestic conditions" is counter to the only decision to have addressed the issue after full argumentation before the court). Similarly, one wonders why the Reporters no longer seem sufficiently concerned about "creating disharmony between the international and the domestic meanings of international agreements" or "serious variance between domestic effect and international effect."[222] This, after all, is the core of the policy problem underlying the "dual" approach. Yet it is as though in moving from earlier positions to the present *Restatement*, the Reporters are encouraging the virus of the "dual" approach to stay hidden.

The immediate predecessor *Restatement*, the *Restatement (Second) of the Foreign Relations Law of the United States*, as revised and published in 1965, clearly adopts the position that informal indicators from Senate treaty consideration are not *ipso facto* effective under national law but are simply to be taken into account "as that of the record of legislative history on the interpretation of a statute." Section 135 of the *Restatement (Second)* provides:

> Effect of Statement of Understanding as Domestic Law
>
> (1) If a statement of understanding as to the meaning of a treaty is either attached at signature by the United States or is included in the instrument of ratification by the United States either because required by the Senate reso-

---

221 AMERICAN LAW INSTITUTE, RESTATEMENT OF THE FOREIGN RELATIONS LAW OF THE UNITED STATES § 138, cmt. b, at 505 (Prop. Off. Draft 1962).

222 For a provision in the *Restatement (Second)* which seems sensitive to the need to only have a single meaning for a treaty obligation of the United States, *see* § 133(3) which is apparently designed to bring informal indications of Senate intent as to the meaning of a treaty into line with the internationally binding meaning. Even this effort, however, fails to understand that many, if not most, of these settings of informal Senate intent as to meaning may arise subsequent to ratification, as in the ABM "broad-narrow" debate. It also fails to meaningfully address the problem as to the standard for ascertaining *any legally binding* Senate intent absent Senate inclusion of the item in the resolution of ratification adopted by the constitutionally required two-thirds vote. *See* RESTATEMENT (SECOND) OF THE FOREIGN RELATIONS LAW OF THE UNITED STATES § 133(3) (1965).

> lution of advice and consent or to reflect a particular meaning that the Senate ascribed to the treaty in giving its advice and consent, the treaty and the understanding become effective as domestic law under the rule stated in Sec. 141.
>
> (2) In the absence of a statement of understanding as described in Subsection (1), an indication from the record of the Senate's consideration of the treaty that the Senate ascribed a particular meaning to the treaty has the same bearing on the interpretation of the treaty as domestic law as that of the record of legislative history on the interpretation of a statute.[223]

And comment *b* to this section says:

> *Interpretative effect of meaning attributed by Senate. If the Senate does not insert an understanding in its resolution of advice and consent and the President does not feel that it is necessary to do so in the instrument of ratification, conclusions based upon the deliberations of the Senate are not controlling in the interpretation of the treaty as the domestic law of the United States.* Under Supreme Court precedents discussed in Sec. 151, Reporters' Note 1, courts in the United States, in interpreting an international agreement, take into account manifestations of intention made during the course of its formation. In the case of a treaty, the deliberations and action of the Senate are a necessary phase of such formation. Moreover, it is clear from Senate practice that the Senate gives its advice and consent in the expectation that its understanding, whether or not included in the resolution of advice and consent, will be taken into account in determining the effect of the treaty as domestic law.[224]

Thus, the immediate predecessor *Restatement* clearly adopted the position that informal indications from the record of Senate intent, as opposed to formal statements of understanding either attached at signature or included in the instrument of ratification, would not *ipso facto* become "effective as domestic law" but rather would only be "taken into account." Moreover, the comment to this section makes it clear that informal "conclusions based upon the deliberations of the Senate are not controlling in the interpretation of the treaty as the domestic law of the United States." The current *Restatement (Third)* cites no authority, and gives no constitutional or policy justification, for departing from this view.

Similarly, the *Restatement (Second)*, in cmt. *b* to § 151 entitled "*Domestic criteria that are not material internationally*," uses the language "is *to some extent* required to take into account domestic sources"[225] as opposed to the unqualified language of its successor statement in Reporters' Note 5 to § 325 of the *Restatement (Third)*, entitled "*Use of domestic sources*" of "is required to take

---

223 American Law Institute, Restatement (Second) of the Foreign Relations Law of the United States § 135, at 422 (1965).

224 *Id.* cmt. b, at 422-23 (emphasis added).

225 Restatement (Second) of the Foreign Relations Law of the United States § 151, cmt. b (1965) (emphasis added).

into account United States materials." Further, Reporters' Note 1 to § 151 in the *Restatement (Second)*, if retained in the *Restatement (Third)*, would have made it far more difficult for the Court in *Stuart*, as expressed in its last sentence in footnote 7, to have mistaken the *Restatement* position as giving priority to preratification Senate materials over a treaty's negotiating history. For Reporters' Note 1 in the *Restatement (Second)*, under a heading entitled: *"United States decisions showing general agreement with the international law standard"* provides in relevant part:

> "'The general rule obtains that the court is to be guided by the intention of the parties. . . .'" Dobrin v. Mallory S. S. Co., 298 Fed. 349, 351 (E.D.N.Y. 1924). "Undoubtedly the intention of the two governments, as gathered from the words of the treaty must control." United States v. Texas, 162 U.S. 1, 36 (1896). See also Geofroy v. Riggs, 133 U.S. 258, 271 (1890). Nielsen v. Johnson, 279 U.S. 47, 51-52 (1929).
>
> "Treaties must receive a fair interpretation according to the intention of the parties, and so as to carry out their manifest purpose." Wright v. Henkel, 190 U.S. 40, 57 (1903). See Asakura v. City of Seattle, 265 U.S. 332, 342 (1924).
>
> "As treaties are contracts between independent nations, their words are to be taken in their ordinary meaning as 'understood in the public law of nations.'" Santovincenzo v. Egan, 284 U.S. 30, 40 (1931).
>
> . . . .
>
> "In ascertaining the meaning of the treaty we may look beyond its written words to . . . their [the parties'] own practical construction of it." Factor v. Laubenheimer, 290 U.S. 276, 294-95 (1933). For a collection of cases indicating the attitude to these problems of the Supreme Court, see 2 Hyde, International Law Chiefly as Interpreted and Applied by the United States 1478-1485 (1945).[226]

Even Philip C. Jessup and Oliver J. Lissitzyn did not state it any better in their opinion prepared for the *Niagara Reservation* case. Indeed, perhaps the clarity of the *Restatement (Second)* on this point benefitted from the service of Philip Jessup on the Advisory Committee.[227]

---

226 RESTATEMENT (SECOND) OF THE FOREIGN RELATIONS LAW OF THE UNITED STATES, Reporters' Note 1, § 151 (1965).

227 According to the *Restatement (Second)*, Philip C. Jessup served on the Advisory Committee "to 1961." This, of course, included the period during which Professors Jessup and Lissitzyn prepared and submitted their ninety-six page analysis as an opinion in the 1957 *Niagara Reservation* case. Restatement (Second) of the Foreign Relations Law of the United States, at iv (1965). The Chief Reporter of the *Restatement (Second)* was Adrian S. Fisher. Associate Reporters were Covey T. Oliver, Cecil J. Olmstead, I. N. P. Stokes (Reporter for Part IV on "Responsibility of States for Injuries to Aliens"), and Joseph M. Sweeney. RESTATEMENT (SECOND) OF THE FOREIGN RELATIONS LAW OF THE UNITED STATES, at *iii* (1965).

It may be further useful to compare the treatment of the *Niagara Reservation* case in the *Restatement (Second)* with its treatment in Reporters' Note 4 to § 303 of the *Restatement (Third)*, as already examined. Thus, the *Restatement (Second)* does not adopt the Henkin-argued Senate power of "conditioning" acceptance on a "domestic condition." It treats the issue of Senate "legislation by reservation" as arising in the setting of agreement by both the President and the other treaty party, and as unsettled even in that setting. And the *Restatement (Third)* also drops the cross-reference to an article by Professor Covey T. Oliver, an Associate Reporter of the *Restatement (Second)*, which includes a discussion of the *Niagara Reservation* case, in favor of a citation *solely* to the Henkin article. The Oliver piece, which was omitted from this Reporters' Note in the *Restatement (Third)*, was more neutral on the issues in the *Niagara Reservation* case, and asks in an implied negative on the concept of "domestic conditions": "[h]ow much actual legislative power is it wise to lodge in one House at the expense of the other, either by Constitutional change or by toleration?"[228] This Reporters' Note to § 134 of the *Restatement (Second)* provides in principally relevant part:

> A special problem arises when a Senate reservation, rather than the treaty as signed, raises the question whether its subject matter (i) is appropriate for settlement by international negotiation or (ii) possibly conflicts with specific limitations on the powers of the government of the United States, and is therefore, as indicated in Sec. 117, outside the scope of an international agreement under the Constitution. Related to the second of these questions is that of the extent to which the Senate (if the President and the other state agree to its reservation) may "legislate by reservation" without the concurrence of the House of Representatives. Litigation involving the Senate's "reservation" in 1950 to the United States-Canadian Treaty Concerning Uses of the Waters of the Niagara River was the first, and, apparently, the only case to raise this question directly. See Sec. 133, Reporters' Note 1.
>
> . . . .
>
> Before any action was taken by the Supreme Court, the Congress enacted legislation dealing with the disposition of the Niagara water flow made available to the United States under the treaty. The Supreme Court thereafter granted *certiorari*, vacated and remanded the judgment of the Court of Appeals, with directions to dismiss it as moot, *sub nom*. American Public Power Assn. v. Power Authority of the State of New York, 355 U.S. 64 (1957). See Henkin, The Treaty Makers and the Law Makers: the Niagara Reservation, 56 Colum. L. Rev. 1151 (1956); Oliver, Treaties, the Senate and the Constitution: Some Current Questions, 51 Am. J. Int'l L. 606 (1957).
>
> . . . .[229]

---

228 Covey T. Oliver, *Treaties, The Senate, and the Constitution: Some Current Questions*, 51 AM. J. INT'L L. 606, 610 (1957) (Editorial Comment).

229 RESTATEMENT (SECOND) OF THE FOREIGN RELATIONS LAW OF THE UNITED STATES, Reporters' Note, § 134 (1965). Omitted portions of the full note, covering approximately

As has been previously noted,[230] the *Restatement (Third)* also rejected the requirement present in the *Restatement (Second)* that the subject of an agreement be "of international concern." Reporters' Note 2 to § 302 of the *Restatement (Third)* which discussed this issue cited the *Power Authority* case, thus suggesting that the issue raised in this case was in the sights of the Reporters as they made this change. The Reporters cited no new authority between the *Restatement (Second)* and the *Restatement (Third)* supporting this change. Nor did they note the position to the contrary in State Department Circular 175, or the many statements in Supreme Court decisions to the contrary. And further, the argument that under international law a subject automatically ceases to be a matter solely of "domestic concern" once an international agreement is concluded about it is, of course, correct but hardly conclusive. For since the issue is one of United States constitutional law, rooted in the structure of our federal system, it is simply a classical logical error known as a *non sequitur*, that is, an inference that does not follow from its premise, to argue that the international law rule answers the domestic constitutional law issue. Most importantly, the core reasoning given for this change, that no subjects are intrinsically "impermissible subjects for an international agreement,"[231] hardly applies to "domestic conditions," which, by definition, are not part of an international agreement. The full Reporters' Note 2, providing justification for rejecting the *Restatement (Second)* requirement that the subject of an agreement be "of international concern" provides:

> *International agreements and "matters of international concern."* It had sometimes been suggested that a treaty or other international agreement must deal with "a matter of international concern." That suggestion derived from a statement by Charles Evans Hughes. See 23 Proc.Am.Soc'y Int'l L. 194-96 (1929). See previous Restatement § 117; also Power Authority of New York v. Federal Power Commission, 247 F.2d 538 (D.C.Cir.1957), *vacated and remanded with directions to dismiss as moot*, 355 U.S. 64, 78 S.Ct. 141, 2 L.Ed.2d 107 (1957). Hughes also used other phrases, referring to treaties as "relating to foreign affairs" and not applying to matters "which did not pertain to our external relations." Hughes's statement may have implied only that an international agreement of the United States must be a bona fide agreement with another state, serving a foreign policy interest or purpose of the United States. That requirement may well be implied in the word "treaty" or "agreement" as used in international law and the United States Constitution. See Comment *c*.

---

two full pages in the *Restatement*, related to the history of the *Niagara Reservation* case, including the majority and dissenting opinions in the Case, and a focus on whether, when a "real" reservation is constitutionally invalid, the treaty as a whole would fail as the law of the land, or the Supreme Court might apply a doctrine of "severability."

230 *See supra* note 186.

231 RESTATEMENT (THIRD) OF THE FOREIGN RELATIONS LAW OF THE UNITED STATES, Reporters' Note 2, § 302 (1987).

> There is no principle either in international law or in United States constitutional law that some subjects are intrinsically "domestic" and hence impermissible subjects for an international agreement. As to international law, it has been authoritatively stated that even a subject that is strictly of domestic concern "ceases to be one solely within the domestic jurisdiction of the State, [and] enters the domain governed by international law," if states conclude an international agreement about it. Nationality Decrees in Tunis and Morocco (Great Britain v. France), P.C.I.J. ser.B. No. 4, p. 26 (1923). Under United States law, the Supreme Court has upheld agreements on matters that, apart from the agreement, were strictly domestic and indeed assumed to be within State rather than federal authority. *E.g.*, De Geofroy v. Riggs, Reporters' Note 1 (rights of inheritance in land); Missouri v. Holland, Reporters' Note 1 (protection of migratory birds). Early arguments that the United States may not adhere to international human rights agreements because they deal with matters of strictly domestic concern were later abandoned. (Introductory Note to Part VII). A treaty or other international agreement must be a bona fide international act with one or more other nations, not a unilateral act dressed as an agreement; no agreement of the United States appears to have been challenged in the courts as not being a bona fide agreement.[232]

In assessing the position of the *Restatement (Third)* in relation to the "dual" approach, apparently a virus it never spots, Reporters' Note 4 to § 325 also includes language which could be interpreted as inconsistent with the *Restatement*'s other language lending aid and comfort to that approach. Thus, Reporters' Note 4 says in discussing *"United States and international interpretive approaches"*:

> The courts seek to avoid giving to an international agreement a meaning in domestic law different from its international meaning.
>
> . . . .
>
> [I]n United States tradition the primary object of interpretation is to "ascertain the meaning intended by the parties."
>
> . . . .
>
> [B]oth the Vienna Convention and the United States approach seek to determine the intention of the parties. . . .
>
> . . . .
>
> The United States and its courts and agencies . . . are bound by an interpretation of an agreement of the United States by an international body authorized by the agreement to interpret it. . . .
>
> The international law on the interpretation of international agreements is binding on the United States, and is part of the law of the United States. Insofar as this section [the interpretive articles 31-33, Part III, Section 3 of the Vienna Convention on the Law of Treaties] reflects customary law [as it

232 *Id.*

> does, at least in general terms], or if the United States adheres to the Vienna Convention, courts in the United States are required to apply those rules of interpretation even if the United States jurisprudence of interpretation might have led to a different result.[233]

The reader should note that this language in Reporters' Note 4, focused on the intent of the parties and the importance of international rules of interpretation, appears *immediately* before the language in Reporters' Note 5, cited in footnote 7 by the majority in the *Stuart* case as support for their conclusion that: "[a] treaty's negotiating history . . . would . . . be a worse indicator of a treaty's meaning . . . [than preratification Senate materials]." The reader will also be forgiven if at this point he or she has no idea as to the real position of the *Restatement (Third)* on the "unitary-dual" issue.[234]

D. THE SOURCE: PROFESSOR HENKIN'S *NIAGARA RESERVATION* ARTICLE

The only authority cited by the current *Restatement* for its position in support of a Senate authority for "domestic conditions" is an article by Professor Louis Henkin, now the Chief Reporter for the *Restatement*, written in 1956 when he was a lecturer in law at Columbia. This article, "The Treaty Makers and the Law Makers: the Niagara Reservation,"[235] was written following the decision of the Federal Power Authority that a reservation at-

---

233 RESTATEMENT (THIRD) OF THE FOREIGN RELATIONS LAW OF THE UNITED STATES, Excerpts from Reporters' Note 4, § 325 (1987) (bracketed material added).

234 To further confuse the issue, cmt. b to § 111 of the *Restatement (Third)* provides: "A rule of international law or a provision of an international agreement derives its status as law in the United States from its character as an international legal obligation of the United States. A rule of international law or an international agreement has no status as law of the United States if the United States is not in fact bound by it. . . ." *Ibid.*

235 Louis Henkin, *The Treaty Makers and the Law Makers: The Niagara Reservation*, 56 COL. L. REV. 1151 (1956). For a subsequent discussion of his "domestic conditions" position, *see* LOUIS HENKIN, FOREIGN AFFAIRS AND THE CONSTITUTION 134-36, 160-61 (1972). In apparent contradiction even to the limitations expressed in the *Restatement (Third)*, Professor Henkin writes in this 1972 pre-current *Restatement* consideration of the issues:

> A different question is whether the Senate can impose conditions unrelated to the treaty itself. While the Senate has never attempted to do so, one may ask hypothetically whether, say, it can tell the President that it will consent to a treaty only if he dismisses his Secretary of State. Perhaps such conditions were not contemplated, perhaps the Senate that made them would be abusing its power, and indeed it seems incredible that a Senate would put such a condition, at least formally and publicly. But since the Senate can withhold its consent for no reason, perhaps it can withhold it for any reason, and a President may have to buy that consent at whatever price and in whatever form the Senate asked. It would be particularly difficult to conclude that when the Senate imposes a condition which is not "proper," the President can disregard the condition, treat the Senate's consent as unconditional and proceed to ratify the treaty.

Id. at 135-36.

tached to the Treaty with Canada Concerning Uses of the Waters of the Niagara River, admittedly a "domestic condition," was "invalid as an attempt to amend or repeal in part the Federal Power Act."[236] As has further been noted, Professor Henkin's view, and the inclusion of this view in the *Restatement*, have been the principal intellectual support for the Senate's "dual" approach to treaty interpretation, and perhaps also for the "Biden Treaty Interpretation Condition" now routinely being applied by the Senate to treaties despite Professor Henkin's expressed reservations concerning the latter practice. As such, it may be useful to at least briefly review Professor Henkin's 1956 arguments in relation to contemporary assertions of the "dual" approach, the "Biden Treaty Interpretation Condition," "domestic conditions" generally, and even, by far the strongest case of a "domestic condition," a Senate "non-self-executing condition" as was presented in the *Niagara Reservation* case itself.

In fairness to Professor Henkin, it should be noted that his article was written *before* the decision of the Court of Appeals in the *Niagara Reservation* case in which the majority of the Court rejected his approach in favor of that taken by his then fellow Columbia senior faculty colleagues, Philip C. Jessup, Hamilton Fish Professor of International Law and Diplomacy, and Oliver J. Lissitzyn, Associate Professor of Public Law.[237] And it should be noted that his article was written *before* the important *I.N.S. v. Chadha*[238] decision in which the Supreme Court set aside a formidable pattern of practice by the House and the Senate in the use of one-House vetoes as inconsistent with the constitutional requirements for legislative action. And it was written *before* the more recent *Clinton, President of the United States v. City of New York*[239] in which the Court showed even heightened sensitivity

---

236 Louis Henkin, *supra* note 235, at 1151.

237 We know that Professor Henkin's approach was available to the Court of Appeals and rejected by the majority since the dissenting Judge cites it in footnote 24 of his dissent as "an excellent and cogently reasoned discussion," even providing the correct article title and *Columbia Law Review* volume and page number. *See* Power Authority v. Federal Power Commission, 247 F.2d 538 (1957), dissenting opinion of Judge Bastian at 544, n.24 at 553. Philip C. Jessup was on the brief for the petitioner in this case. *See* 247 F.2d at 539. Jessup's distinguished career as an international lawyer was, of course, capped by his tenure as a Judge of the International Court of Justice.

Professor Henkin cites the substantial Jessup & Lissitzyn opinion written for the case in the first footnote to his article. Louis Henkin, *supra* note 235, at 1151 n.1.

238 Immigration and Naturalization Service v. Chadha, 462 U.S. 917 (1983).

239 524 U.S. 417 (1998). Professor Henkin's article was also written before the decision in Bowsher v. Synar, 478 U.S. 714 (1986), which also illustrates the vitality of separation of powers for the contemporary Court. In *Bowsher* the Court said:

> Even a cursory examination of the Constitution reveals the influence of Montesquieu's thesis that checks and balances were the foundation of a structure of government that would protect liberty. The Framers provided a vigorous Legis-

to the constitutional lawmaking process. Further, it was written before the "dual" approach or the "Biden Condition" had even been imagined, and when available evidence was to the contrary, as is suggested by Judge Sofaer's unfortunate testimony to the Senate which set off the firestorm. Sadly, however, all the same cannot be said for the *Restatement*, which was published after both the *Niagara Reservation* case and *Chadha*.

In understanding Professor Henkin's arguments in his 1956 article, it is also important to note the strength of the case for the *Niagara Reservation* which Professor Henkin was defending and its differences, as day to night, to the "dual" approach and the Biden Condition. For unlike the "dual" approach and the Biden Condition, and even the asserted "domestic condition" in the *Rainbow Navigation* case, the *Niagara Reservation* case presents a setting of the strongest possible case, indeed I believe the *only* even arguable case, for the lawfulness of "domestic conditions." Thus, the "domestic condition" in question was solely one to prevent domestic implementation of the 1950 Niagara Waters Treaty with Canada until domestic implementing legislation could be passed by the full Congress in the normal legislative process. That is, it essentially related to whether the treaty with Canada was to be self-executing in the United States. And it had been clearly adopted by the Senate, appended to the Treaty as a "reservation," conveyed to Canada by the President with a request that he be "notified whether that reservation is acceptable to the Canadian Government," and the Government of Canada had then explicitly accepted the "reservation." In addition, there had been no effort by the Senate to assert that this condition was simply an interpretation of the treaty or an international condition, but rather it had been

---

> lative Branch and a separate and wholly independent Executive Branch, with each branch responsible ultimately to the people. The Framers also provided for a Judicial Branch equally independent with "[t]he judicial Power . . . extend[ing] to all Cases, in Law and Equity, arising under this Constitution, and the Laws of the United States."

478 U.S. 722. And:

> The dangers of congressional usurpation of Executive Branch functions have long been recognized. "[T]he debates of the Constitutional Convention, and the Federalist Papers, are replete with expressions of fear that the Legislative Branch of the National Government will aggrandize itself at the expense of the other two branches." *Buckley v. Valeo*, 424 U.S. 1, 129 (1976). Indeed, we also have observed only recently that "[t]he hydraulic pressure inherent within each of the separate Branches to exceed the outer limits of its power, even to accomplish desirable objectives, must be resisted."

478 U.S. at 727. And further the Court noted, quoting *Chadha*:

> "the fact that a given law or procedure is efficient, convenient, and useful in facilitating functions of government, standing alone, will not save it if it is contrary to the Constitution. Convenience and efficiency are not the primary objectives—or the hallmarks—of democratic government. . . ."

478 U.S. at 736.

clearly recognized in the report of the Senate Foreign Relations Committee, in the President's diplomatic note to Canada, and in the Canadian statement in the protocol of exchange of ratifications, that it related solely to internal United States applications of the Treaty.[240] That there had been no effort to shoehorn a "domestic condition" into a purported interpretation of the international obligations under the Treaty is clearly reflected in the Canadian statement in the protocol of exchange of ratifications. It provided:

> Canada accepts the above-mentioned reservation because its provisions relate only to the internal application of the Treaty within the United States and do not affect Canada's rights or obligations under the Treaty.[241]

Moreover, the President's transmittal message of the 1950 Treaty to the Senate adverted to the question of domestic implementation of the treaty, and indicated that it would not be appropriate for the international agreement itself to contain a solution to this internal issue. Thus, the President said:

> When the Niagara Treaty has been ratified, the question will naturally arise as to how additional facilities shall be developed to achieve the best use of water to be diverted for power purposes. My own views on this question are a matter of public record; I believe that the additional power facilities should be publicly constructed, in order that the benefits of the hydroelectric power produced there can be passed on to the people at the lowest possible cost to them.
>
> This is a question, however, which is not determined by the treaty itself. It is a question which we in the United States must settle under our own procedures and laws. It would not be appropriate either for this country or for Canada to require that an international agreement between them contain the solution of what is entirely a domestic problem. All this treaty does is to make additional water legally available for power purposes in each of the two countries. This is a step which must be taken in the interest of the United States. It is one which should be left separate from the steps which must be taken in this country in order to convert this water into additional power.[242]

We should remind ourselves that it was even in this strongest possible setting for a "domestic condition," one relating solely to whether the treaty was self-executing in the United States *and* even which had been referred to the other treaty party and accepted, where Circuit Judge Bazelon and a two-to-one majority of the United States Court of Appeals, District of Co-

---

240 *See* Louis Henkin, *supra* note 235, at 1154-58.

241 Louis Henkin, *supra* note 235, at 1158.

242 S. Exec. N., 81st Cong., 2d Sess. (1950). Cited in Louis Henkin, *supra* note 235, at 1155 n.10.

lumbia Circuit, set aside the reservation as an impermissible "domestic condition." And, we should remind ourselves, Circuit Judge Bastian, in dissenting seemed to limit his support for domestic conditions to the strong case before the Court relating solely to a non-self-executing condition as opposed to a setting where the Senate sought to engage in lawmaking on its own apart from the normal legislative process. That is, even his dissenting opinion in *Niagara Reservation* was sensitive to the separation of powers concerns subsequently focused by the Supreme Court in the *Chadha* and *Clinton v. City of New York* cases. He wrote:

> Before turning to petitioner's argument that the reservation in question is beyond the Senate's constitutional power it is important to carefully delineate what is *not* before the court in this case. Doing so should be an aid to a proper understanding of what is. First, the Senate has not by its reservation sought to extort as its price for ratifying the treaty that it be allowed, independently of the Congress at large, to determine the nature and status of domestic legislation or policy. It has not provided that its conditional ratification is to be regarded as withdrawn if the Federal Power Act *is ever applied* to the water in question. It has merely left the question as to whether that Act or some other should be applied open to determination of both houses of Congress and the President. It has not demanded its way. Its reservation is not self-serving, but purports to extend to the Congress and the President a voice in determining how the increased water supply will be developed. This then is a case where the Senate has not sought to limit the participation of the Congress at large and the President in decisions regarding domestic policy. It is a case in which the Senate has sought to enlarge their participation.
>
> Secondly, this is not a case in which the Senate has exacted as a price for its ratification of a treaty that some new, nonexisting legislation become law. Nor is it a situation where ratification is conditioned on nonapplication of some general statute not germane to the subject matter of the treaty.[243]

And in his conclusion he writes:

> The reservation in question is an instance of self-denial, not usurpation. It does not subvert our constitutional system. It was motivated by a desire that the treaty power should not be used in a manner which would exclude the Congress at large and the President from playing their normal roles in making domestic law.[244]

It was in this context that Professor Henkin sought to support the validity of the Niagara "reservation" as a valid "domestic condition." And one can agree with the dissent that, as with most Henkin products, his 1956 article

243 Power Authority of the State of New York v. Federal Power Commission, 247 F.2d 538, 547 (1957) (dissenting opinion of Circuit Judge Bastian).

244 247 F.2d 538, at 552 (1957) (dissenting opinion of Circuit Judge Bastian).

provided "an excellent and cogently reasoned discussion." At least in its broadest implications for consideration of the constitutionality of the "dual" approach, the Biden Condition, and "domestic conditions" generally, however, and, quite possibly, even on its core facts of a "non-self-executing" Senate condition, the Henkin approach is wrong as a modern statement of the law.

With some oversimplification on my part, Professor Henkin made three principal arguments for the constitutionality of the "domestic condition" in the *Niagara Reservation* case. First, he suggests that, based on certain past treaty precedents, this reservation relating to the non-self-executing nature of the Treaty, which was formally incorporated as a reservation to the Treaty and accepted by Canada, was "a proper treaty provision." That is, he says: "[i]t is of bona fide contractual character appropriate to an agreement between States."[245] Second, he argues, in obvious reference to the character of the "domestic condition" in question as of a non-self-executing nature, that: "it is a proper exercise of the constitutional powers of the President and the Senate to give the Congress a role in the treaty process."[246] And finally, reflective of the theory subsequently adopted by the *Restatement*, he broadly poses a Senate power to condition its consent in providing advice and consent to a treaty. Thus, he says, before somewhat limiting his own broad statement, "[i]f the Senate can withhold consent for no reason, or for any bad reason, perhaps it can give its consent on any condition whatever."[247] Immediately, however, perhaps concerned by the audacious breadth of his own surmise, he cautions:

> For present purposes it is not necessary to decide what would be the effect if an irresponsible Senate sought to extract from the President, or from the Congress, as the price of its consent, conditions unrelated to its role in the treaty process, unrelated to the subject matter of the treaty, or unrelated to its legitimate concern for the consequences of its consent to this treaty. That is not this case. Neither is it suggested that by such a "condition" the Senate could automatically repeal a law of the United States. That, again, is not this case. . . .[248]

One wonders where Professor Henkin gets these limitations if the underlying power he posits is simply the power to approve with conditions. But reflecting the powerful influence of its Chief Reporter, at least some of the cautionary points in the first sentence here end up in the *Restatement*, along

245 Louis Henkin, *supra* note 235, at 1176.

246 Louis Henkin, *supra* note 235, at 1176.

247 Louis Henkin, *supra* note 235, at 1176.

248 Louis Henkin, *supra* note 235, at 1177.

with Professor Henkin's underlying "condition to consent" argument.[249] The thrust of Professor Henkin's subsequent discussion in his 1956 article relates to why conditions related generally to a non-self-executing nature are valid.

The remaining paragraphs in this part will discuss why the arguments developed by Professor Henkin in this 1956 article do not support the modern validity of the "dual" approach, the "Biden Senate Treaty Interpretation Condition," "domestic conditions" generally, and, perhaps, even the core non-self-executing "domestic condition" of the *Niagara Reservation* case.

The "dual" approach to treaty interpretation is light years from the stronger case presented in the *Niagara Reservation* case. By definition, the Senate condition sought to be imposed under this doctrine is not only not part of the treaty, it is inconsistent with the treaty. It will neither have been presented to the other treaty party nor accepted by the other treaty party. At least in its specific effect, it will not usually be part of any resolution of advice and consent, nor will it appear as a reservation. Indeed, it will in almost every setting not even be voted on by the Senate to ascertain whether it reflects two-thirds Senate support. Since, by definition, it posits a "domestic condition" that is not *ever* a part of the treaty, Professor Henkin's first argument in his 1956 article is simply irrelevant. Further, by definition, the "dual" approach would not support the role of the President and the Congress in the normal legislative process. For, by definition, the "dual" approach seeks to produce a binding domestic effect solely from the action in the Senate, and always even in opposition to the treaty itself. Thus, it hardly meets Professor Henkin's second argument that it is intended to give the President and the Congress their normal legislative roles in the process. Certainly the President, who objected to the concept in the "broad-narrow" context, would be startled to learn that the doctrine is really intended to protect his role. Rather, in origin and intent, it is, however mistaken in its objective, spun to protect the Senate role. And as to Professor Henkin's third argument, based on a broad Senate power to condition consent, the "dual" approach neither fits the thrust of his cases, which are in the non-self-executing context, nor is it consistent with his own limiting principle. For, the "dual" approach, whenever it would make a legal difference, *always* seeks to alter domestically the treaty law itself. As such, it does seek the equivalent of repeal of not just "a law of the United States," as Professor Henkin says in his article could not be done, but, indeed, departure from a treaty obligation, which is by art. VI, cl. 2 of the United States Constitution, "the supreme Law of the Land." And this, by some form of legal effect which the *Restatement* concedes is not itself "the supreme Law of the

---

249 *See* RESTATEMENT (THIRD) OF THE FOREIGN RELATIONS LAW OF THE UNITED STATES, Reporters' Note 4, § 303 (1987).

Land." And none of this is even to consider the destructive effects for United States foreign policy and the international rule of law from the "dual" approach.

The "Biden Treaty Interpretation Condition" incorporates the "dual" approach so it shares, at minimum, all of its characteristics and shortcomings. As such, it too is clearly not supported by the arguments made by Professor Henkin for "domestic conditions" in his 1956 article. It would seem further suspect by its effort to force the President and the courts to a blanket acceptance of this mode of treaty interpretation espoused by the Senate, in contradiction to their own constitutional roles in treaty interpretation.

"Domestic conditions" generally, that is, for the moment, those other than conditions relating to a non-self-executing effect, are, at least to some extent, which even Professor Henkin was unclear about, supported by Professor Henkin's condition to consent argument, and may further be supported in some cases by Professor Henkin's first argument if incorporated into the treaty itself and accepted by the other treaty party. They are, however, by definition, never supported by Professor Henkin's second argument concerning protecting the role of the normal legislative process, as in every case they *do* seek to create domestic law solely by Senate action. And in cases such as *Rainbow Navigation* where the "domestic condition" thought to be discovered by Judge Harold Greene was never incorporated in a resolution of advice and consent or even voted on, much less conveyed to the other treaty party and accepted by them, these general conditions would also not be supported by Professor Henkin's first argument. Further, just as even the dissent in the *Niagara Reservation* case would seem to have rejected such general "domestic conditions" as encroaching on the normal legislative process even when conveyed to the other treaty party, so too, I believe that the modern law after the *Chadha* and *Clinton v. City of New York* cases would not accept such conditions, whether or not incorporated into the treaty itself. For such general "domestic conditions" assert an undefined unilateral Senate lawmaking power in its consideration of a treaty. Such a lawmaking power does not seem inherent in the advice and consent process and, instead, seems flatly contradictory to the general legislative lawmaking power in accord with "a single, finely wrought and exhaustively considered, procedure" as noted by the Supreme Court in both these cases.

In the conclusion of his article, Professor Henkin does ask an important question with respect to this general "domestic conditions" power. That is:

> And it is the Constitution that is being expounded, a constitutional power that would be limited. To circumscribe a constitutional power should require some basis, some purpose. What in our case is the purpose? What is the basis? What in particular is the purpose in denying the right of those who enjoy a constitutional power to limit the exercise of their power?

> At whose expense is this power of self-restraint being asserted, in favor of whom in the constitutional configuration is this power now being denied?[250]

Quite apart from this passage's question begging assertion of an alleged Senate "constitutional power," both the Framers and, more recently, the United States Supreme Court in the *Chadha* and *Clinton v. City of New York* cases, have given persuasive answers to these questions. It was not by accident that the Framers created a lawmaking process of two Houses and presentment to the President. This more complex process was intended, at its core, as an essential part of the Constitutional framework of checks and balances. In turn, this was intended to lessen the power of "factions," as Madison called them,[251] or special interests, as we would know them today, and to better protect the interests of the citizens of the several states and, indeed, of all the people of the United States. Modern economic theory, with its understanding of "government failure," powerfully endorses this brilliant insight of the Framers.[252] Moreover, it should be noted that while the treaty power, at least in general requires agreement with one or more other nations, a doctrine of "domestic conditions" apart from the underlying treaty does not even have this check. It would be action purely and simply by one house of the legislature. And further, even if the "domestic condition" is embodied formally as a reservation and conveyed to the other party, that party has no incentive other than to accept it while pointing out that it does not affect *their* rights. Indeed, this is precisely what we saw with Canada in the *Niagara Reservation* case. While conveying such "domestic conditions" to the other treaty parties has the considerable advantage of at least being honorable and not violating our Nation's international treaty obligations, it provides no check whatsoever on the asserted domestic lawmaking by a single house. There is at least a touch of this "factions" in the air with respect to the *Rainbow Navigation* case,

---

250 Louis Henkin, *supra* note 235, at 1182.

251 *See generally* the contributions of James Madison to *The Federalist Papers*. As one example, Madison, brilliantly intuiting insights, which with further development would later win the Nobel Prize in Economics, wrote in *Federalist* 10: "The inference to which we are brought is that the *causes* of faction cannot be removed and that relief is only to be sought in the means of controlling its *effects*." THE FEDERALIST PAPERS (1961 ed., Clinton Rossiter ed., with Charles R. Kesler Introduction & Notes 1999). No. 10, at 48.

252 The writings of Professor James M. Buchanan, who was the first to win the Nobel Prize in Economics for this insight, which he called "Public Choice Theory," are a good place to begin on this fundament of good government. *See, e.g.*, JAMES M. BUCHANAN & G. TULLOCK, THE CALCULUS OF CONSENT (1962); JAMES M. BUCHANAN, THE ECONOMICS AND THE ETHICS OF CONSTITUTIONAL ORDER (1991); THE THEORY OF PUBLIC CHOICE—II (James M. Buchanan & Robert D. Tollison eds., 1984). *See* particularly the overview chapter by James M. Buchanan in this work on *The Theory of Public Choice—II* entitled: "Politics without Romance: A Sketch of Positive Public Choice Theory and Its Normative Implications." *Id.* at 11-22.

where the "domestic condition" asserted, and not even voted on or conveyed to the other treaty party, was alleged to be a condition to give certain U.S. Navy carriage contracts to a particular merchant marine company. It is presumably considerably easier to get such special interest provisions in unilateral Senate informal treaty process history than enacted pursuant to the normal legislative process.

In an editorial comment in the *American Journal of International Law* published in 1957, almost contemporaneously with Professor Henkin's article on the *Niagara Reservation* case, Professor Covey T. Oliver, a distinguished international lawyer and Associate Reporter of the *Restatement (Second)*, makes clear that *he* understands the policy question in the *Niagara Reservation* case.[253] He concludes his discussion of that case with the paragraph:

> Despite the lack of any concrete evidence that the House of Representatives does concern itself about the steady increase of Senate power *de facto* throughout the field of lawmaking—an increase sometimes almost as much at the expense of executive power as of the legislative power of the "popular" branch of the national legislature—the policy question, and it is a big one, remains for decision: How much actual legislative power is it wise to lodge in one House at the expense of the other, either by Constitutional change or by toleration?[254]

There is also an additional answer to Professor Henkins's question as to why there is not a unilateral general Senate domestic lawmaking power attached to its advice and consent power. And ironically, this seems to be the converse of Professor Henkin's apparent background concern in his article to ward off the political effort behind the misguided Bricker Amendment to restrict the treaty power in the name of state's rights. For the core check on the legislative power in part to protect state's rights is set out in the limited powers given to the Congress of the United States in Article I of the Constitution. And presumably the limit with respect to the treaty power is that a treaty is an agreement or contract among nations, adopted pursuant to a genuine concern in the Nation's foreign relations. But to permit the Senate unilaterally to make domestic law apart from the obligations of the underlying agreement, and without any limitations on its power, could more easily encroach upon the legitimate interests of the states, though unlikely to do so in the real world of treaty practice. Certainly there seems a stronger argument against a general unilateral Senate "domestic conditions" power in relation to the protection of state's rights than in Pro-

---

253 Covey T. Oliver, *supra* note 228.

254 Covey T. Oliver, *supra* note 228, at 610.

fessor Henkins's implications to the contrary in support of "domestic conditions" in his article.[255]

This article has not been written to inject myself into the ongoing debate about the constitutionality of the peculiar *sui generis* form of "domestic condition," as reflected in the *Niagara Reservation* case, which relates solely to whether the treaty, or part thereof, is non-self-executing within the United States. This is certainly the strongest, indeed, I believe the only even arguable, case for the validity of such "domestic conditions." And, as Professor Henkin's article demonstrates with its examples, this is really the only area with any significant treaty practice reflective of such conditions. Nevertheless, I believe even this category of "domestic condition" is suspect under modern constitutional law. For if the Senate has no "domestic conditions" power in general, that is, a legislative power to alter the law apart from the international meaning of the treaty, then it may not even have this power. Indeed, as has been seen, this was the conclusion of the majority of the Court of Appeals in the *Niagara Reservation* case. Moreover, to the extent that the Senate begins to exercise such a power by unilateral statement, as opposed to conveying it to the other treaty party as a reservation or amendment to be accepted if treaty relations are to be concluded, then it has the potential to put the United States in violation of its treaty obligations, at least if domestic implementing legislation is unreasonably delayed or never enacted. Of course, there is no problem if the Senate statement that a treaty is not self-executing accurately reflects the international meaning of the treaty, or if the reason for subsequent United States domestic legislation is a constitutional requirement which is "manifest and . . . [concerns] a rule . . . of fundamental importance" as reflected in Article 46 of the Vienna Convention, in which case the United States would not be in violation of its international legal obligations while awaiting domestic implementing legislation. These two settings, I believe, reflecting our treaty obligations, are not properly "domestic conditions." Further, since the Senate could, if feasible internationally, *require* that a particular treaty be made not self-executing by the terms of the treaty itself, there would also seem an additional option for the Senate in the event that it had no power to declare treaties not self-executing. The majority of the Court in the *Niagara Reservation* case noted this option available to the Senate. Circuit Judge Bazelon, writing for the Court, said:

> The Senate could, of course, have attached to its consent a reservation to the effect that the rights and obligations of the signatory parties should not arise

255 Professor Henkin's statement on page 1182 about "aid and comfort . . . to those who seek to impose serious limitations on the treaty power" would seem to be written with the damaging Bricker Amendment proposals in mind. *See* Louis Henkin, *supra*, note 235, at 1182. That the Bricker Amendment proposals, and the issue "of international concern," were on the minds of contemporary commentators on the *Niagara Reservation*

> until the passage of an act of Congress. Such a reservation, if accepted by Canada, would have made the treaty executory. But the Senate did not seek to make the treaty executory. By the terms of its consent, the rights and obligations of both countries arose at once on the effective date of the treaty. All that the Senate sought to make executory was the purely municipal matter of how the American share of the water was to be exploited.[256]

There is a further nagging doubt about even this strongest form of "domestic condition"; that is, a "non-self-executing" condition specifically adopted as a reservation solely concerning a "domestic condition" in the Senate resolution of advice and consent and then conveyed to and accepted by the other treaty party, as in the *Niagara Reservation* case. For, in a sophisticated post public choice era, should we accept that the motivation of the Senate in *Niagara Reservation* was purely "neutral" to give the House an opportunity to participate with them in the fashioning of implementing legislation? Or might the Senate not have liked, or wanted to delay for some reason, the legal consequences which would have occurred with the waters of the Niagara River in the absence of its condition? Should we believe that if a majority of the Senate strongly supported the legal effect absent the condition that it would still have pushed for the condition to give the House a participatory role? It is clear that hearings on the Treaty had included hearings on the domestic issue of how additional power should be developed at the Falls and that "[c]onflicting views" had been presented to the Senate Foreign Relations Committee on this issue.[257] It is also clear that the Senate condition altered a legal effect under United States law which otherwise would have governed. Perhaps in this case, the motivation was exactly as expressed in the report of the Senate Foreign Relations Committee, which said:

> Conflicting views as to how the additional power should be developed at the Falls and who should be responsible for that development were presented to the committee. A number of questions raised remain unresolved. This resource is unique and of national interest. The distribution of the Falls is a subject on which opinions differ. It will require careful study. And it is not at all unlikely that additional studies will be sought concerning the relationship of the Niagara power project to the St. Lawrence seaway and power project and to the whole question of power shortage is [sic] northeastern United States.[258]

---

case is most evident in Covey T. Oliver, *supra* note 228 at 608-10 ("Thus, once again the substantive contents of 'of international concern' comes into issue, as does the rôle of the courts *versus* other institutions of government with respect to the making of the determination as to a particular treaty or reservation." *Id.* at 609).

256 Power Authority of the State of New York v. Federal Power Commission, 247 F.2d 538, 542 (1957).

257 *See* Louis Henkin, *supra* note 235, at 1156.

258 S. Exec. Rep. No. 11, 81st Cong., 2d Sess. 6-7 (1950). *See* Louis Henkin, *supra* note 235, at 1156.

As the consideration by the Senate of these domestic issues illustrates, however, at least in the short run even a Senate "non-self-executing" power is a unilateral power to pick and choose concerning the domestic legal effect of a treaty. Should the Senate, acting alone and apart from the normal constitutional legislative process, have such a power to decide even the short run legal effects of a treaty apart from the treaty itself?

On balance, I believe that the best test for whether a treaty is self-executing is the nature of the agreement stemming from the intent of the parties, as seems to be the basis applied by Chief Justice John Marshall in the classic case of *Foster and Elam v. Neilson*.[259] Senate non-self-executing concerns could be dealt with under this approach by either requiring that the treaty itself be non-self-executing, that is, an agreement of the parties that the treaty looks to the political branches for implementation as was the test used by Chief Justice Marshall in *Foster and Elam v. Neilson*, or requiring agreement between the parties that the treaty will only enter into legal effect when subsequently executed by both parties in their domestic law. Further options might include requiring that implementing legislation be simultaneously presented to the Congress with the treaty, rapidly proceeding with implementing legislation on Senate or Congressional initiative, or specifying in the resolution of advice and consent that the President should delay ratification until domestic implementing legislation is enacted.[260]

---

259 Foster and Elam v. Neilson, 27 U.S. (2 Pet.) 253 (1829). Chief Justice Marshall wrote in this case:

> In the United States . . . [o]ur constitution declares a treaty to be the law of the land. It is, consequently, to be regarded in courts of justice as equivalent to an act of the legislature, whenever it operates of itself without the aid of any legislative provision. But when the terms of the stipulation import a contract, when either of the parties engages to perform a particular act, the treaty addresses itself to the political, not the judicial department; and the legislature must execute the contract before it can become a rule for the Court.

27 U.S. (2 Pet.) at 314.

260 Whether or not a treaty is self-executing is not the only issue in its direct application in domestic courts. Other important issues, well understood by domestic courts, include the issue of whether the treaty, while creating an obligation between nations, is intended to create "standing" for private litigants to either invoke the treaty against a Government or other private litigants, the "political question" doctrine, particularly if the treaty is invoked against Presidential conduct of foreign policy, and the usual panoply of what Professor Bickel called "the passive virtues," including the classic meaning of "standing" as to the Article III requirement of adequately presenting a case or controversy, and associated doctrines of ripeness and adversariness. For a discussion of these latter concepts, *see The Justiciability of Challenges to the Use of Military Forces Abroad*, Chapter XIII *in* JOHN NORTON MOORE, LAW & THE INDO-CHINA WAR 570 (1972). And for the classic positions on the "political question" and related doctrines, *see* ALEXANDER M. BICKEL, THE LEAST DANGEROUS BRANCH (1962); Fritz W. Scharpf, *Judicial Review and the Political Question: A Functional Analysis*, 75 YALE L.J. 517 (1966); Herbert Wechsler, *Toward Neutral Principles of Constitutional Law*, 73 HARV. L. REV. 1 (1959); and, of

It should further be noted that, at least for me, there is nothing in Professor Henkin's article, fairly read for his support for the limited "non-self-executing" Niagara reservation, which would support the wrong-headed and destructive notion that a treaty should be interpreted by the intent of the Senate, as opposed to the intent of the treaty parties, or its silly fellow traveler espoused by Professor Tribe that only materials before a Senate in its consideration of a treaty could be considered in the interpretive process. Despite the breadth of his argument for a Senate power to impose "domestic conditions" as part of the advice and consent process, which I believe is not part of modern law, I cannot believe that Professor Henkin, as a strong adherent to the international rule of law, would have intended any such positions, as he made the "domestic conditions" argument in what was, as should be fairly recognized, the much stronger context of the *Niagara Reservation* case.

E. MORE RIGHT STUFF

> ***"The least initial deviation from the truthis multiplied later a thousandfold."***
>
> *Aristotle, On the Heavens, bk. I, ch. 5*

The structure of the Constitution, authority and policy suggest that the *Restatement* is wrong in its view that the Senate power of advice and consent includes a power to attach "domestic conditions" to treaties. Such "domestic conditions" are not part of the advice and consent power. The *Restatement* is further wrong in its view that such "domestic conditions" can be implied simply from deliberations of the Senate absent any provision in the resolution of advice and consent or even a Senate vote. Even more clearly, the "dual" approach to treaty interpretation, and the effort to write it large in the Biden Condition, are unconstitutional even if the Senate did have a "domestic conditions" power.

---

course, Baker v. Carr, 369 U.S. 186 (1962), reflecting the judicial resolution of this debate as to the legitimacy of judicial consideration of prudential and systemic considerations.

V.
Into the Fray and Damn the Torpedoes: The Original Great Case, Senate Intent and Perverse Conclusion of the "Dual" Approach

A. FOCUSING THE ISSUE

The "broad-narrow" dispute about the correct interpretation of the ABM Treaty may well have been the most contentious legal issue in the history of United States foreign policy, and it was certainly the most complex. It is not the intention of the author to engage on the merits of that dispute in this article nor to take a stand here on the "correct" international interpretation.[261] Indeed, I will seek to avoid, as much as possible, getting caught up in the emotion of this debate, or subjecting the reader to the intensity of it, which intensity and deep feeling, I believe, is largely responsible for the "great cases make bad law" emergence of the "dual" approach. It is for that reason that this article will sometimes refer to the meanings as "X or Y" rather than the "narrow" and "broad" interpretations. Since, however, this "broad-narrow" debate was the "great" case which produced the "dual" approach to treaty interpretation, I believe that it will be useful to discuss the original Senate advice and consent process. I will examine this original process to demonstrate the difficulty of ascertaining the *real* intent of the Senate in settings subsequently presenting the "dual" interpretation issue, a difficulty that I believe is underestimated by the proponents of the "dual"

261 The author served the Director of the former Arms Control and Disarmament Agency (ACDA) in preparing an exhaustive 4000 page, 4000 hour, study on this issue, with full access to the record and interviews of many of the principal ABM negotiators in an effort to assist the Director in sorting out the respective views of the then Legal Adviser of the Department of State, Judge Sofaer, supporting the "broad" view and Senator Sam Nunn supporting the "narrow" view. Classified portions of this study, prepared within ACDA, remain classified and have never been publicly released. An unclassified Volume IV in this study, entitled "The National Law of Treaty Implementation," dealing solely with constitutional issues in treaty interpretation, is being published. *See* John Norton Moore, *supra* note*.

approach, and which perversely can result in that approach undermining, rather than supporting, the intent of the original consenting Senate, as I believe it would have as asserted in this case.[262]

This discussion will first examine intent as to the treaty *meaning*; that is, whether a two-thirds majority of the Senators present supported a particular interpretation of the ABM Treaty (an interpretation X). It should be noted in this connection that we will apply the Constitutional standard of "two thirds of the Senators present" as reflected in art. II, § 2, cl. 2, and the *Fourteen Diamond Rings*[263] case previously discussed.

The discussion will then turn to the question of intent as to the treaty *bargain*; that is, whether, if the original understanding by the requisite majority of the Senate was X, would that majority have intended to hold the United States to a higher standard than that binding on the Soviet Union under the Treaty if the correct international interpretation of the Treaty turned out to be Y? The reader should not read into this discussion the conclusion that the correct international legal interpretation of the ABM Treaty is Y, rather, this is simply one possible question which arises whenever the "dual" approach is invoked, and, thus, to examine the independent legal effect of the "dual" approach as a modality of treaty interpretation, this question must also be examined. That is, the "dual" approach, whenever it has any independent effect apart from the underlying treaty, will inevitably either require violation of our national treaty obligations or holding the Nation to a standard not bargained for or not binding on the other treaty party. In the case of the "broad-narrow" interpretation of the ABM Treaty, the variant of these two logical consequences of the "dual" approach is to require national adherence to the "higher standard," since interpretation Y, the "broad" interpretation, would internationally permit testing and development of mobile ABM systems based on other physical principles (OPP). That is, the "dual" approach is presented as an independent legal ground in the "broad-narrow" debate only if we assume a difference between the Senate understood meaning, presumably the "narrow," or more restrictive, meaning, and the internationally correct meaning, assumed for purposes of our exercise to be the "broad," or more permissive, meaning. To fully

---

262 This analysis will draw on an unclassified "Summary Chart of Congressional Consideration of the 'Broad-Narrow' Issue in Initial Consideration of the ABM Treaty" prepared by the author as an Annex to the study for the ACDA Director, and released to the author by the Director of ACDA on December 7, 1992. The "Summary Chart," in turn, was based on a detailed analysis of each document, meeting, statement or exchange related to initial Senate consideration of the Treaty. This full analysis remains part of the unreleased ACDA study. The Summary Chart is being published along with the unclassified Volume IV in this study, entitled "The National Law of Treaty Implementation." *See* JOHN NORTON MOORE, *supra* note*.

263 Fourteen Diamond Rings v. United States, 183 U.S. 176 (1901).

pursue this question of ascertaining Senate intent, then, in the context of the ABM "broad-narrow" dispute and an asserted "dual" approach legal effect, we must assume for purposes of our analysis that the correct international meaning and the Senate intent were different, for if they were the same, then the "dual" approach produces no effect. Similarly, we examine the question here because, as previously discussed, the intent of the Senate in approving a treaty is always a double intent. That is, the Senate believes that the meaning is X *and* that X is the internationally correct meaning binding on both parties. Not to understand that *both* of these intents, intent as to the *meaning* and intent as to the *bargain*, are always simultaneously present, and to understand that the issue when the Senate is mistaken on one of these is the more complex issue of what would the Senate have wanted under the circumstances in which, inevitably, only one of the two intents can be met, is to miss the real problem of ascertaining Senate intent in settings where the "dual" approach is presented.

Finally, we will briefly discuss the Executive Branch testimony to the Senate in initial Senate consideration of the ABM Treaty since some variants of the "dual" approach seem to seek binding legal effect from Executive Branch statements to the Senate. The purpose, again, will be to demonstrate that the issues, assumed simple by proponents of the "dual" approach, in real world settings may be less clear cut than they may first appear.

B. INTENT AS TO TREATY *MEANING*

The "broad-narrow" issue is sufficiently complex that characterization of views from statements, hearings, or documents is far from an exact science. As has been earlier noted, this abstruse technical issue is made all the more difficult for even the expert observer by the ease with which it can be confused with closely associated issues concerning research, fixed land based systems, mobile systems not based on OPP, deployment or theater systems.[264] Further, the potential for confusion or uncertainty among all these related issues is even greater during oral testimony or exchanges—and in this case no prepared testimony of any Executive Branch witness clearly addresses the issue. In an effort to characterize the record as accurately as possible, however, the author undertook to characterize all relevant documents, meetings, statements or exchanges during the initial Senate (and Congressional) consideration of the ABM Treaty as part of the study for the ACDA Director. Such statements or exchanges were divided into five categories. These were: "unambiguous for narrow," "ambiguous: leans to nar-

264 For a more precise discussion of these potentially confusing or closely associated issues, *see supra* note 20.

row," "ambiguous neutral or does not address," "ambiguous: leans to broad," and "unambiguous for broad."

This analysis showed that Senator Nunn and the proponents of the "narrow" interpretation were correct in their assessment that statements and exchanges were made during the Senate consideration of the ABM Treaty, which unambiguously reflected the "narrow" interpretation. My overall analysis scores five such instances, with none scored as unambiguous for the "broad" interpretation.[265] These include one statement by General Bruce Palmer, the Acting Chief of Staff of the Army, in an exchange with Senator Jackson in the Senate Armed Services Committee, two statements by Senator Jackson during Senate Armed Services Committee hearings, and two statements by Senator Buckley, one made in testimony before the Senate Foreign Relations Committee and the second during Senate consideration of the Treaty.

It is less clear from the record, however, whether two-thirds of the members of the Senate present shared an understanding of this "narrow" interpretation, or even adverted to the interpretive issue. Thus, this issue was not addressed in the Senate Resolution of Advice and Consent, which contained no reservation, understanding, or condition of any kind. Nor was it addressed in Committee reports, including the Report of the Senate Foreign Relations Committee. Indeed, in putting the congressional consideration of the "broad-narrow" issue in context, it was not a central issue in either Executive Branch presentation or congressional consideration of the ABM Treaty. The ABM Treaty was considered with the Salt I Interim Agreement, together presenting a host of central strategic issues including overall limits on offensive forces, non-inclusion of MIRV's, the appropriateness of unequal aggregate national limits on offensive forces, the number of ABM sites, the definition of heavy missiles, and verification and compliance issues. The "broad-narrow" issue was not specifically defined or presented to the Congress in either the President's transmittal letter, including the Secretary of State's accompanying analysis, or the opening statements of the principal administration witnesses, including Ambassador Gerard C. Smith as the leader of the United States SALT Delegation, or in Dr. Kissinger's White House briefing for Members of Congress on June 15, 1972.

On no occasion does a White House, National Security Council (NSC), State Department, Arms Control and Disarmament Agency (ACDA), or participating member of the SALT Delegation, personally make a state-

---

265 Footnotes in my Summary Chart, however, note that several statements or exchanges can be argued as "unambiguous for broad," including the statement of Ambassador Smith, the head of the ABM Treaty U.S. negotiating team, before the Senate Foreign Relations Committee.

ment or participate in an exchange before the Senate or House in initial consideration of the ABM Treaty that can even be reasonably regarded as leaning toward the "narrow" interpretation. In over four hearings and the brief one day floor debate the issue seems to have been unambiguously addressed by only two Senators, and one middle level administration witness who had not participated in the negotiation. And even these unambiguous statements for the narrow interpretation occurred in a broader context of considerably less clarity on the issue. My overall analysis scored statements by Executive Branch officials or other Executive Branch actions as: one unambiguous for narrow; four ambiguous: leans to narrow; thirteen ambiguous neutral or does not address; five ambiguous: leans to broad; and zero unambiguous for broad. Statements by members of Congress or other congressional actions (largely, but not exclusively, in the Senate), were scored as: four unambiguous for narrow; two ambiguous: leans to narrow; twelve ambiguous neutral or does not address; seven ambiguous: leans to broad; and zero unambiguous for broad. Further, as a measure reflecting the considerable uncertainty of making these characterizations, the study also provided an analysis of arguable additional characterizations, producing a combined total from both Executive Branch and Congressional sources, when added to original scoring, of: ten unambiguous for narrow; nine ambiguous: leans to narrow; thirty-one ambiguous neutral or does not address; seventeen ambiguous: leans to broad; and eight unambiguous for broad. The head of the United States SALT I Delegation, Ambassador Gerard C. Smith, with repeated opportunities to clarify the issue and accompanied by other SALT I Delegation principals, on three occasions, once in an exchange before the Senate Foreign Relations Committee and twice in exchanges before the Senate Armed Services Committee, makes remarks that can at least be regarded as ambiguous but leaning toward the broad interpretation.

Of course, simply adding together these indications, without reference to where in the treaty advice and consent process they occurred, and particularly whether made by Executive Branch or Senate sources, or other context of the statements, is not an appropriate test, taken alone, for seeking the intent of an at least two-thirds majority of the Senate on a matter of treaty interpretation. How, for example, would one weigh the fact that the only unambiguous statement for the narrow interpretation from an Executive Branch spokesman came from General Palmer, who was not a member of the ABM negotiating team, that when he was pressed earlier in testimony by Senator Goldwater who, at least initially, seemed to lean toward believing that the broad interpretation was correct, he gave testimony scored by me as "ambiguous: leans to broad," and that his testimony scored as "unambiguous for narrow" came in testimony before the Senate Armed Services Committee in response to Senator Jackson, a tough questioner who apparently then believed that the narrow interpretation was correct?

How should this "unambiguous for narrow" testimony of General Palmer in the Armed Services Committee, whose Chairman repeatedly stressed that the ABM Treaty was "not before our committee," be weighed against that of the head of the ABM Delegation (technically the Salt I Delegation), Ambassador Smith, accompanied by other senior Salt I Delegation members, testifying before the Senate Foreign Relations Committee, with principal jurisdiction over the Treaty, which I have scored as "ambiguous: leans to broad"?

Perhaps it is reasonable on this record to conclude that a two-thirds majority of the United States Senate adverted to the "broad-narrow" issue and believed that it was the correct interpretation of the ABM Treaty as the Senate initially considered that Treaty. Certainly the record could not be persuasively cited for the opposite interpretation. But if we are embracing a new doctrine of Senate domestic lawmaking, which can as a matter of domestic law compel a President to set aside the internationally binding meaning of a treaty, and which must depend on a concurrence of two-thirds of the members of the Senate present, does this record truly establish that? Indeed, for the Senate to be adopting a "domestic condition" on this meaning apart from the underlying treaty, should we not also require evidence that the members of the Senate holding this view believed that a particular interpretation was so central that it should be binding on the President as a matter of domestic law quite apart from the treaty? But do we have any evidence of this more complex legislative intent simply from the record as to understandings about meaning? To the contrary, there seems to be no evidence in the record that the Senate, or even any member thereof or Executive Branch spokesman, intended that the ABM Treaty should receive Senate advice and consent *conditioned* on adoption of the "narrow" interpretation under national law regardless of the correct international interpretation of the ABM Treaty. And there was neither a vote on this issue nor a condition adopting it as part of the resolution of advice and consent.

This analysis is presented here simply to suggest that the effort to ascertain *a domestic lawmaking* intent of two-thirds of the Senate from "legislative history" materials may be more difficult than initially perceived by proponents of the "dual" approach.[266]

---

266 During the initial ABM Treaty interpretation debate, Professor Eugene V. Rostow, former Director of the Arms Control and Disarmament Agency, expressed his view as to the difficulty of ascertaining the intent of the Senate consenting in 1972 to the ABM Treaty from the record of "legislative history." He writes:

> In any case, "the truth" is not always easy to know. . . . The application of the A.B.M. Treaty to novel technologies was not a major issue in the ratification process in 1972; what was said on the subject by various witnesses then is quite as diverse as what is being said and written today. A few exchanges before a committee, a few

C. INTENT AS TO TREATY *BARGAIN*: THE REST OF THE STORY

We will now turn to the question of Senate intent as to the treaty *bargain*. That is, in the event that a Senate shared interpretation was not the correct international meaning, would a two-thirds majority of the consenting Senate have preferred the United States to follow their original interpretation, thus imposing greater restrictions on the United States than on the Soviet Union, or would they have preferred the United States to follow their simultaneously held original understanding, and its congressionally expressed sense of importance, as to equality of obligation with the Soviets?

As has been seen, there is evidence in the record of Senate consideration of the ABM Treaty supporting the "narrow" interpretation of the Treaty. We can, however, say with equal confidence that the evidence suggests, both on the part of individual Senators, and the Senate as a whole (and the Congress as well), that far greater importance was attached to the principle of equality in SALT relations with the Soviet Union *and* maintenance of a "vigorous research and development and modernization program," *and* that the ABM Treaty was assumed to be reflective of "the principle of equality." As such, it seems highly likely that the ABM Treaty Senate, and Senator Jackson particularly, would have preferred adherence to the less restrictive internationally binding meaning, which would have bound the United States and the Soviet Union under a continuing principle of equality, and which would have simultaneously permitted greater United States system development and modernization, *if the "broad" interpretation later turned out*

> sentences in prepared statements or speeches on the floor, may of course have been among the factors persuading a Senator to vote "yea" or "nay" on the Resolution giving the Senate's advice and consent to ratification. But the larger meaning of A.B.M. and the Interim SALT agreement together was quite different. Those agreements were considered to have been a matter of great importance to the future of Soviet-American relations and to the Republican Party in the 1972 elections. As many judges have said, however, they cannot and should not assume that legislators vote in reliance on any particular statement made in the course of debate. After all, many remain silent. Justice Jackson once acidly remarked that it is not yet the rule that a judge can examine the text of a statute or a treaty only if the legislative history is ambiguous.

E. Rostow, *supra* note 12, at 1459.

Even Professor Koplow, a principal proponent of the "dual" approach, writes in relation to the "legislative history" of the ABM Treaty interpretation issue that: "[o]ne could argue . . . that the 1972 testimony supporting the original interpretation was too ambiguous or too contradictory to entrench any durable Senate understanding." D. Koplow, *supra* note 12, at 1430 (footnote omitted). Professor Koplow cites the statement of Senator Hollings in the ABM debate *Joint Hearings* as one who apparently held this view. D. Koplow, *supra* note 12, at 1430 n.282. Note that, as with the *Restatement*, Professor Koplow fails to focus clearly on the standard for any such "domestic condition" understanding, that is, that a *two-thirds majority* of the Senate *both* held the understanding and intended it to be domestically binding on the United States regardless of the correct international meaning of the treaty.

to be the correct international meaning rather than the "narrow" interpretation. The "dual" approach, however, would have tilted toward the particular meaning locked in from a few statements in initial Senate consideration, even if the consequences of doing so ran directly counter to that Senate's most importantly expressed concerns of equality and development, overwhelmingly adopted and clearly expressed by both the Senate and the House in formal resolutions.

While one can only speculate about such a preferred Senate choice, it seems reasonable to assume that the issue they seemed to attach greatest importance to would have been their preference in a setting where no choice could restore their original double assumption that the meaning is X and that X is also the internationally correct meaning binding on the other party to the treaty. If this is correct, then the "dual" approach not only presents harsh costs for United States foreign policy and the rule of law, but it could, in individual cases, subvert rather than support the intent of the consenting Senate, as it would seem to in this case, if relevant at all.

A brief look at the central Senate and congressional action in relation to SALT I, including the ABM Treaty, may be in order concerning the greater interest of the Senate, and Congress as a whole, in the principle of United States-Soviet equality and a program of vigorous development and modernization. Congress as a whole, by joint resolution of September 30, 1972, authorized the President "to approve on behalf of the United States" the SALT I Interim Agreement with respect to the limitation of strategic offensive arms. The general "floor" debate on the Interim Agreement lasted sixteen days in the Senate. The joint resolution, approved September 30, was a product of a revised House Joint Resolution 1227, Senate Joint Resolution 241, and various Senate amendments. The most important of these Senate amendments leading to the joint resolution was the so-called "Jackson Amendment." The Jackson Amendment was originally introduced on August 7, 1972, co-sponsored by twenty-four senators, including Senators Jackson, Buckley, Fong, Thurmond and Hollings. A "revised" Jackson Amendment of September 13, was co-sponsored by 44 Senators, including Senators Jackson, Buckley, Dole, Dominick, Ervin, Fong, Goldwater, Hollings, Magnuson, Stennis, Stevens, Thurmond and Tower. The Jackson Amendment was principally aimed at ensuring United States-Soviet equality in future SALT treaty limits in reaction to the unequal limits within the Interim Agreement and at ensuring a vigorous research and development program for a prudent strategic posture. Both the original and revised Jackson amendments contained the following relevant language:

> Congress recognizes the principle of United States-Soviet Union equality reflected in the antiballistic missile treaty. . . .

> Congress considers that the success of these agreements and the attainment of more permanent and comprehensive agreements are dependent upon the maintenance of a vigorous research and development and modernization program leading to a prudent strategic posture.

With minor amendments to this latter provision proposed by Senators Cranston and Taft and Senators Javits and Mathias and accepted by Senator Jackson, the modified Jackson Amendment was adopted on September 14 by a vote of 56-35 and ultimately became section 3 of the joint resolution of September 30, 1972. Proposals offered by Senator Muskie and Senator Fulbright, which would have softened the Jackson Amendment's principal thrust on equal limits, failed respectively by votes of 35-55 and 38-48. Following adoption of the Jackson Amendment, and several other amendments to S.J. Res. 241, the modified joint resolution was passed by the Senate on September 14, by a vote of 88-2. The Senate then moved to insist on its amendment in conference with the House. The House agreed to the Senate amendment on September 25, by a vote of 307-4, and the joint resolution was signed into law on September 30, 1972.

The Joint Resolution provided, in language almost identical to the original Jackson amendment:

> [T]he Congress recognizes the principle of United States-Soviet Union equality reflected in the antiballistic missile treaty, and urges and requests the President to seek a future treaty that, inter alia, would not limit the United States to levels of intercontinental strategic forces inferior to the limits provided for the Soviet Union; and the Congress considers that the success of these agreements and the attainment of more permanent and comprehensive agreements are dependent upon the maintenance under present world conditions of a vigorous research and development and modernization program as required by a prudent strategic posture.[267]

Senator Jackson spoke at length during the August 3 debate and said in his segment on "The Objective of Equal Limits in SALT II": "In the treaty covering anti-ballistic-missile defenses we and the Soviets have clearly established the principle of equal limits on both countries. . . . we and they have undertaken to live by identical limitations. . . ." Similarly, speeches made by Senator Jackson and placed in the *Record* included the statement: "We should support the principle of equality on which the ABM treaty is based. . . ." and referred to "the principle that was applied in the case of the ABM treaty—the principle of equality. . . ." And his speeches included the statement: "My amendment . . . simply points to the need for a vigorous program of research, development and modernization leading to a prudent strategic posture. . . . [I]t is useful for the Senate to go on record to the

---

267 *Section 3 of Public Law* 92-448, 86 STAT. 746 (Sept. 30, 1972).

effect that we must continue our efforts in the research, development and modernization area. . . ."[268]

In light of this effort by Senator Jackson, culminating in overwhelming acceptance of the Jackson Amendment as the principal response of both the Senate and the House to the SALT I Agreements, including the ABM Treaty, it simply does not pass the straight face test to believe that Senator Jackson, or Senator Buckley who was a co-sponsor of the Amendment and an opponent of the Treaty (together the only two Senators scored as "unambiguous" for the "narrow" interpretation), would have preferred, in a setting where the correct international interpretation turned out to be the "broad" interpretation, to have restrictively applied the "narrow" interpretation to the United States while the Soviet Union was free to test and develop mobile OPP based ABM systems. In such a setting, if the purpose of the "dual" approach to treaty interpretation is to protect the intent of the original Senate, then it is likely quite mistaken about that intent in the *real* setting which spawned the new doctrine.[269]

---

268 This history of Senate and congressional action on the SALT I Agreements is drawn from my more detailed description in JOHN NORTON MOORE, *supra* note*.

269 When imposing greater restrictions on the United States than on our treaty partners in arms control settings, a "dual" approach to treaty interpretation, which depends on informal indications from the record of Senate intent for its asserted binding effect, would also seem suspect under § 33 of the Arms Control and Disarmament Act of 1961. That section provided in relevant part:

> [N]o action shall be taken under this chapter or any other law that will obligate the United States to disarm or to reduce or to limit the Armed Forces or armaments of the United States, except pursuant to the treaty making power of the President under the Constitution or unless authorized by further affirmative legislation by the Congress of the United States.

ARMS CONTROL AND DISARMAMENT ACT OF 1961, 22 U.S.C. § 2551 (1988), at 22 U.S.C. § 2573 (1992). An interpretation not part of the Senate resolution of advice and consent and not conveyed to our treaty partners which is inconsistent with the correct international meaning of the treaty is neither part of the treaty nor legislation. Note that, as legislation, this Act embodied an interest of the House as well as of the Senate. Indeed, a subsequent effort by the Senate to remove the referent to treaties *and legislation* and substitute in its stead the language: "in accordance with the constitutional processes of the United States" was rejected by the House. *See* Phillip R. Trimble & Jack S. Weiss, *The Role of the President, the Senate and the Congress with Respect to Arms Control Treaties Concluded by the United States*, 67 CHI.-KENT L. REV. 645, 656-57 (1991). Note also that this original § 33 referred to the treaty making power as "of the President under the Constitution."

The 1994 Amendment to § 33 provides:

> No action shall be taken pursuant to this chapter or any other Act that would obligate the United States to reduce or limit the Armed Forces or armaments of the United States in a militarily significant manner, except pursuant to the treaty-making power of the President set forth in Article II, Section 2, Clause 2 of the Constitution or unless authorized by the enactment of further affirmative legislation by the Congress of the United States.

22 U.S.C. § 2573 (1995).

Since, when the "dual" approach has an effect it always requires either that the United States violate its treaty obligations or be held to an obligation not bargained for or binding on the other party, a reasonable question can be raised as to whether any Senate, much less the required two-thirds majority of any Senate, would ever, in a specific case known to that Senate to present such a split in meaning and bargain, prefer either of these outcomes simply to domestically preserve a meaning not binding internationally? While any answer would be mere speculation, my instinct is that more often than not a consenting Senate would find mutuality and legality more compelling than the specific interpretation, in the event of a future eventuality of a mistake as to the correct international meaning of the treaty.[270]

D. A POSTSCRIPT ON THE NATURE OF THE EXECUTIVE BRANCH TESTIMONY

Since some variants of the "dual" approach seek to have Executive Branch statements made to the Senate during advice and consent declared "authoritative," presumably meaning that they would bind the President domestically regardless of the correct international interpretation of the treaty, it may be useful to also briefly review the Executive testimony in the "great" case which gave rise to the "dual" approach. The purpose of this brief postscript is again to suggest that frequently the real world of Senate "legislative history" in consideration of a treaty is more ambiguous and complex than many proponents of the "dual" approach would assume.

As has been seen, the only Executive Branch testimony scored by me as "unambiguous for the narrow interpretation" was that of General Bruce Palmer, the Acting Chief of Staff of the Army. Contextual ambiguities in relation to this testimony relate both to the nature of General Palmer's knowledge and authoritativeness on the issue, and the interface of his testimony with that of other Executive Branch officials.

With respect to General Palmer's testimony, a number of features of the record at least somewhat reduce its effect. Most importantly, he was not a member of the ABM Delegation likely to have firsthand knowledge of the

---

270 One interesting analogy, is that even at the height of the Senate emotionalism about the Biden Condition, an amendment to require that: "[t]he United States shall not be bound to or constrained by any interpretation of this treaty that is not equally binding or constraining upon the Soviet Union . . . ," offered in opposition to the Biden Condition by Senator Wilson, quoting "Scoop" Jackson on the SALT I Agreements, was defeated by a vote of less than two-thirds of the Senate. Thus, the Wilson Amendment failed in a close, largely party line vote of 53-45. That is, the record conclusively shows on the Biden Senate Treaty Condition itself that a two-thirds majority of the Senate could not be found to prefer preservation of the meaning over mutuality in any future dispute arising under the condition. *See* 134 CONG. REC. S6804-05, 09 (daily ed., May 26, 1988).

issue, particularly given its complexity and the apparent failure of testifying ABM Delegation members themselves to clearly expound on the issue. Second, in an earlier exchange with Senator Goldwater, who may at that time have leaned toward believing that the "broad" interpretation was correct, I have scored General Palmer's testimony as "ambiguous: leans to broad." A footnote to this characterization, however, says:

> It can reasonably be argued that the statements of all three Generals in this exchange with Senator Goldwater, by not specifically being qualified by a "fixed land-based" referent, should be regarded as "unambiguous for 'broad.'"[271]

Thus, it is quite possible, if not even likely, that General Palmer agreed with Senator Goldwater who seemed to support the "broad" interpretation when the issue initially arose, and then agreed again with Senator Jackson, an even tougher questioner, who seemed to believe the "narrow" interpretation was correct. That General Palmer initially gave testimony characterized as "ambiguous: leans to broad" at least casts doubt as to his real knowledge of the issue. Third, in an interview with the author on the ABM interpretation issue, Admiral Thomas H. Moorer, former Chairman of the Joint Chiefs of Staff, took the position that General Palmer's testimony as to the "narrow" approach was simply wrong in so far as it invoked the Chiefs. Similarly, a contemporaneous report by Mr. James L. Malone of ACDA reported "some confusion" by General Palmer during his testimony. Fourth, General Palmer's statement was not part of a prepared statement, but rather was given during an oral exchange, and such exchanges are not always known for their accuracy. And finally, General Palmer's statement was made in the Senate Armed Services Committee hearings, whose Chairman, Senator John C. Stennis, had repeatedly said the ABM Treaty was "not before our committee."

General Palmer's testimony should also be placed in context with the totality of other Executive Branch testimony. Most importantly, no prepared statement or legal analysis from the President, the Secretary of State, ACDA, the NSC, or Members of the SALT I Delegation addressed the "broad-narrow" issue and adopted either the "broad" or "narrow" interpretations. And, as has been seen, testimony of the Head of Delegation, Ambassador Smith, three times is scored as "ambiguous: leans to broad," including his testimony before the Senate Foreign Relations Committee, the Committee with principal jurisdiction over the ABM Treaty. Similarly, Admiral Thomas Moorer also gave testimony characterized as "ambiguous: leans to broad."

---

271 *See* John Norton Moore, *Summary Chart of Congressional Consideration of the "Broad-Narrow" Issue In Initial Consideration of the ABM Treaty*, printed as an Annex to John Norton Moore, *supra* note *.

None of these features remove the fact that an Executive Branch official did give testimony to the Senate that I believe is fairly scored as unambiguous for the narrow interpretation. These features of the broader context do, however, give further pause to the wisdom of declaring any Executive Branch statement made to the Senate as, by itself, automatically creating binding domestic law capable of overriding a treaty. And again, none of these contextual complexities are pointed out for the purpose of adopting a position on the merits of the "broad-narrow" issue. My report on that complex issue has been communicated to the Director of ACDA and remains confidential. The point is, however, to illustrate that the real world complexities of Senate "legislative" or "treaty consideration" history suggest yet further serious difficulties with adopting any of the versions of the "dual" approach to treaty interpretation which emerged from this unfortunate debate.[272]

272 These complexities, rooted in ascertaining Senate intent from "Senate consideration treaty history," suggest that Executive Branch testimony, considering all its possible dimensions, is neither automatically an indication of a meaning shared by two-thirds of the Senate, nor an indication of such a Senate intent as to the nature of the bargain, nor an indication of such a Senate intent to require a legally binding "domestic condition." Indeed, in some possible settings, perversely such testimony could even be counter to Senate intent on any of these elements.

VI.
A Brief Excursion: More Ships in the Night

A. THE VORTEX EXPANDS

Like the vortex in the Wizard of Oz, the contentious "broad-narrow" dispute between a powerful Chairman of a Senate Committee and a former federal judge serving as the Legal Adviser of the Department of State expanded even to the judiciary. This was particularly evident in two cases decided in 1988 and 1989, during the height of the storm. The first of these cases was *Rainbow Navigation, Inc. v. Department of the Navy,*[273] decided by Judge Harold H. Greene, District Judge in the United States District Court for the District of Columbia, on November 15, 1988. The second was *United States v. Stuart,*[274] decided by the United States Supreme Court on February 28, 1989.

In neither of these cases, which will be examined below, were the constitutional and policy issues concerning "domestic conditions" and the "dual" approach fully identified and effectively joined in briefs by opposing counsel, and in both cases the Court seems to have been drawn into the vortex on its own initiative. Indeed, both cases are testaments to the dangers of dealing with issues not fully addressed through the adversarial process. And both bear unmistakable marks that the judicial initiative may have been triggered or influenced by the ongoing "broad-narrow" storm.

Thus, in *Rainbow Navigation,* issues concerning Executive Branch statements and informal Senate conditions became more prominent in Judge Greene's opinion on the merits written after his opinion in the case at the preliminary injunction stage was cited approvingly in connection with the "broad-narrow" issue in an editorial in the *New York Times* on May 25,

273 699 F.Supp. 339 (D.D.C. 1988), *rev'd and vacated,* Rainbow Navigation, Inc. v. Department of the Navy, 911 F.2d 797 (D.C. Cir. 1990), *cert. denied* 499 U.S. 906 (1991).

274 489 U.S. 353 (1989).

1988,[275] and the next day entered into the *Congressional Record*[276] with a long laudatory comment by Senator Nunn.[277] Indeed, Judge Greene's opinion on the merits written after this heady experience in the vortex seems barely to address any issues of treaty interpretation as were addressed in his earlier May 17, 1988, opinion in the case,[278] and focuses instead on the effect of Executive Branch representations and informal Senate understandings. Similarly, footnote 18 in Judge Greene's November 15 decision bears unmistakable marks of the vortex. It says:

> The Senate Committee on Foreign Relations has stated in connection with the debate over the ABM treaty, the Executive's unilateral reinterpretation of treaties "assaults the Constitution's allocation of the treaty power," "disparages the Constitution's requirement that the President take care that the laws be faithfully executed" and "denigrates the central precept of international order—the principle that treaty obligations are to be carried out in good faith." Senate Committee on Foreign Relations, The ABM Treaty Interpretation Resolution, S.Rep. No. 164, 100th Cong., 1st Sess. 47 (1987).

It would be hard to miss the drift, and the righteous sense of the writer that the Senate approach to treaty interpretation in the ABM interpretation dispute is compelled by the rule of law. Indeed, it is as though Judge Greene were the chorus in a Greek tragedy.

In *United States v. Stuart* we need not speculate about the power of the vortex since Justice Scalia's opinion concurring in the Judgment of the Court points it out for us, along with the involvement of the *Rainbow Navigation* case. Thus, Justice Scalia writes:

> It can hardly have escaped the Court's attention that the role of Senate understanding in the treaty ratification process has recently been the subject of some considerable dispute between the Senate and the Executive. See Washington Post, Mar. 19, 1988, p. A11, col. 1 (discussing disagreement on the importance to be accorded to Senate understanding of the Anti-Ballistic Missile Treaty at the time of advice and consent to the President's ratification); Washington Post, Feb. 17, 1988, p. A17, col. 1 (same); Washington Post, Feb. 6, 1988, p. A1, col. 6 (same). [Justice Scalia then adverts in this same

---

275 *The Treaty and Its Enemies*, N.Y. TIMES, May 25, 1988, at A26, col. 1 (editorial desk, late city final ed.).

276 *See* 134 CONG. REC. S6756-58, S6772-90 (daily ed. May 26, 1988).

277 134 CONG. REC. S6774-75 (daily ed. May 26, 1988)(statement of Sen. Nunn).

278 The May 17 decision is 686 F. Supp. 354 (D.D.C. 1988). *See* particularly Judge Greene's two footnotes on the standards for treaty interpretation featured in this May 17 decision before his opinion was directly drawn into the vortex of the "broad-narrow" issue. They are at 359 nn.25-26. These footnotes clearly adopt the conventional view of the "intent or expectations" of the parties, and even emphasize the rules of interpretation in the Vienna Convention on the Law of Treaties as "authoritative."

paragraph to the *Rainbow Navigation* decisions of Judge Harold Greene in May and November mentioned above].[279]

It seems equally obvious that footnote 7, in the opinion of the Court, which is the only part of the opinion of the Court to engage these issues, is both unnecessary to the decision of the Court and has the impression of simply an add on. It seems highly likely that counsel in this case had no idea that any issue relevant to the issues discussed in this article were presented in the *Stuart* case. Such was the power of the vortex.

Great cases make bad law had now leaped from the Senate to the Courts. The virus of the "dual" approach, however, continued to remain largely hidden.

B. THE *RAINBOW NAVIGATION* CASE AND THE MOMENTARY REAPPEARANCE OF "DOMESTIC CONDITIONS"

Rainbow Navigation does not present or address the "dual" approach. Judge Harold Greene, however, in a somewhat ambiguous opinion, does seem to embrace the concept of "domestic conditions" and seems to hold what he finds to be such a condition binding on the Department of the Navy in a dispute about transit of military cargo to Iceland on a particular United States carrier. Moreover, he seems to find such a binding "domestic condition" incident to Senate approval of the United States-Icelandic Treaty on the Carriage of Military Cargo solely from the testimony of an Executive Branch witness, a floor statement from a Senator, and language in the Senate Report. Thus, he finds a binding "domestic condition" solely from informal indicators in the record of Senate ratification consideration in the absence of any such condition in a Senate resolution of ratification. Quite apart from the constitutional issue of "domestic conditions," one considerable problem with this finding is, of course, deciding whether such policy statements about implementation in the informal record were intended by two-thirds of the Senators present to be legally binding domestic law, or rather whether they were simply intended as a good faith indication as to the intentions of the Executive Branch. And it should be noted that quite apart from the constitutionality of "domestic conditions," an issue never addressed in the opinion, this domestic lawmaking intent carries a burden on *two* separate intent issues. First, was the intent of the Senate to create a legally binding domestic obligation, or merely to put pressure on the Executive Branch by way of precatory statements in the record? And second, was the intent shared by two-thirds of the Senators present, the only way *anything* could be legally binding from the advice and consent process?

---

279 United States v. Stuart, 489 U.S. 353, 376 (1989) (opinion of Justice Scalia concurring in the judgment).

Both intent elements would seem particularly difficult to ascertain in the absence of inclusion of the condition in a Senate resolution of advice and consent. Judge Greene also appears enamored with what he seems to regard as a legally binding effect of Executive Branch witnesses in testifying during the advice and consent process. In effect, Judge Greene's November 15 decision is a party line acceptance of the arguments being made by the supporters of the Biden Condition, without either adverting to or ruling on the specifics of the "dual" approach. Standing as testament to the lack of wisdom of deciding important issues without full identification, briefing and argumentation, Judge Greene seemed blissfully unaware in all of his *Rainbow Navigation* decisions that the only such fully briefed and argued case addressing the issue of "domestic conditions" was by his own Court of Appeals in the *Niagara Reservation* case, and that his Court of Appeals had decided two-to-one against such conditions. Indeed, with respect to the form of "domestic condition" asserted by Judge Greene, which goes far beyond the "non-self-executing" condition in *Niagara Reservation, all* of the judges in the case would seem to be in opposition.

The reawakening of the doctrine of "domestic conditions" by Judge Harold Greene, after Judge Bazelon had driven a stake through its heart in the1957 *Niagara Reservation* case, was but momentary. On appeal, the United States Court of Appeals for the District of Columbia Circuit reversed in a sensible and traditional treaty analysis.[280] In an opinion for the Court filed by Circuit Judge D.H. Ginsburg, and joined by Judge Sentelle and Judge Ruth Bader Ginsburg, the Court makes it clear that it looks to the language of the treaty and the intent or expectations of its signatories as the appropriate normative basis for treaty interpretation.[281] And it dismisses the argument that the Executive Branch statements during consideration by the Senate are "binding interpretations," on the dual ground that it is not clear that these statements were "interpretations of what the Treaty requires, as opposed merely to representations about how the Administration then intended to implement the Treaty,"[282] and ambiguity in those remarks and the Senate Committee Report as to whether they were aimed at protecting the plaintiff carrier in the case, Rainbow Navigation, "as opposed to the

---

280 Rainbow Navigation, Inc. v. Department of the Navy, 911 F.2d 797 (D.C. Cir. 1990).

281 911 F.2d 797, 801 (D.C. Cir. 1990). The Court begins by quoting the *Sumitomo* case [457 U.S. 176, 180 (1982)], quoting the famous language of the *Maximov* case [373 U.S. 49, 54 (1963)] that:

> The clear import of treaty language controls unless "application of the words of the treaty according to their obvious meaning effects a result inconsistent with the intent or expectations of its signatories."

911 F.2d 797, at 801.

282 911 F.2d 797, 802.

U.S. flag service in general."[283] The Court then concludes: "Ambiguous ratification history cannot be allowed to obscure the meaning of clear Treaty language."[284]

C. THE *STUART* CASE AND THE BEGINNING OF A NON-DEBATE ABOUT THE USE OF SENATE MATERIALS

United States v. Stuart[285] presents a garden variety treaty interpretation issue which the courts have handled since the beginning of the Republic. It involved whether the 1942 Convention Respecting Double Taxation between the United States and Canada required "the IRS to attest that a Canadian tax investigation has not reached a stage analogous to a Justice Department referral by the IRS in order to obtain enforcement of a summons issued pursuant to a request by Canadian authorities under the . . . Convention."[286] It did *not* involve either an asserted "domestic condition" or the "dual" approach to treaty interpretation.[287]

In resolving this straightforward interpretation issue the Court clearly applied the traditional rule of looking to the language of the treaty and the intent and expectations of the parties. Thus, it began its analysis by quoting the *Sumitomo* case quoting *Maximov* that:

> The clear import of treaty language controls unless "application of the words of the treaty according to their obvious meaning effects a result inconsistent with the intent or expectations of its signatories."[288]

And subsequently, in the context of discussing "[n]ontextual sources" in aid of interpretation, such as "a treaty's ratification history and its subsequent operation," the Court said they "often assist us in 'giving effect to the intent of the Treaty parties . . . ,'" again citing *Sumitomo*.[289] In two further statements, the Court also implied that the intent of the parties is the controlling standard. Thus, in reviewing the subsequent practice of the treaty parties, the Court wrote: "The practice of treaty signatories counts as evidence of the treaty's proper interpretation, since their conduct generally

283 911 F.2d 797, 802.

284 911 F.2d 797, 802.

285 489 U.S. 353 (1989).

286 489 U.S. at 353 (quote from headnote as to the holding).

287 Professor Kenneth S. Gallant also concludes, in his article on "Treaty Interpretation after the Biden Condition," that *Stuart* is not an acceptance of the Biden Condition. He writes: "*Stuart* cannot be viewed as the Court's acceptance of the theory of the Biden Condition." Kenneth S. Gallant, *supra* note 131, at 1100.

288 489 U.S. at 365-66.

289 489 U.S. at 366.

evinces their understanding of the agreement they signed."[290] And it also wrote: "a treaty should generally be 'construe[d] . . . liberally to give effect to the purpose which animates it."[291] The separate opinions of Justices Kennedy and O'Connor concurring in part and concurring in the judgment, and Justice Scalia concurring in the judgment, also supported the traditional standards for treaty interpretation. Thus, the separate opinion of Justices Kennedy and O'Connor referred to "what the signatories to a treaty intended."[292]

Similarly, the Court's opinion implicitly rejects the extreme view, which as we have seen is inconsistent with a long line of treaty interpretation decisions, which would restrict interpretive materials to those before the Senate at the time of advice and consent. It examines and repeatedly discusses the subsequent practice of the parties, which, by definition, is unlikely to be before a Senate during consideration of advice and consent.[293]

Indeed, *Stuart* would have drawn no notice, and perhaps even no separate opinions, had it not been for what almost seems a gratuitous inclusion of footnote 7 in the opinion of the Court, quite possibly a product of the "broad-narrow" vortex. Footnote 7, looking elaborated as a result of interaction with Justice Scalia's separate opinion, provides in full:

> Contrary to JUSTICE SCALIA'S suggestion, see *post*, at 377, the Government relied on the preratification Senate debate in its brief, see Brief for United States 29, and n. 11, pointing out that the only reference to intergovernmental exchanges of information came in the following colloquy:
>
> "Mr. TAFT . . .
>
> "In other words, if an American citizen were using a Canadian bank deposit to evade income taxation, I think the convention would permit the United States Government to ask the Canadian Government to obtain information from its own bank and furnish it to this Government in connection with the enforcement of our internal-revenue laws.
>
> "Mr. GEORGE. It does provide for exchange of information, as the Senator from Ohio points out." 88 Cong. Rec. 4714 (1942).
>
> Nor is reliance on the Senate's preratification debates and reports improper. As JUSTICE SCALIA acknowledges, the American Law Institute's most recent Restatement counsels consideration of such materials. See Restatement (Third) of Foreign Relations Law of the United States Sec. 314, Comment *d*

---

290 489 U.S. at 369.

291 489 U.S. at 368.

292 489 U.S. at 370. The separate opinion of Justices Kennedy and O'Connor concurring in part and concurring in the judgment is 489 U.S. 370, and the separate opinion of Justice Scalia concurring in the judgment is 489 U.S. 371.

293 *See* 489 U.S. at 366 & 369.

> (1987) ("indication that . . . the Senate ascribed a particular meaning to the treaty is relevant"); *id.*, Sec. 325, Reporters' Note 5 ("A court . . . is required to take into account . . . (i) Committee reports, debates, and other indications of meaning that the legislative branch has attached to an agreement . . ."). Consultation of these materials is eminently reasonable. *Pace* JUSTICE SCALIA , reviewing preratification Senate debates and reports is not akin to "determining the meaning of a bilateral contract between two corporations on the basis of what the board of directors of one of them thought it meant when authorizing the chief executive officer to conclude it." *Post*, at 374. Senate debates do not occur behind closed doors, out of earshot of proposed treaty partners, nor are preratification Senate reports kept under seal. Both are public statements. They therefore bear no resemblance to the private deliberations of a board of directors prior to the board's decision whether to authorize the chief executive officer to sign an agreement. Insofar as the contract analogy is apt, the better comparison is to a meeting of the board whose minutes and position papers the other corporation's board and chief executive officer are invited to peruse. It is hornbook contract law that the proper construction of an agreement is that given by one of the parties when "that party had no reason to know of any different meaning attached by the other, and the other had reason to know the meaning attached by the first party." Restatement (Second) of Contracts Sec. 201 (2)(b) (1981). See also E. Farnsworth, Contracts 487-488 (1982). A treaty's negotiating history, which JUSTICE SCALIA suggests would be a better interpretive guide than preratification Senate materials, see *post*, at 374, would in fact be a worse indicator of a treaty's meaning, for that history is rarely a matter of public record available to the Senate when it decides to grant or withhold its consent.[294]

The thrust of footnote 7 is simply to support the well established proposition that it is not improper to *use* preratification Senate materials in treaty interpretation. Indeed, the footnote refers four times to this issue. Thus, it says: "Nor is *reliance* on the Senate's preratification debates and reports improper"; "[a]s JUSTICE SCALIA acknowledges, the American Law Institutes's most recent Restatement counsels *consideration* of such materials"; and "*[c]onsultation* of these materials is eminently reasonable"; and again, "*reviewing* preratification Senate debates and reports. . . ." Moreover, in quoting the *Restatement* § 314, cmt. *d*, the Court quotes *only* that part of cmt. *d* which seems to stand for the proposition that Senate preratification materials may be relevant in treaty interpretation. Importantly, it *does not* quote the controversial paragraph which constitutes the principal authority within the *Restatement* which can be at least construed as supportive of the "dual" approach. Thus footnote 7 does not endorse a Senate power of "domestic conditions," either with or without inclusion of the condition in a formal resolution of advice and consent. It does not endorse the concept that Executive Branch statements made during the process of advice and

---

294 489 U.S. 367 n.7.

consent are *ipso facto* binding. And it does not endorse the "dual" approach to treaty interpretation.

Sadly, however, the final sentence of footnote 7, which is flatly wrong, can be interpreted as giving aid and comfort to the "dual" approach. To suggest, as this sentence does, that preratification Senate materials are a better guide to a treaty's meaning than the negotiating history is, for an international lawyer familiar with both treaty negotiation and Senate consideration of treaties, simply nonsense on stilts.[295] And, of course, this would not be consistent with the rules of interpretation reflected in the Vienna Convention on the Law of Treaties, widely regarded as customary international law in the interpretation of international agreements, and, thus, part of our law.[296] Nor would it even seem consistent with the *Restatement* itself, which does not take the position anywhere in § 325 that preratification Senate materials should be weighed more heavily in interpretation than context, subsequent practice, *travaux*, or multiple language texts. Moreover, this final sentence, which vaguely suggests that the touchstone for interpretation perhaps should be Senate intent rather than the intent of the parties, is inconsistent with the opinion's clear reliance on the language of the treaty and the intent and expectations of the parties. And its implications of the extreme Tribe view that only materials before the Senate could be taken into account in treaty interpretation is both inconsistent with a long history of the Court's own jurisprudence and the opinion's reliance itself on subsequent practice of the parties. It seems likely that footnote 7 is simply a product of the vortex, mysteriously appearing and seemingly contradicting the opinion of the Court, in a setting in which the virus of the "dual" approach remained hidden to most observers.[297]

---

295 The reader who doubts this is invited, as one example, to review any of the interpretive texts on the 1958 Geneva Conventions on the Law of the Sea and compare it with the brief Senate consideration of these treaties.

296 *See, e.g.*, The Paquete Habana, 175 U.S. 677 (1900). The classic statement from this case is:

> International law is part of our law, and must be ascertained and administered by the courts of justice of appropriate jurisdiction as often as questions of right depending upon it are duly presented for their determination.

175 U.S. at 700.

297 John O. McGinnis, a Deputy Assistant Attorney General, indicated to the author that "the issue of their relevance ["preratification deliberations"] was obviously not fully briefed" to the Court. Letter from John O. McGinnis to John Norton Moore (Mar. 21, 1989). Similarly, Justice Scalia's separate opinion notes: "It is odd, to say the least, that in the present case, where the language of the Treaty is clear, where the role of Senate reports and debates has not even been argued, and where the Solicitor General has not been requested to give us the benefit of his views on that subject, we should reach out to use such materials for the first time in two centuries of treaty construction." 489 U.S. at 377. Lawrence J. Block, Lee A. Casey and David B. Rivkin, Jr., three Senior-Attorney

Probably the problem with footnote 7, perhaps as well the fact that these issues were neither fully briefed to the Court nor presented for decision by the context, prompted Justices Kennedy and O'Connor to prudently submit a separate opinion concurring in part and concurring with the judgment, but not joining Part II-C of the Court's opinion, which is the part dealing with treaty interpretation. The thrust of their short separate opinion was:

> The intent of the Treaty's signatories is manifest from the language of the document itself. I agree with JUSTICE SCALIA that we should not reach, either in a direct or an implicit way, the question whether Senate debates on ratification are authoritative or even helpful in determining what the signatories to a treaty intended. That determination should be reserved until we confront a case where the language of the treaty itself does not yield a clear answer to the question before us.[298]

Justice Scalia also filed a separate opinion, concurring only in the judgment of the Court. His opinion is in two parts. Part I focuses, in the treaty context, on what has long been a focus of Justice Scalia in statutory interpretation; that is, the importance of relying on the language of the written instrument as the principal embodiment of intent and expectations, as opposed to a liberal reliance on legislative history.[299] Here he urges that "our traditional rule of treaty construction is that an agreement's language is the best evidence of its purpose and its parties' intent."[300] And "[o]nly when a treaty provision is ambiguous have we found it appropriate to give authoritative effect to extratextual materials."[301] International lawyers familiar with treaty interpretation practice will immediately realize that while this may not be the majority view in United States statutory construction, or among

---

Advisors in the Department of Justice, also noted in their 1989 Commentary against the "dual" approach and the Biden Condition:

> having reviewed the briefs submitted to the Court and the record of the oral arguments in *Stuart*, we have found no evidence that the issue of whether, as a matter of constitutional law, a treaty may generate domestic obligations at variance with international obligations assumed by the United States was briefed by the parties or considered by the Court.

Lawrence J. Block, Lee A. Casey & David B. Rivkin, Jr., *supra* note 12, at 1495 n.44.

298 489 U.S. at 370.

299 The rule in the United Kingdom, by way of comparison, is that generally it is impermissible to rely on legislative history in statutory construction. As has earlier been discussed in this article, while continuing to follow this rule in treaty interpretation with respective to the *legislative proceedings* necessary in the United Kingdom for the incorporation of treaties into domestic law, the House of Lords has considered the *foreign language texts and travaux* relating to the *treaty negotiating history*. *See* Fothergill v Monarch Airlines Ltd, [1980] 2 All E.R. 696 (July 10, 1980).

300 489 U.S. at 372.

301 489 U.S. at 373.

United States scholars of treaty interpretation, it is the predominant European and perhaps World view, that has been largely embodied in the Vienna Convention on the Law of Treaties, as the principal international law approach to treaty interpretation. Thus, the thrust of this approach appears in Article 31 "General Rule of Interpretation" of the Vienna Convention on the Law of Treaties. Whether one agrees or disagrees with this approach, it is certainly a widely shared position about treaty interpretation internationally.[302]

Before leaving Part I of Justice Scalia's opinion, it may be worth noting that the problem of "domestic conditions," as supported by the *Restatement* in settings even in the absence of a Senate resolution of advice and consent, and implicitly part of the debate in the *Stuart* case, presents a special and unique problem with "legislative history." And since we are talking—in the doctrine of "domestic conditions"—about something by definition not part of the treaty, it *is* an issue of "legislative history." That is, normally we look to legislative history for the purpose of clarifying the language of a specific legislative enactment clearly intended to have at least some governing legal effect. If that effect is ambiguous, we then examine the legislative history. But asserting, as the *Restatement* does, that the Senate has a power of "domestic conditions" even in the absence of any resolution language agreed by the Senate, that is, a power which can create a binding legal effect solely from informal indications in the record (or, as some assert, any Executive Branch statement), really means that the problem of "legislative history" is far more difficult than in the normal Article I legislative process. Thus, we must first ascertain with the asserted doctrine of informal "domestic conditions" whether the Senate had *any* domestic lawmaking intent at all before we then ascertain what it was. And we must do that with no language (or vote) of the Senate for this intent to attach to. Indeed, this turned out on appeal to be one of the problems the Court of Appeals had with the opinion of Judge Harold Greene in *Rainbow Navigation.* Did the Senate intend by its expressed views to create a legally binding restraint, or were those views (or those expressed by an Executive Branch spokesman) merely precatory? We must also ascertain, whether or not the "domestic conditions" are embodied in a resolution of advice and consent, that the intent is that of

302 This is an area in which the author would adopt a different emphasis, while recognizing the importance of language as the culminating event in an agreement, also remaining receptive to the complete context of agreement, in the search for the shared intent of the parties. *See, e.g.*, M. McDougal, H. Lasswell & J. Miller, The Interpretation of Agreements and World Public Order (1967). Professor McDougal was one of the members of the United States Delegation to the Vienna Conference which produced the Vienna Convention on the Law of Treaties, and he remained disappointed at the interpretive provisions of that Treaty. I continue to regard this work of Professor McDougal as the best work on the general international law of treaty interpretation and one of his best works on any subject.

two-thirds of the Senators present, which is the only constitutional standard for any effective Senate action in the advice and consent process. For these reasons, Justice Scalia's concern about "legislative or treaty history" has a special resonance concerning the "dual" approach to treaty interpretation or "domestic conditions" more broadly.

Part II of Justice Scalia's separate opinion focuses on the nature of the extratextual materials relied on by the Court. Here he strongly objects to use of the Senate preratification record in treaty interpretation. The core of his concern here, in the context of *Rainbow Navigation* and the broader vortex of the "broad-narrow" dispute, which he adverts to in his opinion, is that we may abandon the intent of the treaty parties as the normative standard for treaty interpretation domestically, in favor of the intent of the Senate. Thus he writes:

> The question before us in a treaty case is what the two or more sovereigns agreed to, rather than what a single one of them, or the legislature of a single one of them, thought it agreed to. And to answer that question accurately, it can reasonably be said, whatever extratextual materials are consulted must be materials that reflect the mutual agreement (for example, the negotiating history) rather than a unilateral understanding.[303]

And he says:

> This is not the case in which to commit ourselves to an approach that significantly reduces what has hitherto been the President's role in the interpretation of treaties, and commits the United States to a form of interpretation plainly out of step with international practice.[304]

Justice Scalia is clearly indicating that for him the virus of the "dual" approach is not hidden, there are most serious foreign affairs, separation of powers, and rule of law issues inherent in "domestic conditions," efforts to make Executive Branch statements "authoritative," and the "dual" approach to treaty interpretation. He, and I believe Justices Kennedy and O'Connor, are quite concerned at a footnote 7 containing *any* implications for these fundamental issues without full briefing and argumentation, including, as Justice Scalia notes, the views of the Solicitor General. In these points, which I regard as the central thrust of Justice Scalia's opinion, I think he is clearly correct and that his alertness to the shortcomings of what was at the time a popular approach, deserves the gratitude of the international law community.

Alas, however, gratitude is not frequently the reward of those tasked with making decisions on the Supreme Court. In his opinion, Justice Scalia had

---

303 489 U.S. at 374.

304 489 U.S. at 376.

been critical of the *Restatement* which, of course, had been cited in the infamous footnote 7. Thus, he referred to § 314, cmt. *d*, and § 325, Reporters' Note 5, and then noted the quote presented earlier in this article from the Proposed Official Draft of the *Restatement* in 1962, which noted: "There is virtually no precise decisional authority on this matter. . . ."[305] Earlier, in overly broad language, Justice Scalia had said, "I have been unable to discover a single case in which this Court has consulted the Senate debate, committee hearings, or committee reports." Never mind that it seems reasonably clear from the context of Part II of his separate opinion, where this language appears, as opposed to Part I focused on the general issue of legislative or treaty history, that Justice Scalia had in mind here such materials consulted for the purpose of ascertaining the intent of the Senate, as opposed to the intent of the parties to the treaty or the views of the Executive on the correct interpretation of the treaty. That this was his intent is also reflected in his statement only thirteen lines later in the same paragraph that: "whatever extratextual materials are consulted must be materials that reflect the mutual agreement (for example, the negotiating history) rather than a unilateral understanding." That is, consistent with this statement, Justice Scalia would seem to have had no Part II objection to consulting Senate preratification materials which provided references to negotiating history or other indicators as to the mutual intent of the treaty parties. Similarly, to anyone familiar with the "broad-narrow" vortex, which seemed to be stimulating the relevant debate in the *Stuart* case, it was highly significant that Justice Scalia, in the same paragraph adverting to the ABM interpretation dispute between the Senate and the Executive, singled out the opinions by Judge Harold Greene in the *Rainbow Navigation* cases for the observation: "The first (and, as far as I am aware, the only) federal decisions relying upon preratification Senate materials for the interpretation of a treaty were issued by the District Court for the District of Columbia, in successive phases of the same controversy, last May . . . and last November. . . ."[306] Since these decisions were quite unique in seemingly asserting binding "domestic conditions" simply from Executive Branch statements and informal Senate preratification treaty history, it was apparent that Justice Scalia was shooting broader game. Moreover, unlike his original broadest statement, this one was qualified with the phrase "*relying* upon preratification Senate materials *for the interpretation of a treaty*."[307] This suggests more clearly that he had in mind relying on such materials for their own authoritative legal effect in interpretation of a treaty, rather than simply relying on them as one would a law review article for the information contained therein. Most importantly, his critical reference to the *Restate-*

305 489 U.S. at 375-76.

306 489 U.S. at 376.

307 489 U.S. at 376 (emphasis added).

ment included a reference, not just to Reporters' Note 5 to § 325 on "Use of domestic sources," but first in his list to § 314, cmt. *d*. That comment includes the language:

> indication that the President or the Senate ascribed a particular meaning to the treaty is relevant to the interpretation of the treaty by a United States court in much the same way that the legislative history of a statute is relevant to its interpretation. . . .

and:

> Although the Senate's resolution of consent may contain no statement of understanding, there may be such statements in the report of the Senate Foreign Relations Committee or in the Senate debates. In that event, the President must decide whether they represent a general understanding by the Senate and, if he finds that they do, must respect them in good faith.[308]

The language here, ascribing "a particular meaning to the treaty . . . in much the same way that the legislative history of a statute is relevant to its interpretation," is more than a claim that one refers to legislative history like a law review article or treatise for the information contained therein. Rather, it is at least implicitly asserting an authoritativeness of the Senate-ascribed meaning. Indeed, the very reference to "Senate . . . meaning" even suggests this conclusion. And if there is any doubt from the first paragraph of cmt. *d*, all doubt vanishes with the second paragraph. Here the *Restatement* directs that a "general understanding by the Senate" must be respected, which is hardly a reference to consult preratification history like a law review article or scholarly treatise purely for the information contained therein. I believe that a fair interpretation of Justice Scalia's principal Part II concern, taken in context by someone knowledgeable about the treaty law issues at stake in the *Stuart* case, would have been that his focus was on not examining preratification treaty materials for the purpose of ascertaining the intent of the Senate, as opposed to the traditional, and well established rule in the jurisprudence of the United States Supreme Court, that a treaty was a contract or compact among nations to be interpreted by the intent of the parties.[309] Thus, even his broad language, when taken in

---

308 AMERICAN LAW INSTITUTE, RESTATEMENT (THIRD) OF THE FOREIGN RELATIONS LAW OF THE UNITED STATES § 314, cmt. d (1987).

309 Yet another indication that Justice Scalia had in mind broader game, particularly the *Restatement* position on "domestic conditions" and its interface with the ABM Treaty interpretation vortex and the *Rainbow Navigation* case, is the single footnote in his separate opinion, made in his discussion of the opinions of Judge Harold Greene in *Rainbow Navigation*. This footnote provided:

> The court [the District Court in *Rainbow Navigation*] relied in part upon testimony—reproduced in The ABM Treaty Interpretation Resolution, Report of the Committee on Foreign Relations of the United States Senate, S. Rep. No. 100-164,

its full context, and particularly when it is noted that it was not in Part I, but rather Part II of the Scalia opinion, with that Part's focus on the international contractual nature of a treaty, would seem most fairly to refer to consulting Senate materials as the Court would consult them in interpreting domestic legislation; that is, to establish from the congressional intent itself a legally binding "authoritative" interpretation.

Nevertheless, Justice Scalia's broad language almost immediately produced an attack. The attack was apparently stimulated by a felt need of one of the distinguished Associate Reporters of the *Restatement* to mount an

---

> p. 49 (1987)—by none other than the reporter for the Restatement of Foreign Relations Law, Professor Louis Henkin. Thus, by self-exertion, so to speak, there is now at least one case that the Restatement *almost* restates. The qualifier is needed because, as I discuss later in text, even that case does not go as far as the Restatement (and the Court's opinion today) would do.

Professor Henkin's support for "domestic conditions" in the context of the *Niagara Reservation* case, and his testimony seeming to support what I have termed in this article the "dual" approach to treaty interpretation, in the context of the "broad-narrow" vortex, is well known. *See, e.g.*, the Statement of Louis Henkin, University Professor at Columbia University in New York, New York, *in* THE ABM TREATY AND THE CONSTITUTION, *supra* note 12, at 81-83. He has expressed reservations, however, with respect to the Senate Treaty Interpretation Condition now routinely being attached to treaties by the Senate. It is less clear to me whether Professor Henkin, certainly a leader of the international law community in supporting the rule of law, has fully adverted to the disastrous consequences of the "dual" approach for that rule of law.

Professor Henkin's testimony during the ABM Treaty interpretation debates, like the controversial positions on these issues adopted in the *Restatement (Third)*, seems to this author to obscure the real issues at stake in the "dual-unitary" debate with overly simple conclusory statements. Thus, Professor Henkin told the Senate hearing:

> For present purposes, we may reduce that constitutional provision [the treaty power of Article II, section 2, clause 2] to a simple proposition: the President can make a treaty if the Senate has consented to it. Of course, the President can only make the treaty to which the Senate consented. He cannot make a treaty other than the one to which the Senate consented.
>
> It follows that the President cannot make a treaty with a text different from the one to which the Senate consented; he cannot make a treaty with a meaning different from the one to which the Senate consented. . . .
>
> . . . . The President can only make a treaty that means what the Senate understood the treaty to mean when the Senate gave its consent. . . . The same principle governs when the Senate's understanding of a treaty provision is not expressed in a formal resolution, but is apparent from the Senate's deliberations leading to its expression of consent.

THE ABM TREATY AND THE CONSTITUTION, *supra* note 12, at 81-82. Professor Henkin's testimony also suggests that he may have adverted to the possible costs to the rule of law and the foreign relations practice of the United States in the event that the domestic and international meanings of a treaty were not congruent under the approach he was espousing as the foreign relations law of the United States. For he went on to say: "Nor am I addressing the extent to which, as a matter of international law, the Senate's understanding of a treaty, if not communicated to other states parties to the treaty, is binding on those other states." *Id.* at 82.

exuberant defense of the *Restatement,* which he did by singling out this single sentence. When removed from context, its broad language presented an easy target. And perhaps most ironically, when removed from context it paints a target for Professor Vagts, which, in its implications, is also almost certainly not the view of Justice Scalia or any other Justice on the Court. In the process, the critical core focus of Justice Scalia's opinion in *Stuart,* for a focus on treaty interpretation rooted in the shared expectations of the parties, and its important implications for the rule of law, was lost. And the issues of "domestic conditions" in all its permutations, the core questionable *Restatement* positions, reflected in § 314 and its cmt. *d,* also remained invisible, along with the hidden virus of the "dual" approach.[310]

D. AN EXUBERANT DEFENSE OF THE *RESTATEMENT*: WINDMILLS FALL WHILE THE VIRUS STAYS HIDDEN

> ***"Parturient montes, nascetur ridiculus mus."***[311]
> *[The mountain labored and brought forth a mouse.]*
>
> *Horace, in* De Arte Poetica

---

310 Subsequent to *Stuart,* the Supreme Court decided another important treaty interpretation case, Eastern Airlines v. Floyd, 499 U.S. 530 (1991). The issue in *Floyd* was whether Article 17 of the Warsaw Convention allowed recovery for purely mental injuries. In interpreting the Convention to answer this question, a *unanimous* Court examined the English and French texts of the Convention, its negotiating history, subsequent practice, the meaning of the treaty terms in question under French law (including an analysis of French treatises and scholarly writing) and even interpretation of the Convention by the Supreme Court of Israel, a "sister" signatory. After pointing out that the English *American translation* of the "authentic" French text was "employed by the Senate when it ratified the Convention in 1934" [499 U.S. 535] the Court said "[b]ecause the only authentic text of the Warsaw Convention is in French, the French text must guide our analysis." 499 U.S. 535. Thus, despite noting that the English translation of the text had been "employed by the Senate," the Court specifically determined "the French text must guide our analysis." Moreover, there is no indication that the Court sought to ascertain whether any of the interpretive materials it used in its textbook analysis (generally congruent with international interpretive principles) were "employed" by the Senate when it ratified the Convention. Further, the Court specifically referred to "the signatories' intent" [499 U.S. 551], and it said: "treaties are construed more liberally than private agreements, and to ascertain their meaning we may look beyond the written words to the history of the treaty, the negotiations, and the practical construction adopted by the parties." 499 U.S. 535. Footnote 7 in the *Stuart* case seems to have disappeared as quickly and quietly as it appeared.

311 H. Rushton Fairclough, Horace Satires, Epistles and Ars Poetica 462 (1970). The following phrase from Horace in Latin is "quanto rectius hic, qui nil molitur inepte." The two phrases are translated by Professor Fairclough as:

> Mountains will labour, to birth will come a laughter-rousing mouse! How much better he who makes no foolish effort.

Id. at 463. *See also* John Bartlett, Familiar Quotations 98 (Justin Kaplan, ed., 16th ed. 1992). "The mountains will be in labor, and a ridiculous mouse will be brought forth." *Ibid.*

In an editorial comment published in the *American Journal of International law* in 1989, Professor Detlev F. Vagts, an Associate Reporter of the *Restatement (Third),* attacks the broad language of Justice Scalia in his *Stuart* opinion to the effect that: "I have been unable to discover a single case in which this Court has consulted the Senate debate, committee hearings or committee reports."[312] Professor Vagts indicates that one of his reasons for the public response, in addition to assisting future researchers, is to defend against the attack on the *Restatement*. Thus, he says:

> [T]he opinion [of Justice Scalia] goes on from these research errors to attack my long-time collaborator, Louis Henkin [the Chief Reporter of the *Restatement (Third)*]. I cannot let that attack on him and, by application of the principles of the Uniform Partnership Act, on myself go unanswered. Under the engraving of the porcupine in a French book on animals appears the legend "cet animal est bien méchant; quand on l'attaque il se défend." Loosely translated, that means that this very nasty animal, when attacked, has a tendency to defend itself.[313]

With his usual élan, Professor Vagts establishes that truly the courts have consulted preratification materials in treaty interpretation cases. As has been seen, however, this is, in truth, a trivial point not really at issue in treaty law, and not the core of Justice Scalia's concern in the *Stuart* case. The real point, and again, highly likely what Justice Scalia had in mind despite his broad language, is that these materials were not consulted for the purpose of overriding the intent of the parties to a treaty by the intent of the Senate, or of finding a binding "domestic condition" from informal Senate advice and consent history, as with Judge Harold Greene's opinions

---

312 Detlev Vagts, *Senate Materials and Treaty Interpretation: Some Research Hints for the Supreme Court* 83 Am. J. Int'l L. 546 (1989) (editorial comment).

313 Detlev Vagts, *supra* note 312, at 550. That Professor Vagts is not simply neutrally seeking to provide "research hints" for the Supreme Court, but rather is seeking to defend the *Restatement (Third),* which he may assume supports footnote 7 in the majority opinion in *Stuart*, is also suggested by his comment that an episode ending in a statement by Charles Evan Hughes to be presented to the German Foreign Office to the effect that general debate in the Senate "cannot be regarded as affecting the interpretation" of the Treaty of Berlin, also supports "the suspicion of the *Stuart* majority that sophisticated foreign states are quite aware of what is said during the advise-and-consent process." Detlev Vagts, *supra* note 312, at 548. On the merits, of course, that "sophisticated foreign states" will sometimes seek to use statements made in Senate debate hardly shows that they are broadly aware of all such internal exchange and its nuance in the foreign relations law of the United States, much less that the great majority of nations have a "sophisticated" capability in this respect or even that the United States has such a capability in respect to all other nations. And, of course, where other nations *are* aware of relevant internal statements, an approach giving binding legal effect to such statements gives those nations the ability to pick and choose against the United States in the future. If things turn out to favor the internationally correct interpretation, they can argue that interpretation; if not, they can argue the internal statement made during Senate proceedings.

in *Rainbow Navigation*. None of Professor Vagts's cases contradict this apparent core concern of Justice Scalia.[314] Nor would those cases seem to support the implications of § 314, cmt. *d* of the *Restatement* concerning "domestic conditions." And that seems to be the reality for *all* of the cases triumphantly revealed by Professor Vagts.[315]

Professor Vagts's "Research Hints for the Supreme Court," though written with considerable wit, would not merit much more than a footnote in this article—as yet another treaty law issue that is not the real issue—were it not that his porcupine defense of the *Restatement* may give some the impression that the *Restatement* view of "domestic conditions," including cmt. *d* to § 314, has been adequately defended. Since I suspect this was really the bigger game that Justice Scalia had noticed in the underbrush, I believe that it is important to point out that this editorial comment by Professor Vagts has not tamed it, nor changed the fact that there is no authority for such conditions cited in the *Restatement*, and that, as this article explores the issue, such advice and consent "conditions" as a mode of domestic lawmaking apart from the treaty bargain itself are structurally unconstitutional as a mode of lawmaking under the United States Constitution. And even worse, the "dual" interpretation mode of treaty interpretation, one variant of such "conditions," is extraordinarily harmful to United States foreign policy and the rule of law. Having great respect for Professor Vagts and Professor Henkin, I am only saddened that they are not both leading the fight on this side of the issue, *with* Justice Scalia, instead of one of these

---

314 Modern communication theory reminds us that language takes meaning from context. And a sentence can be taken out of context as well as a word or phrase. In this respect, in posing the issue, Professor Vagts does so in a way which is flatter than the full context of Justice Scalia's language. Thus, Justice Scalia's sentence, in context in Part II of his opinion, reflecting a core concern against overriding the intent of the parties by the intent of the Senate, was: "I have been unable to discover a single case in which this Court has consulted the Senate debate, committee hearings, or committee reports." To this sentence, Professor Vagts simply added the phrase "to interpret a treaty," thus effectively presenting a new sentence clearly posing the issue in the broadest general terms, as opposed to the use of the original sentence in its overall context of the sentences following it as well as those preceding it. And the following sentences clearly reflect that Justice Scalia's core concern is a rule of interpretation "in a treaty case . . . [determining] what the two or more sovereigns agreed to, rather than what a single one of them, or the legislature of a single one of them, thought it agreed to." 489 U.S. at 374.

315 Professor Malvina Halberstam, after reviewing the Vagts editorial comment and cases cited, also concludes that Professor Vagts missed the core issue to which the Scalia opinion was addressed. She writes: "[w]hile Justice Scalia's statement quoted by Professor Vagts was not so limited, that clearly was the issue in the ABM controversy (i.e., whether the legislative or negotiating history was controlling), and the issue to which both Justice Scalia's statement in his concurring opinion and Justice Brennan's statements in a footnote to the majority opinion in *Stuart*, were clearly addressed." Malvina Halberstam, *supra* note 140, at 1651 n.23.

distinguished scholars picking a fight by singling out broad language on a peripheral issue in defense of the *Restatement* with the one Justice who seems most clearly to have the beast in his sights. One would have hoped, for example, that a scholar of such distinction as Professor Vagts, who also serves as an Associate Reporter of the *Restatement*, would have, in a balanced critique of treaty issues in the *Stuart* case, at least have attacked the extraordinarily silly—and harmful—last sentence of footnote 7 in the majority opinion to the effect that preratification Senate material would be a better interpretive guide to treaty interpretation than the negotiating history between the parties. And he might have pointed out that Reporters' Note 5 to § 325 of the *Restatement*, cited in this footnote, contains no such ranking, nor, more centrally, does it, in its overall context as part of § 325, support such a conclusion. Even more importantly, I hope, as Professor Vagts and the other *Restatement* Reporters consider these issues in the future, they will indeed change the erroneous *Restatement* positions and speak out on the real issues in treaty law.[316]

The line of cases cited by Professor Vagts will be discussed in the next section. It may be useful here, however, to briefly note Professor Vagts's discussion of the *Restatement (Third)*. For one who is lecturing a Supreme Court Justice on how to do legal research, who is an Associate Reporter of the *Restatement*, and who is defending that *Restatement*, Professor Vagts's discussion of the *Restatement* is, to say the least, disappointing. He writes in critiquing Justice Scalia's criticism of the *Restatement (Third)*:

> A check from the *Restatement (Third)* back to the *Restatement (Second)* would have shown that sections 314 and 325 were not Professor Henkin's "proposal for change" but a nearly word-for-word reproduction of comment *a* to

316 In his defense of the *Restatement* Professor Vagts notes what he seems to regard as the collective responsibility of all of the Associate Reporters, in addition to the responsibility of the Chief Reporter. The narrow focus of his article attacking Justice Scalia's insightful support for the international rule of law in treaty interpretation cases, however, and his surprising ignoring of the core issue raised by footnote 7 and Justice Scalia's rejoinder, suggests that he himself may not have been fully aware of the real nature of this dispute or the consequences being read by others into the *Restatement* position on "domestic conditions." If so, it is to be hoped that the Reporters, as well as all the Advisors to the *Restatement*, all of whom are among the Nation's finest international lawyers, will rethink the implications of these previously obscure provisions of the *Restatement*, if they have, in fact, been meaningfully consulted on these issues. Indeed, should we assume from Professor Vagts's collective responsibility reference in footnote 14 to the three Associate Reporters of Professors Andreas F. Lowenfeld, Louis B. Sohn and Detlev F. Vagts, and his non-inclusion of the distinguished Advisers, that *all* of the Associate Reporters, including Professor Vagts, were meaningfully consulted on these controversial provisions of the *Restatement* and share the apparent position of the Chief Reporter, and that the Advisers may not have been so consulted? *See* Detlev Vagts, *supra* note 312, at 550 n.14.

> section 151 of the *Restatement (Second)* as it was written in 1965 by a different set of reporters."[317]

Presumably the reference here to §§ 314 and 325 is made by Professor Vagts because Justice Scalia specifically identified § 314, cmt. *d* and § 325, Reporters' Note 5, in his critique of the *Restatement (Third)*.[318] It should be recalled that § 314, cmt. *d* supports the approach that statements of understanding reflected in informal Senate treaty history (that is, material not incorporated in the Resolution of Ratification and voted on by the Senate) may create a binding obligation on the President to "respect them in good faith." And § 325, Reporters' Note 5, counsels that a United States court "is required to take into account United States materials relating to the formation of an international agreement . . . [which] may include . . . [c]ommittee reports, debates, and other indications of meaning that the legislative branch has attached to an agreement. . . ." The thrust of Professor Vagts's treatment of the *Restatement* is to convince the reader that the *Restatement* has not incorporated a "proposal for change" under its new Chief Reporter, Professor Henkin, but rather merely reflects the *Restatement (Second)* "written in 1965 by a different set of reporters."[319] But sadly, Professor Vagts's description is both wrong and misleading.

Professor Vagts is flatly wrong that §§ 314 and 325 incorporate "a nearly word-for-word reproduction of comment *a* to section 151 of the *Restatement (Second)*." Indeed, comment *a* is not even close to either § 314, cmt. *d* or Reporters' Note 5 to § 325. Comment *a* provides in full:

> *General*. Courts and administrative agencies in the United States are frequently called upon to interpret international agreements, because they contain the rules of law applicable to litigation or administrative matters before them. There are many judicial decisions in the United States dealing with proper criteria for the interpretation of international agreements. The principal decisions are collected in Reporters' Note 1. These cases conform to the international standard for interpretation stated in § 147. They also show the concern of the courts and agencies to avoid

---

317 Detlev Vagts, *supra* note 312, at 549.

318 489 U.S. at 375-76. The majority of the Court also identified these two sections in footnote 7, but the majority seems to limit its invocation of cmt. *d* to a softer statement in the first paragraph of that comment, whereas the Scalia reference is to cmt. *d* without qualification.

319 Strictly speaking, the *Restatement (Second)* was not "written in 1965" but is dated May 26, 1962, with "[r]evisions adopted and promulgated by The American Law Institute at Washington, D.C., on May 20, 1964 and May 20, 1965," and was *published* in 1965. Presumably most of the writing even predated May 1962. There is, of course, no *Restatement (First)*.

> differences between the international and the internal legal effects of international agreements.[320]

Presumably, Professor Vagts means cmt. *b* to § 151, but here again he is wrong in two major respects. First, cmt. *b* is not even close to the language or content of § 314, cmt. *d*[321] and second, while new § 325 Reporters' Note 5 is largely drawn from cmt. *b* to old § 151, even here the old comment included important language which was omitted from the new Reporters' Note 5 to § 325. For the old comment qualified the obligation by the language "to some extent" before the language "required to take into account," and this qualification is omitted from Reporters' Note 5. Comment *b* to old § 151 provides in full:

> *Domestic criteria that are not material internationally.* In determining the effect of an international agreement as domestic law, a court or agency of the United States is to some extent required to take into account domestic sources in the formation of an international agreement that an international body, such as the International Court of Justice, would not consider under the factors stated in § 147. These may include:
>
> (i) Committee reports, debates, and any other indications of the meaning that the legislative branch has attached to an international agreement in cases where the agreement, as a matter of internal law, requires the assent of the Senate or Congress. See § 133 dealing with the obligation of the President with respect to qualifications upon such assent.
>
> (ii) Aspects of the history of the negotiations leading to the agreement, including unilateral statements of understanding, not included in the President's proclamation or otherwise communicated to the other party and,

---

320 RESTATEMENT (SECOND) OF THE FOREIGN RELATIONS LAW OF THE UNITED STATES § 151, cmt. a (1965).

321 Professor Vagts seems to even contradict himself on this point when in his footnote 9 concerning missing *Restatement (Third)* cross-references, he connects *only* new § 325 to old § 151, and not also to new § 314. Footnote 9 provides: "I am partly to blame for this. Because it involved a mere Reporters' Note, I did not in the cross-reference table, 2 RESTATEMENT (THIRD) OF FOREIGN RELATIONS LAW OF THE UNITED STATES 477 (1987); cross-reference old § 151 to new § 325." Detlev Vagts, *supra* note 312, at 549 n.9. Professor Vagts should also note that the critical change in treatment of the *Niagara Reservation* case and "domestic conditions" as set out in the *Restatement (Third)* in § 303 Reporters' Note 4, also was not cross-referenced in this table to the Reporters' Note in § 134, or even to § 134 generally. Nor is the new § 314, embodying the critical change with respect to domestic conditions from informal Senate materials, cross-referenced to old cmt. *b* to § 135 which was reversed in § 314 in its key conclusion that "the deliberations of the Senate are not controlling in the interpretation of the treaty or the domestic law of the United States." Since elsewhere in the table of cross-references, Reporters' Notes and comments are specifically cross-referenced, it suggests that the compiler may not have been fully aware of the major changes being proposed in the treaty interpretation law of the United States between the *Restatement (Second)* and the *Restatement (Third)*. *See* 2 RESTATEMENT (THIRD) OF THE FOREIGN RELATIONS LAW OF THE UNITED STATES, tbl. III, 477 (1987).

> probably, internal official correspondence and position papers prepared for the use of the United States delegation to the negotiation that produced the agreement. Although internationally much of this evidence of intention may not be material under the factors stated in § 147, it may be necessary for domestic courts to consider it in view of the essentially legislative internal effect of treaties, and to some extent, executive agreements.[322]

Even more important than these errors, Professor Vagts's statement is seriously misleading in relation to the *Stuart* case treaty interpretation issues. First, in citing old § 151, cmt. *a*, apparently erroneously in relation to the point he is making, paradoxically he fails to note that cmt. *a* specifically refers to a collection of cases in Reporters' Note 1 to that section described as "dealing with proper criteria for the interpretation of international agreements." We have already seen that these cases, which embody the international standard of "the intention of the parties" rather than the intent of the Senate, were omitted from the *Restatement (Third)*. Further, the last sentence of cmt. *a* reflects the concern "to avoid differences between the international and the internal legal effects of international agreements," which is a point made in an early draft of the *Restatement (Second)*, which Professor Vagts chastises Justice Scalia for noting.[323] Most seriously in misleading the reader as to the difference between the *Restatement (Second)* and the *Restatement (Third)* concerning the core treaty interpretation points in *Stuart*, Professor Vagts never tells us of the major changes between the *Restatement (Second)* and the *Restatement (Third)* which precisely reflect Justice Scalia's point that the *Restatement (Third)* reflects "a proposal for change rather than a restatement of existing doctrine." These include, as previously discussed:

- Drafts of the *Restatement (Second)*, and the *Restatement (Second)* itself, reflect a concern in treaty interpretation to avoid differences between the international and internal legal effects of international agreements. This concern, a core of the hidden virus of the "dual" approach, seems to have disappeared in the *Restatement (Third)*;

---

322 RESTATEMENT (SECOND) OF THE FOREIGN RELATIONS LAW OF THE UNITED STATES § 151, cmt. b (1965).

323 Professor Vagts says: "Ironically, what causes Justice Scalia difficulty here is that he consulted the legislative history of the old *Restatement*, that is its Proposed Official Draft, but not the completed product. The passage he quotes was dropped from the final version." Detlev Vagts, *supra* note 312, at 549. But, of course, Justice Scalia referred to the Proposed Draft precisely *to show the change*. Moreover, one of the core points made in this excerpt cited by Justice Scalia, that of "disharmony between the international and the domestic meanings," *is* reflected in the *Restatement (Second)* and *not* in the *Restatement (Third)*.

- The *Restatement (Third)* seems to have dropped the important list of cases in Reporters' Note 1 to § 151 indicating that the proper criteria for the interpretation of international agreements under the foreign relations law of the United States is the intent of the parties;
- The *Restatement (Third)* departs from the *Restatement (Second)* position that informal indications from the record of Senate intent, as opposed to formal statements of intention either attached at signature or included in the instrument of ratification, would not *ipso facto* become "effective as domestic law" but rather would only be "taken into account";
- The *Restatement (Third)* departs from the *Restatement (Second)*, which made it clear that absent an understanding in the Senate Resolution of Advice and Consent or the instrument of ratification, "conclusions based upon the deliberations of the Senate are not controlling in the interpretation of the treaty as the domestic law of the United States";
- The *Restatement (Third)* departs from the *Restatement (Second)* in dropping the "international concern" standard in reference to the scope of treaties;
- The *Restatement (Third)* departs from use of the qualifying language "to some extent" in relation to taking into account domestic materials; and
- Most importantly, the *Restatement (Third)* drops the earlier more neutral discussion of the *Niagara Reservation* case in the *Restatement (Second)* and newly adopts the "conditionality" argument on domestic conditions of its Chief Reporter.

Since these collectively are *the* core issues in the *Restatement* of relevance to the "dual-unitary" and "domestic conditions" debates, surely it is disingenuous to lead the reader to believe that the *Restatement (Third)* was "a nearly word-for-word reproduction" of the decisions of an earlier set of *Restatement* reporters and advisers.[324]

Windmills tilted were toppled, but despite Justice Scalia's good effort to reveal the virus of the "dual" approach, it, and its associated doctrine of "domestic conditions," remained thoroughly hidden in Professor Vagts de-

---

324 Professor Vagts also says in relation to this *Restatement* discussion: "All of this shows that the *Restatement* rule has passed the scrutiny of two sets of reporters and two sets of advisers. . . ." Detlev Vagts, *supra* note 312, at 549.

Even more important than that the *Restatement (Third)* was indeed "a proposal for change" from the *Restatement (Second)*, is the question of underlying judicial authority for the *Restatement (Third)* core changed positions. There seems to be no such authority and, thus, no change from the state of the law at the time of the *Restatement (Second)*. Nor does the new *Restatement* offer any coherent policy arguments as to why its proposals for change are desirable.

fense of the *Restatement.* In the process, an important good deed by a Supreme Court Justice in the struggle for the international rule of law was rewarded by the equivalent of a legalistic "Ni" from the "Knights who say 'Ni'" of Monty Python and the Holy Grail.[325]

---

325 Although Professor Vagts, unlike the "Knights who say 'Ni,'" did not ask the Justice to produce a "shrubbery" in order to pass, one might question whether the nature of his attack made on a Justice of the Supreme Court, who by the tradition of his Office is not easily able to respond, was seemly in its nature. The structure of the piece was as a lecture on legal research and standards of scholarship, much as one might lecture a first year student, none of which would remotely be new for a Supreme Court Justice, particularly a former Professor of Law and Assistant Attorney General. Indeed, the tone seems calculated to disparage. And its entire premise was based on Justice Scalia intending a broad statement quite literally, rather than in the context of his expressed core concerns. Thus, it was hardly a fair response to the serious points he was raising, which were simply ignored in the rush to the soft target.

Moreover, Professor Vagts's "Research Hints for the Supreme Court" contained unnecessary slights on minutiae. To use one example of such minutiae, Professor Vagts attacks Justice Scalia's use of the word "self-exertion," saying he cannot be sure of its meaning because "that word appears in none of the six dictionaries I consulted." Detlev Vagts, *supra* note 312, at 549. Professor Vagts might want to check the Random House College Dictionary (rev. ed. 1975), which on page 1194 lists "self-exertion" as one self compound in a long list of such compounds. But more to the point, why would one expect all "self" compounds—a compound potentially almost limitless—to be defined in dictionaries apart from the meaning of the individual words in the compound, or have a real problem in understanding the meaning of "self-exertion" in the context in which Justice Scalia used it where its pointed meaning was quite obvious? To further beat this dead pony, Professor Vagts might also want to check THE NEW FOWLER'S MODERN ENGLISH USAGE (Third Edition 1996), which at 698-99 describes the general, and largely discretionary, rule about self compounds. It provides:

> **Self—**. Such compounds are of unlimited number. . . . The rule is quite simple: make a lightning decision about whether the *self-* adds anything essential to the proposed second element of a compound. It usually does. . . .

Id. at 698-99. Similarly, THE RANDOM HOUSE DICTIONARY OF THE ENGLISH LANGUAGE (2d ed. unabridged 1987), lists "self-exertion" on page 1736 in a long list of such compounds following the note:

> The lists at the bottom of this and following pages provide the spelling, syllabification, and stress for words whose meanings may easily be inferred by combining the meanings of SELF- and an attached base word. . . .

Id. at 1735. And this note further says by way of explanation as to which self compounds are specifically defined and which not: "[w]ords prefixed by SELF- that have special meanings or uses are entered in their proper alphabetical places in the main vocabulary . . . ." *Id.* at 1735. That is, apparently, only those meanings of self-compounds which are viewed as not of easily inferred meaning are specifically defined in the dictionary.

To risk being ungracious, perhaps Professor Vagts, who lectured Justice Scalia on the utility of "modern technology" in computer searches, if still puzzled by the meaning of "self-exertion," might today benefit from further self-instruction. A search of "self-exertion" on several popular search engines turned up over 200 hits. The "Google Search," with about 198 hits, took the computer 1.06 seconds. Professor Vagts would learn, for example, that the compound is used in the literary works of Thomas Carlyle, Nathaniel Hawthorne and Charles Lamb. And, without the need to consult six dictionaries, he

E. A FRESH LOOK AT THE CASES: THE VINDICATION OF JUSTICE SCALIA'S VIEW OF INTERNATIONAL AGREEMENTS AS COMPACTS AMONG NATIONS

Having reviewed the cases cited by Professor Vagts in his critique of Justice Scalia's broad language in the Justice's separate opinion in the *Stuart* case, I am not going to inflict them in full upon the reader. For the trivial, they do show, as Professor Vagts says, that courts sometimes do consult preratification materials and Senate records in treaty interpretation cases, just as they sometimes consult law review articles or scholarly treatises in these same cases. More importantly for treaty law, however, these cases also reflect the traditional approach to treaty interpretation. That is, the courts are looking to the intent of the parties, and to some extent the views of the Executive Branch, which are entitled to "great weight" in treaty interpretation. Thus, preratification materials, when consulted, are consulted, as would be expected, for information relevant to determination as to the meaning agreed between the parties, and the views of the Executive on that agreed meaning. They are *not* consulted for the purpose of overriding the intent of the parties by the intent of the Senate. They are *not* consulted for the purpose of the "dual" approach to treaty interpretation. There is simply no evidence in these cases that any court is seeking to substitute the intent of the Senate for the intent of the parties, under domestic or any

---

would turn up the following explanatory note from *Webster's Revised Unabridged Dictionary*:

> Note: self is used in the formation of innumerable compounds, usually of obvious signification, in most of which it denotes either the agent or the object of the action expressed by the word with which it is joined. . . .

Following this note is a short list of self compounds ending with the phrase "and many others."

Professor Vagts also reports Justice Scalia's failure to get the apostrophe right on the *Restatement* Reporters' Notes. The author, knowing the propensities to human error of all of us, resisted placing a [sic] on Professor Vagts's quotation of Justice Scalia's broad general language when Professor Vagts left out the comma after "committee hearings" which appeared in Justice Scalia's original. The reader should not, however, be overwhelmed by the author's generosity, since the West Publishing Company Supreme Court Reporter, from which Professor Vagts may have taken his quote, also made the same mistake. *Compare* the official U.S. cite at 489 U.S. 373 with the West version at 109 S. Ct. 1183, at 1195. More to the point, Professor Vagts might also have noted, but he did not, that the majority in *Stuart* also got the apostrophe wrong in its discussion of these issues in footnote 7 in the West Supreme Court Reporter version he may have relied on. *See* 109 S. Ct. 1183, 1191 n.7 at 1192. To add to the mystery surrounding footnote 7, however, this misplaced footnote 7 apostrophe was corrected in the official U.S. version. *See* 489 U.S. 353, 367 n.7. In any event, Vagts cannot have it both ways. If he relied on the West version then he might decently have noted that the majority had the apostrophe misplaced as well, and if he relied on the U.S. version, which likely would not then have been available, he might have correctly included the comma in the Scalia quote. The very fact of the printing errors here underscores the triviality of such points as serious revelations.

other law. And they are *not* consulted for the purpose of demonstrating a legally binding "domestic condition" from informal indications of Senate intent or an Executive Branch statement during the process of advice and consent.[326] As such, I believe they do *not* support the broad implications of the *Restatement* position expressed in § 314 and its cmt. *d.*

It is what these cases *do not support* that I believe were the core concerns of Justice Scalia in Part II of his separate opinion in the *Stuart* case. In short, these cases vindicate Justice Scalia's core concern of the traditional view of treaties, that they are contracts or compacts among nations, not domestic lawmaking by the Senate or even the Senate and the President. And these cases are completely consistent with a long line of Supreme Court cases to the same effect that we have reviewed.

Earlier we noted that United States courts have cited or referred to Senate materials in treaty interpretation cases. Before turning to a closer look at the cases revealed by Professor Vagts in this connection, it may be useful to further differentiate such "consultations" of "Senate materials."[327] Indeed, by not clarifying these distinctions for the reader, Professor Vagts may have inadvertently added to the confusion surrounding the treaty interpretation debate. These differentiations are first, a court may refer to Senate materials as a convenient source for the treaty, the President's transmittal message to the Senate with accompanying Executive Branch analysis, or information concerning the negotiating history of the treaty. Consultation in this first sense is not to the view of the Senate, but rather is to relevant interpretive material preceding any Senate consideration in order to ascertain the intent of the parties or the view of the President entitled in the interpretive process to "great weight." This is a standard sense in which "consultation" of such materials takes place. Materials consulted in this sense may be from the President's transmittal message to the Senate or its accompanying documents, or sometimes to information revealed in a hearing or committee report and, thus, in this latter setting, from Senate consultation history. Use of the President's transmittal message and accompanying documents is fa-

---

326 An independent review of Professor Vagts's cases by Professor Malvina Halberstam, a fellow former Counselor on International Law to the Department of State, reaches the same conclusion as the author about these cases. She writes: "[n]one of these cases . . . rely on legislative history to support an interpretation of the treaty that is contrary to, or differs from, the meaning of the treaty as determined by reference to the negotiating history." Malvina Halberstam, *supra* note 140, at 1650. She further notes: "Nor has research, following Professor Vagts's suggestions, disclosed a case in which a court relied on legislative history of a treaty to impose obligations domestically that were not required by the treaty as interpreted internationally." Malvina Halberstam, *supra* note 140, at 1650-51.

327 *See* the related general discussion in Part II of this article. The analysis here is, in part at least, a further division, among many such possible divisions, of the first of the issues discussed in Part II.

cilitated by the Senate practice of printing the treaty and the transmittal statement, with relevant documents transmitted therewith, as a Senate "Executive" or "Treaty" Document upon receipt by the Senate.[328] This "Executive" or "Treaty" document thus becomes a natural focal point of important information about a treaty. And such a reference is *not* normally to Senate debates, committee hearings or committee reports, unless the Senate "Executive" or "Treaty" document, or information contained therein, is incorporated, for example, in a committee report or hearing document, as is sometimes the case. And even in this latter case, citation to such an incorporated *Executive* document is functionally really a consultation of the *Executive* document itself, rather than the Committee report or hearing. It should be noted that consultations to transmittal documents themselves, at least when the citation is to an Executive or Treaty Document, and functionally to wherever such documents are reprinted, are thus not even of "Senate debate, committee hearings, or committee reports" within Justice Scalia's sentence attacked by Professor Vagts. This first sense in which Senate materials are consulted in treaty interpretation cases, that is, as a source of information arising prior to and beyond the Senate consideration process itself as to the intent of the treaty parties, overwhelmingly captures the bulk of such consultative practice. As discussed earlier, this sense is somewhat like consulting a law review article or treatise for relevant information in a case, as well, of course, as obtaining the views of the Executive Branch, which are entitled to great weight.

A second sense in which "Senate materials" may be consulted is for information revealed in a Senate hearing or report or in the Senate debate which may be relevant in ascertaining the intent of the treaty parties but which is generated during Senate consideration. Consultations in this sense are, as with the first sense, still not for the purpose of overriding the intent of the parties by the intent of the Senate or in ascertaining a binding Senate "domestic condition." This category of consultation of Senate materials is always from Senate consultation history. The treaty debate issue in *Stuart* itself, concerning a floor colloquy between Senators Taft and George as to the meaning of the United States—Canada Tax Treaty, seems principally to be this sense of "consultation," at least as reflected in the overall opinion of the majority, rather than its inconsistent last sentence in footnote seven.

---

328 Normal Senate practice is for the *Senate* to print the treaty and President's transmittal message (with any materials accompanying the transmittal) as an *Executive* or *Treaty* document for the Senate, simultaneous with the referral to Committee. Such *documents* are to be distinguished from Committee *hearings* or *reports* or *records of Senate debate*. As has earlier been noted, the old *Executive Documents* series was replaced with *Treaty Documents* beginning with the 97th Congress in 1981. *See* the Introduction to the *CIS Index*, *supra* note 48.

A third sense, and I can find *no* support in *any* of Professor Vagts's cases for such a consultation, is consultation of "Senate materials," whatever the category, for the purpose of ascertaining the intent of the Senate as the governing source of authority as opposed to the intent of the parties as to the meaning of a treaty or in establishing a legally binding "domestic condition" apart from the treaty.[329]

Turning to consideration of some of the cases identified by Professor Vagts, the first to be considered is *Factor v. Laubenheimer*,[330] decided by the Supreme Court in 1933. This case involved interpretation of a number of treaties, most centrally Article X of the Webster-Ashburton Treaty of 1842, in an extradition case. The core issue before the Court was whether a proviso to Article X meant that extradition could only occur if the crime for which extradition was requested by Britain was also a crime under the law of the State of Illinois, the place of refuge, or whether it merely referred to evidentiary or procedural requirements not barring the extradition. Mr. Justice Stone, writing for the Court, applied a traditional normative standard for treaty interpretation, reflecting both a concern for honoring "the good faith of treaties" and effecting the "intention of the parties." Thus, he wrote:

> In choosing between conflicting interpretations of a treaty obligation, a narrow and restricted construction is to be avoided as not consonant with the principles deemed controlling in the interpretation of international agreements. Considerations which should govern the diplomatic relations between nations, and the good faith of treaties, as well, require that their obligations should be liberally construed so as to effect the apparent intention of the parties to secure equality and reciprocity between them.[331]

Not only was this normative standard squarely within the long line of Supreme Court cases previously noted, which looked to the "intent of the parties" for treaty interpretation, but, of special relevance to the recent assertion of a "dual" approach, the Court emphasized "the good faith of treaties" and interpretation "to secure equality and reciprocity." There is *nothing* in this case suggesting that the Court was even considering Senate preratification history, much less that the intent of the Senate, as espoused in the "dual" approach, was to be the controlling standard in treaty interpretation. Nor does this case present any issue of "domestic conditions."

---

329 There are other senses, as well, in which "Senate materials" might be consulted. For example, amendments, understandings or international conditions attached to a Senate resolution of advice and consent may *directly* enter into the international treaty process itself, as subsequently transmitted or renegotiated by the President.

330 290 U.S. 276 (1933).

331 290 U.S. at 293. The Court also said: "The question presented here, therefore, is one of the construction of the provisions of the applicable treaties in accordance with the principles governing the interpretation of international agreements." *Id.* at 287.

With respect to the extreme Tribe view that only materials before a consenting Senate can be taken into account in interpretation, there is no hint of such an approach. Thus, with no inquiry as to whether the materials were before the consenting Senate, and some such as the Blaine-Pauncefote Convention of 1889[332] and the cited dispatch and letter of 1885 and 1905, respectively,[333] clearly were not, the Court relied on subsequent treaty practice of the parties, the negotiations and diplomatic correspondence and practical construction of the treaty by the parties, and several treatises on extradition, among other evidence. And specifically on the propriety of consulting *travaux* and subsequent practice, the Court said:

> In ascertaining the meaning of a treaty we may look beyond its written words to the negotiations and diplomatic correspondence of the contracting parties relating to the subject matter, and to their own practical construction of it.[334]

Further, the Court noted:

> But the exhaustive search, by counsel, through available diplomatic records and correspondence, in response to the invitation of the Court in its order for reargument of this cause, has disclosed nothing in diplomatic history which would afford a basis for any different conclusion.[335]

That is, the Court even requested counsel to undertake an exhaustive search of "diplomatic records and correspondence" in an effort to determine the intent of the parties.

The Court also noted the classic foreign relations law of the United States, as has earlier been noted, that the views of the Executive, were entitled to weight. Thus, the Court said:

> in resolving doubts the construction of a treaty by the political department of the government, while not conclusive upon courts called upon to construe it, is nevertheless of weight.[336]

And in its subsequent treatment of "[t]he political department," the Court referred exclusively to the Department of State and Executive Branch actions and views. Again, there is not a hint of looking to the intent of a consenting Senate as the normative standard for treaty interpretation.

Finally, even with respect to any consultation of Senate "debate, committee hearings or committee reports" by the Court, which is presumably the nar-

---

332 290 U.S. at 286.

333 290 U.S. at 300 n.8.

334 290 U.S. at 294-95.

335 290 U.S. at 295.

336 290 U.S. at 295.

row point of Professor Vagts in referring to this case, there is, quite simply, *no consultation here whatever of any such Senate "debate, committee hearings or committee reports." Nor is there any Senate consideration history reflected in the opinion of the Court.* Rather, the Court's consultation was clearly to the President's message transmitting the treaty to the Senate, as printed in *Executive Documents* of the Senate. Indeed, the 1842-43 cite was to a pre-1919 era in which treaties were considered in closed session, and was to a time apparently even well before the first printed hearing in 1902. That is, the Court's reference was to the President's transmittal message in an era in which *there was not even a public record of Senate consideration history as we would understand it today.*

Professor Vagts said he located this case "the old way," that is "by simply reading treaty interpretation cases until one finds opinions that use Senate materials."[337] And specifically with respect to *Factor v. Laubenheimer* he says:

> Rather randomly, I found an old case, *Factor v. Laubenheimer*, that used a document that would now probably be in a committee report. LEXIS would not have turned it up since it did not use the modern citation form.[338]

The actual footnote six reference in the Court's opinion to President Tyler's transmittal message is in full:

> President Tyler, in his message transmitting the Treaty of 1842 to the Senate for consideration, referred to Article X as "carefully confined to such offenses as all mankind agreed to regard as heinous and as destructive to the security of life and property. In this careful and specific enumeration of crimes, the object has been to exclude all political offenses, or criminal charges, arising from wars or intestine commotions." Executive Documents, Vol. 1, 1842-3, Doc. No. 2, p.22.[339]

Having tracked down the particular Executive Document referred to by the Court in the Library of Congress, I can attest that the document contains no reference whatever to Senate consideration history. Further, it is *not* a debate, committee hearing, or committee report, but rather is a Senate printed confidential transmission of the Webster-Ashburton Treaty to the Senate from President John Tyler, together with the associated transmittal message of August 11, 1842, and over one hundred pages of diplomatic correspondence related to the negotiation of the treaty between the parties. And the Court is clearly providing simply a citation to the Court's footnote quo-

---

337 Detlev Vagts, *supra* note 312, at 548.

338 Detlev Vagts, *supra* note 312, at 548 (footnote omitted).

339 290 U.S. at 299 n.6.

tation from the transmittal message of the President.[340] Further, with reference to Professor Vagts's comment that this document "would now probably be in a committee report" and was not turned up because "it did not use the modern citation form," I believe that he, or his research assistant, has likely missed the distinction, even in modern Senate treaty practice, between Executive or Treaty *Documents* and Executive *Reports*. *Executive Documents*, or, today, *Treaty Documents*, are printed by the Senate and are used to provide for the Senate as a whole the transmittal message from the President, together with the treaty and related documents.[341] *Executive Reports* submit the Report of the Committee on Foreign Relations to the Senate concerning a treaty. They are said "to accompany a particular Executive or Treaty Document"[342] and only sometimes do they reprint the full treaty and transmittal message. The document referred to by the Court in *Factor v. Laubenheimer* was an *Executive Document* with the full treaty, transmittal message and accompanying negotiating history, not an *Executive Report*.

---

340 *See* 1 EXECUTIVE DOCUMENTS, 1842-43, Doc. No. 2 in Congressional Information Service No. 27-2-11 (quotation of the Court at page 12 in President Tyler's transmittal message—Treaty and message labeled "Confidential"); U.S. SERIAL SET NO. 413 (quotation of the Court at page 24 in President Tyler's transmittal message, transmittal message at pages 19-26, treaty at pages 27-33, and associated diplomatic correspondence at pages 34-145) (It might be noted that the Court's quotation varies in four insignificant ways from the original quote in both microfiche series).

This document from *Factor* is described as a "Senate" document and was printed by the "Senate." It is neither a Committee Report nor a record of Senate consideration of the Treaty.

341 *Executive Documents* became *Treaty Documents*, with revised numbering, in 1981 during the 97th Congress. After that date they are included in the Serial Set and the depository library program and are thus more widely available. Conversation of the author with Gregory Harness, Librarian of the United States Senate, November 8, 2000.

342 By way of examples, *compare* "Convention on the Service Abroad of Judicial and Extrajudicial Documents in Civil or Commercial Matters: Message from the President of the United States transmitting . . . [the Treaty]," Executive C, 90th Cong., 1st Sess. (1967) (CIS Microfiche NO: 90-1-D3); "Tax Convention with the Netherlands: Message from the President of the United States transmitting . . . [the Treaty]," Treaty Doc. 103-6, 103d Cong., 1st Sess. (1993); "Two Protocols Amending the OAS Charter: Message from the President of the Untied States transmitting . . . [the 'Protocol of Washington']" Treaty Doc. 103-22, 103d Cong., 2d Sess. (1994); "United Nations Convention on the Law of the Sea, With Annexes, and the Agreement Relating to the Implementation of Part XI of the United Nations Convention on the Law of the Sea, With Annex: Message from the President of the United States transmitting . . . [The 1982 United Nations Law of the Sea Treaty]" Treaty Doc. 103-39, 103d Cong., 2d Sess. (1994); *with* "Convention on the Service Abroad of Judicial and Extrajudicial Documents," Report from the Committee on Foreign Relations, Exec. Rept. No. 6, 90th Cong., 1st Sess. (1967) (CIS Microfiche NO: 90-1-R6) (This report prints on its cover page "To accompany Ex. C, 90th Cong., 1st Sess."); "Income Tax Convention with the Czech Republic," Report from the Committee on Foreign Relations, Exec. Rept. 103-22, 103d Cong., 1st Sess. (1993) (This report prints on its cover page "To accompany Treaty Doc. 103-17").

Of course, a Committee report or hearing could choose to reprint some or all of the Executive document concerning a treaty, and some do.

While it may be true that this document *might* today "be in a committee report," as Professor Vagts says, I believe that he is wrong that the full report and transmittal message, as was the document here, *probably* would be. Rather, it *probably* would be in the *Executive* or *Treaty* document rather than the Senate report.[343] And, in any event, in *Factor*, it was *not* in a committee report. Nor is it a matter of not using "the modern citation form." This document does not use the "modern citation form" to a committee report, not just because it is not modern, but centrally because *it is not a committee report*.[344]

As one would expect in a treaty interpretation case, the Court in *Factor* is looking to the President's transmittal message of the Treaty to the Senate, a source entitled, according to the Court, to "weight" in interpretation, and here cited from Executive Documents of the Senate where such transmittal messages are printed per the usual treaty practice. This case provides *zero* support for the "dual" approach to treaty interpretation, or the permissibility of Senate imposed "domestic conditions." It is a standard Supreme Court treaty interpretation case in a long line of such cases looking to the intent of the parties and, where applicable, according weight to the view of the President.

A second case turned up by Professor Vagts, this time using computer assisted search, is the 1951 case *Warren v. United States*.[345] In *Warren* the Supreme Court looked to the language and purpose of the Shipowners' Liability Convention, proclaimed by the President in 1939, to interpret that Convention.[346] No issue of the "dual" approach nor "domestic conditions" is presented in the case, and there is not the slightest hint that the Court is

---

343 The Librarian of the United States Senate confirms that the full report and transmittal message, as was the document in *Factor*, today *probably* would be in the Executive or Treaty *document*, although it *might* be in the Executive *Report*. Conversation of the author with Gregory Harness, Librarian of the United States Senate, November 8, 2000.

344 Although a technical distinction in Senate treaty practice, this is a not inconsiderable lapse for one giving "research hints" to the Supreme Court and indicating that assisting future researchers was an object of his effort. Professor Vagts might want to review the discussion of the distinction between *Executive Documents* and *Executive Reports* in Laurence F. Schmeckebier & Roy B. Eastin, Government Publications and Their Use 166 (2d rev. ed. 1969).

As a "research hint" for Professor Vagts and future researchers seeking treaty materials using LEXIS, understanding the importance of *Executive Documents* and *Treaty Documents*, as well as *Executive Reports*, will lead to a more effective search. For example, searching with "treaty and 'Exec! Doc!' or 'Treaty Doc!'" will produce additional cases not found with the search "'Treaty' and 'S. Exec. Rep.'" used by Professor Vagts. Indeed, Professor Vagts would have found *Factor v. Laubenheimer* with this additional search as well as *Volkswagenwerk* and *Aérospatiale*, all cases he said he found "the old way." *See* Detlev Vagts, *supra* note 312, at 548.

345 340 U.S. 523 (1951).

346 340 U.S. at 526-27.

applying a standard of interpretation looking to the intent of the Senate as opposed to the intent of the treaty parties. Indeed, *there is no reliance whatsoever on any Senate treaty consideration history*. The computer search turns up this case because of a footnote cite to a Senate report using the LEXIS "S. Exec. Rep." input of Professor Vagts.[347] But the Court makes this cite *solely in reference to the report of Secretary of State Cordell Hull to President Franklin D. Roosevelt* recommending ratification, and transmitted by the President to the Senate, which the Court does rely on, along with the *Proceedings* of the International Labor Conference and one scholarly article and two scholarly treatises, at least one of which, dated 1942, is subsequent to Senate consent to the Treaty.[348] Moreover, the Court also cites the report of the Secretary of State to the President concerning the need for implementing legislation, citing a House of Representatives report on the source.[349] Hearings are cited for *implementing legislation* before the Senate, which legislation passed the House but not the Senate.[350] In short, Professor Vagts's use of "modern technology" in this case merely turned up a use by the Court in treaty interpretation of a report of the Secretary of State recommending ratification of the Convention and transmitted to the Senate by the President. Even at the level of minutiae the Vagts critique represents, this is a pretty good stretch to suggest that a reliance by the Court on a Secretary of State report, merely cited to a Senate report where it can be found, is a consultation of: "'the Senate debate, committee hearings or committee reports' to interpret a treaty."[351]

The report of the Secretary of State, "consulted" in *Warren*, is an enclosure sent to the Senate with the President's message of transmittal. It appears in the Report of the Senate Foreign Relations Committee simply because the President's transmittal message and relevant enclosures were reprinted in the Committee Report to the Senate. Indeed, as would be expected, the report of the Secretary of State is reprinted in the Committee report from the Executive Document transmitting the Shipowner's Liability Convention (and five other treaties and two recommendations all adopted by the International Labor Conference at its twenty-first session) from President Franklin D. Roosevelt to the Senate.[352] As has been noted, sometimes such trans-

---

347 Detlev Vagts, *supra* note 312, at 547 and 547 n.5. Professor Vagts cites only page 527 n.5 on this case, the reference in the Senate Report to the report of the Secretary of State, and does not refer to the Senate hearings on implementing legislation cited on the preceding page.

348 *See* 340 U.S. at 527 and 527 nn. 3-5.

349 *See* 340 U.S. at 526 n.2.

350 *See* 340 U.S. at 526 n.2.

351 Detlev Vagts, *supra* note 312, at 546-47.

352 U.S. SENATE, SIX DRAFT CONVENTIONS AND TWO RECOMMENDATIONS CONCERNING EMPLOYMENT OF SEAMEN, ADOPTED AT THE INTERNATIONAL LABOR CONFERENCE,

mittal messages, printed as Executive Documents, are reprinted in a committee report or hearing. The citation of the Court to page three of the Committee Report is *solely* to the report of the Secretary of State making the points noted by the Court in the footnote for which the cite is provided. There is *no* reference by the Court to the one-and-one-half page report of the Committee on Foreign Relations that begins this report. Thus, the consultation in *Warren* is *solely* to information contained in an enclosure with the President's transmittal message to the Senate and reprinted from an Executive Document.[353]

A third case turned up by Professor Vagts, this one taken from Justice Scalia's opinion with the Justice being instructed to "[r]ead widely in what one cites"[354] is *Maximov v. United States*.[355] This 1963 decision of the Supreme Court presents for decision whether a United States trust, all of the beneficiaries of which are residents of the United Kingdom, is entitled to exemption from U.S. capital gains taxes by virtue of the 1945 Income Tax

---

October 6-24, 1936, *Executive Doc. V to CC Inclusive*, 75th Cong., 1st Sess. (Aug. 19, 1937) (CIS Microfiche NO: 75-1-D22). The report of Secretary of State Cordell Hull to President Roosevelt, subsequently reprinted in the report of the Senate Foreign Relations Committee where it was cited by the Court in *Warren*, is at 2-5 in this Executive Document.

It seems likely that the Senate Foreign Relations Committee chose to reprint the President's transmittal message and Secretary of State Report, and other materials relevant to the Shipowner's Liability Convention, because the original Executive Document transmitted *six* treaties and *two* recommendations and the Committee Report only related to one of the treaties, technically transmitted singly as a stand alone treaty in Executive X without the President's transmittal message, the Secretary of State's report, or other relevant materials. Thus, an incorporation of Executive X by the Committee would not include the relevant materials accompanying the treaty, and an incorporation of Executive V to CC inclusive would incorporate materials related to five treaties and two recommendations not part of the Committee's action. *See* Draft Convention (No. 55) Concerning the Liability of the Shipowners in Case of Sickness, Injury, or Death of Seamen, Adopted by the International Labor Conference At Its Twenty-First Session Held at Geneva, October 6-24, 1936, *Executive X*, 75th Cong., 1st Sess. (Aug. 19, 1937) (Executive X contains only the draft convention text).

353 *Draft Convention (No. 55) Concerning the Liability of the Shipowner in Case of Sickness, Injury, or Death of Seamen, Adopted by the International Labor Conference at its Twenty-First Session Held at Geneva, October 6-24, 1936, Report from the Senate Committee on Foreign Relations Executive Rept. No. 8*, 75th Cong., 3d Sess. (1938) (Pages 1-2 of this report contain the report of the Committee and Subcommittee of the Committee to the Senate. Pages 2-23, the remaining pages in this report, reprint the President's message of transmittal and accompanying documents concerning Executive Branch views and negotiating history). (The report also contains the note: "[To accompany Executive X, Seventy-fifth Congress, first session].") This report was located courtesy of the United States Senate Library.

354 Detlev Vagts, *supra* note 312, at 549.

355 373 U.S. 49 (1963). Certiorari was granted in this case to resolve a conflict between the Ninth and Second Circuits as to the interpretation of the Tax Convention.

Convention between the United States of America and the United Kingdom. In deciding this straightforward treaty interpretation case, a unanimous Court looked to "[t]he plain language of the Convention"[356] and the "intent or expectations of its signatories"[357] as, we have seen, is the historic approach within the Court to treaty interpretation. More specifically in regard to the intent of the parties the Court says:

> there is no indication that application of the words of the treaty according to their obvious meaning effects a result inconsistent with the intent or expectations of its signatories. It appears from the relevant materials instructive as to the intent of the parties to the Convention that the general purpose of the treaty was not to assure complete and strict equality of tax treatment—a virtually impossible task in light of the different tax structures of the two nations—but rather, as appears from the preamble to the Convention itself, to facilitate commercial exchange through elimination of double taxation resulting from both countries levying on the same transaction or profit; an additional purpose was the prevention of fiscal evasion.[358]

Nothing in this case presents for decision the "dual" approach or "domestic conditions," or suggests that the Court even adverted to the possibility of interpreting a treaty by the intent of the Senate as opposed to the intent of the parties. Moreover, even on Professor Vagts's trivial point, as to whether the Court can consider Senate ratification history in treaty interpretation, *there is nothing in this case suggesting that the Court was even considering Senate views* in aid of interpretation.

Professor Vagts said of this case in critiquing the single sentence of Justice Scalia:

> While the Justice quotes from the text of one page at some length, a more comprehensive reading of that page would show in a footnote that the Court consulted hearings before a subcommittee of the Committee on Foreign Relations.[359]

And Professor Vagts identifies this page in *Maximov* as page 54 and the footnote as note 2 on that page. But footnote 2 on page 54 provides in full:

> The preamble [to the U.S.-UK Income Tax Convention] recites that the parties desired "to conclude a Convention for the avoidance of double taxation

---

356 373 U.S. at 52.

357 373 U.S. at 54.

358 373 U.S. at 54. Note the location of the Court's footnote 2 in this text, which will be relevant in evaluating Professor Vagts's critique.

In footnote 3 on page 55 the Court also said that its interpretation "is not only mandated by the terms of the treaty itself, the apparent intention of its signatories, and the context in which negotiated, but is consistent with long-standing administrative practice and regulations. . . ." *Id.* at 55 n.3.

359 Detlev Vagts, *supra* note 312, at 550.

> and the prevention of fiscal evasion with respect to taxes on income." See also Hearings before a Subcommittee of the Committee on Foreign Relations, on Conventions with Great Britain and Northern Ireland Respecting Income and Estate Taxes, S. Exec. Docs. D and E, 79th Cong., 1st Sess. 1-2.[360]

The reader should note that this footnote cites two things, presumably for the purpose of showing that an "additional purpose" of the U.S.-UK Tax Convention was the prevention of fiscal evasion. The first was the preamble to the Convention, hardly a reliance on Senate "hearings" as suggested by Professor Vagts. And the second was not a *see also* cite to the record of the Senate subcommittee hearings, as apparently assumed by Professor Vagts, but rather was specifically a *see also* cite *only* to pages 1-2 of the Committee print. An examination shows this to be a reference to the President's transmittal message to the Senate and the first parts of the report of the Secretary of State to the President on the Convention, both of which specifically make the Court's point as to an "additional purpose" of the Convention being the prevention of fiscal evasion. That is, this two page reference was, again, to a President's transmittal message and accompanying analysis of the treaty, clearly entitled to weight in the interpretive process as long established in the foreign relations law of the United States. Moreover, the reference was *not* to pages 29-82 of this report which contained the record of additional materials submitted, witnesses, and discussion by members of the Senate concerning the Convention. Further, the "Hearing" record cited by the Court has simply reprinted the text of Senate Executive Document D, which is the full treaty and transmittal message from the President. Thus, as has been previously discussed, this is functionally a cite by the Court to the treaty Executive Document rather than to the hearing. Again, it is a pretty good stretch to refer to this *reference to the President's transmittal message merely reprinted in a Senate report*, as consulting "hearings before a subcommittee of the Committee on Foreign Relations," as does Professor Vagts. Perhaps Professor Vagts, or his research assistant, should have taken Professor Vagts's own research advice to "read widely in what one cites."

A fourth case identified by Professor Vagts is *Trans World Airlines, Inc. v. Franklin Mint Corp.*,[361] decided by the Supreme Court in 1984. In *Trans World Airlines*, the Court considers the liability limit under the Warsaw Convention, an international air carriage treaty ratified by the United States in 1934. Justice O'Connor, in the opinion of the Court holding that the limit remains enforceable in United States courts, states: "A treaty is in

---

360 373 U.S. at 54 n.2.

361 466 U.S. 243 (1984).

the nature of a contract between nations."[362] Again she states: "our task is to construe a 'contract' among nations."[363] Disagreeing with the majority's interpretation of the Treaty as said to be made by the purposes and subsequent practice of the parties, the dissent insists on even more rigorous application of what he believes to be the intent of the parties. Thus, Justice Stevens, dissenting, repeatedly stresses that a treaty is a contract between nations to be interpreted by the intent of the parties: "A treaty is essentially a contract between or among sovereign nations"; "International agreements, like 'other contracts, . . . are to be read in the light of the conditions and circumstances existing at the time they were entered into, with a view to effecting the objects and purposes of the States thereby contracting'"; and "[t]he great object of an international agreement is to define the common ground between sovereign nations." He further uses the language "intention of the parties"; "[w]e are to find out the intention of the parties" (quoting Justice Story); and "solemn compact of nations."[364] And of relevance for the total non-support of the language of his opinion for the *Restatement*'s "domestic conditions" concept, Justice Stevens variously says:

> The frame of reference in interpreting treaties is naturally international, and not domestic. Accordingly, the language of the law of nations is always to be consulted in the interpretation of treaties;
>
> "As treaties are contracts between independent nations, their words are to be taken in their ordinary meaning 'as understood in the public law of nations.'" [citing the *Santovincenzo v. Egan* case];
>
> Construction of treaties yielding parochial variations in their implementation are anathema to the *raison d'etre* of treaties, and hence to the rules of construction applicable to them; [and]
>
> "It is a general principle of construction with respect to treaties that they shall be liberally construed, so as to carry out the apparent intention of the parties to secure equality and reciprocity between them. As they are contracts between independent nations, in their construction words are to be taken in their ordinary meaning, as understood in the public law of nations, and not in any artificial or special sense impressed upon them by local law, unless such restricted sense is clearly intended" [quoting *Geofroy v. Riggs*].[365]

There is not the slightest hint in this case of a "dual" approach to treaty interpretation, or of binding "domestic conditions" from informal Senate preratification history or Executive Branch statements. This case is also clearly inconsistent with the extreme view that only materials before a Sen-

---

362 466 U.S. at 253.

363 466 U.S. at 260.

364 466 U.S. at 262-64.

365 466 U.S. at 262-63.

ate in consideration of advice and consent can be taken into account in interpretation, since the majority opinion relies on subsequent practice of the parties and refers to the Warsaw Convention Conference Minutes. Scholarly treatises and law review articles were referenced in the opinion of the Court far more than any Senate records, and presumably not because they were regarded as "authoritative" in treaty interpretation apart from their scholarly merits.

Senate materials were referred to, in the Opinion of the Court, principally for the purpose of showing that the Fourth Montreal Protocol to the Warsaw Convention had not been consented to by the Senate. This, it might be noted, is not a reference to the record of the initial Senate consideration of the Warsaw Convention itself. Indeed, if the Senate record consulted is taken as referring to the original Senate record of the treaty being construed, then this case seems to be more consistent even with Justice Scalia's broad language than the Vagts characterization. Perhaps there are risks to computer assisted searches as recommended by Professor Vagts.

A fifth case, this one also turned up by Professor Vagts using computer assisted search, apparently simply looking for cases using both the terms "treaty" and "S. Exec. Rep" (a dangerous practice without more, as the *Warren* and *Trans World Airlines* cases would seem to suggest), is *Air France v. Saks*,[366] decided by the Supreme Court in 1985. In this case, the Supreme Court was determining the meaning of "accident" within the same Warsaw Convention of 1934 as was construed in the *Trans World Airlines* case discussed above. Justice O'Connor, in delivering the opinion of the Court, took a thoroughly traditional approach to treaty interpretation, consistent with a long line of such Supreme Court interpretation cases. Thus, in identifying the normative standard for interpretation, she said:

> [T]reaties are construed more liberally than private agreements, and to ascertain their meaning we may look beyond the written words to the history of the treaty, the negotiations, and the practical construction adopted by the parties. (citing *Choctaw Nation of Indians v. United States*); [and]
>
> it is our responsibility to give the specific words of the treaty a meaning consistent with the shared expectations of the contracting parties.[367]

And the opinion of the Court referred to the text of the treaty, its negotiating history, and the subsequent conduct of the parties, as the appropriate references in making its interpretive judgement. The Court did cite a Senate report, and it liberally referred to scholarly book and law review materials as well. Again, there was not the slightest hint in this case of a "dual"

366 470 U.S. 392 (1985).

367 470 U.S. at 396, 399.

approach to treaty interpretation, or binding "domestic conditions" from preratification Senate materials or Executive Branch statements during the Senate process of advice and consent. And again, the case was completely inconsistent with the extreme view that only materials before the Senate at the time of advice and consent could be used in treaty interpretation, because the Court liberally used negotiating history and subsequent practice without making the slightest inquiry as to whether they had been before the Senate. Moreover, the Court particularly pointed out that the *English* text of the treaty had been before the Senate but that it would use the *French* text because "the Warsaw Convention was drafted in French by continental jurists."[368]

And, as with *Trans World Airlines*, it is useful to review the Senate materials referred to by Professor Vagts in selecting this case to call to Justice Scalia's attention. He cites Senate sources used on pages 397 and 403 of the opinion.[369] His citation to page 397 Senate materials is stretching just a bit since there is no such report on that page (to have been located by computer or otherwise), and he must have been referring simply to the Court's own *statement* that the "official American translation of this portion of the text . . . was before the Senate when it ratified the Convention in 1934," or the English version of the text of these relevant articles itself that appears on the page, but are cited on the next page to 49 Stat. 3018-19, hardly a cite to original Senate materials. As an even greater stretch here, the Court sets out the English text it says was before the Senate and then sets out and uses, and says it is using, the French text, which presumably was not before the Senate. Not good, Professor Vagts. And to compound the problem, the one reference to Senate materials on page 403, which must have been identified in the computer search, refers, as in the *Trans World Airlines* case above, to a 1983 Senate report cited for the proposition that Montreal Protocols Nos. 3 and 4 have yet to be ratified by the Senate, hardly a reference to the original 1934 Senate record of advice and consent to the Warsaw Convention being construed. Again, if the reference is to the Senate original advice and consent record of the treaty being interpreted, then this case does not seem to qualify even to make the Vagts trivial point; tricky thing those computer searches.

A sixth case is *Volkswagenwerk Aktiengesellschaft v. Schlunk*,[370] decided by the Supreme Court in 1988. The issue for decision in this case involved interpretation of the Hague Service Convention, particularly whether it applied when process is served on a foreign corporation by serving a domestic sub-

---

368 470 U.S. at 399.

369 Detlev Vagts, *supra* note 312 at 547 n.5.

370 486 U.S. 694 (1988).

sidiary, which under state law, is the foreign corporation's involuntary service agent. The opinion of the Court, delivered by Justice O'Connor,[371] is a textbook example in treaty interpretation. Thus, the opinion declares:

> When interpreting a treaty we "begin 'with the text of the treaty and the context in which the written words are used.'" (quoting *Societe Nationale* quoting *Air France v. Saks*). . . . Other general rules of construction may be brought to bear on difficult or ambiguous passages. "'Treaties are construed more liberally than private agreements, and to ascertain their meaning we may look beyond the written words to the history of the treaty, the negotiations, and the practical construction adopted by the parties'"[quoting *Air France v. Saks*]. . . .[372]

The Court then carefully examines the language of the treaty, including the equally authentic French text, the negotiating history of the Convention in depth, and the general purposes of the Convention. The opinion of Justice Brennan, concurring in the judgment and joined by Justices Marshall and Blackmun, examines the negotiating history of the Convention in depth to reach a contrary conclusion. The materials cited by both majority and separate opinions examine a wide range of materials, particularly regarding the negotiating process, with no hint of anyone wanting to know whether such materials were before the Senate during advice and consent.[373] Indeed, the contrast between this traditional and excellent Supreme Court interpretation case, and the bizarre footnote 7 in the *Stuart* case less than nine months later, is staggering evidence of the effect of the "broad-narrow" vortex and the power of "great" cases to make bad law. Once again, there is not a hint of a "dual" approach to treaty interpretation, or an effort to set aside the intent of the parties for the intent of the Senate, or a doctrine of "domestic conditions" from informal preratification Senate materials or Executive Branch statements during advice and consent.

Professor Vagts is correct that Senate materials are reviewed, and this time for the treaty being interpreted. The majority opinion, however, merely cites one such brief reference, apparently for the purpose of citing a statement of the head of the United States delegation as to the meaning of the

---

371 Justice O'Connor, it should be noted, authored the opinion of the Court in three of these most recent treaty interpretation cases of the Supreme Court and is thus certainly one of the Court's top experts on the treaty interpretation practice of the Court. It is significant that in *Stuart* she did not join Part II-C of the Court's opinion dealing with treaty interpretation.

372 486 U.S. at 699-700.

373 Both the opinion of the Court and the separate opinion of Mr. Justice Brennan relied heavily on an international conference report for detailed discussion of the negotiating history of the Convention. The report is 3 *1964 Conférence de la Haye de Droit International Privé, Actes et Documents de la Dixième Session* (Notification) (1965) (3 Actes et Documents). Mr. Justice Brennan's opinion gives the cite here as "3 1965" rather than "3 1964."

civil-law procedure called "*notification au parquet*." Justice Scalia, who joined in the opinion, could certainly have been forgiven for overlooking the three lines in the over twelve page majority opinion which briefly makes this cite. Further, there is no cite to or discussion of the views of any member of the consenting Senate. Rather, the Court's cite is to a statement of an Executive Branch official. The separate opinion makes somewhat greater use of such cites, apparently also for the purpose of describing the views of members of the United States delegation, a letter of submittal from Dean Rusk, a Statement of President Johnson, and the views of the State Department Legal Adviser.[374] Indeed, as a former Counselor on International Law to the Department of State, this is precisely the sort of material I would have expected to find in carefully analyzed treaty interpretation, and in use of Senate materials where such information is easily available. It should be kept in mind, after all, that the views of the Executive Branch are, under hornbook foreign relations law of the United States, entitled to "Great Weight." And it should be kept in mind that Senate documents are frequently good sources for a variety of relevant information, much as are law reviews and treatises. The important point is that both opinions seriously sought to address the intent of the treaty parties, and there is no evidence that any of these references were for any other purpose. It should also be noted, again, as with any good treaty interpretation analysis in a truly ambiguous setting, that the discussion and references to the negotiating history of the Convention far overwhelmed the few references to Senate materials. And I don't believe any of the Senate references were referring to, or were for the purpose of, ascertaining the intent of the Senate as opposed to the intent of the parties.

In fairness to Professor Vagts, it might be useful also to end this brief examination of some of the cases he has cited by reviewing *Immigration and Naturalization Service v. Stevic*,[375] which he selects in his critique of Justice Scalia, saying: "If one had to choose a single example, it would probably be *INS v. Stevic*, which heavily uses those materials, including Senate floor debates."[376] The issue before the Court in *Stevic* was the proper standard for

---

374 The separate opinion of Mr. Justice Brennan makes five citations to *Executive Document* C, the Senate treaty transmittal document, and four citations to *S. Exec. Rep. No.* 6, the Committee report. The opinion's principal citations (five of the above nine) are references to the United States delegation's report or Executive Branch spokesmen following a statement by Mr. Justice Brennan including the phrase: "... our own negotiating delegation, whose contemporaneous views are 'entitled to great weight' ... " 486 U.S. at 713. The other four references concerned a general discussion of the meaning and operation of "*notification au parquet*," including references to a statement of the head of the United States delegation and the letter of submittal from Secretary of State Rusk. 486 U.S. at 709 & 709 n.1.

375 467 U.S. 407 (1984).

376 Detlev Vagts, *supra* note 312, at 547-48.

deportation claims under § 243(h) of the Immigration and Nationality Act of 1952, as amended by § 203(e) of the Refugee Act of 1980. Since the core issue for decision was one of statutory construction, Mr. Justice Stevens, writing for the Court, did not set out a standard for treaty interpretation. Senate preratification materials concerning the compatibility of the United Nations Protocol Relating to the Status of Refugees with existing United States law were referred to and examined as one of the factors looked at in statutory construction of § 243(h), since one of the objectives of the Congress in amending that section in 1980 was, according to the Report of the House Judiciary Committee, so that "U.S. statutory law clearly reflects our legal obligations under international agreements."[377] The Court seemed to find no variance between United States law under § 243(h) and the requirements of the Protocol, but if it had found a clear difference, it would seem that under normal United States foreign relations law, the later in time implementing legislation would prevail, even if the Protocol had been self-executing. The Protocol, then, was relevant as one factor among a variety of factors in legislative history generally, which the Court examined. This case is not itself a treaty interpretation case, though the question of whether a treaty was largely consistent with existing law when approved by the Senate was relevant. Certainly this case neither adopts a "dual" approach to treaty interpretation nor adopts a position that Senate preratification materials or Executive Branch statements during advice and consent hearings create binding "domestic conditions." Nor is there any evidence that the Court is setting aside the intent of the parties to the Protocol as overridden by the intent of the Senate. That the Senate meaning and the subsequent correct interpretation with respect to that meaning were the same in the view of the Court is reflected in the footnote sentence: "The point is not, however, that the Senate was merely led to *believe* accession would work no substantial change in the law; the point is that it did not work a substantial change in the law."[378]

With respect to Professor Vagts's Senate preratification materials, they were examined, along with a great deal of other history relevant to the statutory interpretation issues. By my rough count, consideration of what happened on the United Nations Protocol before the Senate accounts for approximately a paragraph of a little less than a page out of a total of about seventeen pages of relevant overall history of relevance to the statutory interpretation issue. Further, concerning examination of the Protocol, there were four cites to Executive Document K, one of these to President Lyndon

---

377 467 U.S. at 426-27.

378 467 U.S. at 429, n.22. The Court also noted that the President and the Senate *shared* the view adopted by the Court concerning the Protocol. Thus, the Court said in its opinion: "The President *and* the Senate believed that the Protocol was largely consistent with existing law." 467 U.S. at 417 (emphasis added).

B. Johnson's transmittal message to the Senate and three of these to Secretary of State Dean Rusk's Letter of Submittal to the President. There were five cites to Executive Report No. 14, the Report of the Senate Foreign Relations Committee to the Senate. Three of these Report cites were to the statement of Laurence A. Dawson, the principal Executive Branch official testifying before the Committee on the treaty. One was to an exchange between Senator Sparkman and Mr. Dawson and one was to the report of the Foreign Relations Committee. And there were two cites to *Congressional Record* statements by members of the Senate. Thus, of these overall eleven cites, seven related solely to the views of the Executive, and four of these from Executive Document K preceded real Senate consideration. One reference was to the Report of the Senate Foreign Relations Committee, two were statements of members of the Senate and one was a colloquy in testimony with the principal Executive Branch witness. I believe it is fair to say for Professor Vagts that this case met the test of the Court consulting preratification Senate materials, and even for interpretation, indirectly, of the treaty being considered. In fairness to Justice Scalia, however, this case was *not* really a treaty interpretation case. And even in examining the Protocol, the preponderance of cites by the Court are to the views of the Executive Branch. If Professor Vagts regards this as his "example" case, it confirms the essential trivia of the point he is making.

Nothing in these cases pointed out by Professor Vagts is inconsistent with the long line of precedent in Supreme Court practice, or the view of Justice Scalia in the *Stuart* case, that treaties are international compacts among nations. Indeed, where relevant, these cases confirm *that* is precisely the foreign relations law of the United States.

VII. Conclusion: Reclaiming the Rule of Law in United States Treaty Practice

> ***If a Government could set up its own municipal laws as the final test of its international rights and obligations, then the rules of international law would be but the shadow of a name. . . .***[379]
>
> *United States Secretary of State Bayard, 1887*

The integrity of agreement is a cornerstone of the rule of law nationally and internationally. In the international system, with its more diffuse law-making, a robust protection of agreement is particularly central. The United States should not lead the world toward the disgraceful "dual" approach to treaty interpretation. That approach, which, whenever it makes a difference, would either require the United States to breach its treaty obligations or hold the Nation to higher requirements than internationally agreed, should be consigned to the ash can of a history which never should have been. And if followed by other nations, so that they would place interpretations in their own internal approval process above the agreement between the parties, it would degrade the critical modality of agreement and the rule of law for all nations.

Paradoxically, the "dual" approach arose in an effort by good people devoted to the rule of law to ensure that their own Nation adhered to its international obligations. Their reasonable slogans in this effort, such as the President can only make the agreement understood by the Senate, concealed, in the mistake settings where the approach would arise, a hidden virus which turned their solution of the "dual" approach both against the rule of law and potentially even against the intent of the approving Senate. As with Plato's exile of the poets from his Republic, the purpose was high,

379 [1887] U.S. Foreign Rel. 751, 753.

the arguments logical, yet the result was both wrong and counter to the high purpose itself.[380]

The setting that produced the "dual" approach also stimulated the continuing struggle between the branches in the conduct of foreign policy. That struggle, periodically erupting throughout American history, had encompassed a wide variety of issues, from the scope of the treaty power, executive agreements, war powers, information flow and executive privilege, the control of secrecy and intelligence, and the treaty termination power, before embracing the struggle over treaty interpretation triggered by the "broad-narrow" debate in interpretation of the ABM Treaty.[381] In that setting, and riding a crest of conviction that it was serving the rule of law, the Senate began a practice of appending the "Biden Treaty Interpretation Condition" to its resolution of advice and consent, thus seeking to eternalize the "dual" approach throughout United States treaty practice. This condition, like many of the other measures unilaterally advanced by Congress in its struggles with the Executive for the control of foreign relations, is almost certainly unconstitutional, as well as perversely upside down in harming rather than serving the rule of law. Certainly, if allowed to stand, it would damage the United States in its international relations and would interfere with the legitimate constitutional roles of the President as the Chief Executive of the Nation in the conduct of foreign relations, and of the courts as the chief interpreters of the Nation's treaties in cases and controversies of judicial cognizance.

As sometimes happens in "great" cases, the effects of actions may be different than initially understood or anticipated. This seems likely also to be the case for the Senate, as the issue of its asserted power of domestic lawmaking through "domestic conditions" attached to treaties in the advice and consent process, becomes more visible as a result of this debate and its actions in espousing the "dual" approach and attaching it as a "domestic condition" to numerous treaties. It seems likely that when this issue is again squarely addressed by the courts that they will rule against any such Senate power, as has already been the case in the only Court of Appeals deci-

---

380 *See* PLATO, THE REPUBLIC 84-85, for the banishment of the poets from the commonwealth, and Part V, at 321-40, for the logical arguments in support of this decision. (Translated with introduction and notes by Francis MacDonald Cornford 1945; The Legal Classics Library, Special Edition 1991). *See also* PAUL FRIEDLÄNDER, PLATO: 3 THE DIALOGUES, SECOND AND THIRD PERIODS 75-79, 86-87 (Translated from the German by Hans Meyerhoff, Bollingen Series LIX 1969). Critical theory in literature has had a field day with this Platonic recommendation and reasons given for it.

381 *See, e.g.*, on this continuing struggle, *Executive Agreements and Congressional Executive Relations, Treaty Termination: Hearings Before the Senate Comm. on Foreign Relations*, 96th Cong., 1st Sess. 400, 414 (1979) (Appendix to Statement of John Norton Moore).

sion to have the issue fully identified and argued by counsel before the court. In recent years, the Supreme Court has begun importantly to focus on structural issues under the Constitution, including the integrity of the lawmaking process and the separation of powers. In the *Chadha* and *Clinton* cases in particular, the Court has firmly stressed the "single, finely wrought" requirements of art. I, § 7 of the Constitution as critical structural requirements for domestic lawmaking. Since it is conceded even by supporters of this asserted Senate "domestic conditions" power that such conditions are neither part of the treaty being considered nor the "supreme Law of the Land," this strange asserted power seems highly likely to fail judicial scrutiny as did the one House and even line-item vetoes before it.

The "broad-narrow" dispute about the proper interpretation of the ABM Treaty is not the first heated struggle about the proper interpretation of a treaty in United States history. Nor will it be the last. Sometimes in these struggles the Executive will be right, and sometimes he or she may be wrong. But throughout American history, no President has argued that he has the power as a matter of interpretation simply to ignore the correct international interpretation of a treaty to create a parallel domestic interpretation binding within the United States. Ironically, however, the Senate, perhaps only dimly aware of the consequences of its position, has asserted precisely that and in the name of the rule of law.

During the 1950s a heated dispute arose over the scope of the federal treaty power. A proposal by Senator Bricker during the 83d Congress to amend the Constitution to restrict the treaty power was narrowly defeated.[382] Today it is generally accepted that the Bricker Amendment would have been a malignancy for the Nation in its conduct of foreign policy. And its core motivation, fear of human rights treaties expressed by some during the civil rights struggle, seems quaintly dated. So too, the "dual" approach, whatever the merits of its original motivation, would severely harm the ability of the Nation in its foreign policy. This latest "impulse of sudden passion," as with the earlier Bricker Amendment, should not be permitted to do permanent harm to our international constitutive processes in an even more global world.

---

382 *See, e.g.*, for the nature of the Bricker Amendment controversy and Administration arguments in opposition, Statement by the Honorable Herbert Brownell, Jr., *supra* note 29. *See also* COMM. ON THE JUDICIARY, 83D CONG. 1ST SESS., PROPOSALS TO AMEND THE TREATY-MAKING PROVISIONS OF THE CONSTITUTION: VIEWS OF DEANS AND PROFESSORS OF LAW (Comm. Print 1953).

The United States and the international community are powerfully served by the rule of law.[383] Protecting and strengthening it should be a primary concern as we continue to examine issues of treaty law under the Constitution. The "dual" approach to treaty interpretation, however, is a deep disservice to the rule of law and an abomination whose time should never come.

383 For development of this theme, and the great importance of democracy and the rule of law, *see* John Norton Moore, *Toward a New Paradigm*, 37 VA. J. INT'L L. 811 (1997).